VALLEY FORGE
The Making of an Army

★

BOOKS BY ALFRED HOYT BILL

☆

The Ring of Danger

Rehearsal for Conflict,
The War with Mexico, 1846-1848

The Campaign of Princeton, 1776-1777

The Beleaguered City,
Richmond, 1861-1865

VALLEY FORGE

THE MAKING OF AN ARMY

BY ALFRED HOYT BILL

HARPER & BROTHERS ✶ PUBLISHERS NEW YORK

9748
B

VALLEY FORGE

Copyright, 1952, by Alfred Hoyt Bill
Printed in the United States of America
By The Haddon Craftsmen, Inc., Scranton, Pa.

974.6
B

Library of Congress catalog card number: 52-5420

To

Mary and Edward Pierce

*

CONTENTS

The purpose of this book is not so much to tell once more the story of Valley Forge as to elucidate the sequence of military events of which it was the central phase. The brilliant operations of the army under Washington's personal command in 1777-78 have been largely eclipsed by the campaign in the North that ended in the surrender of Burgoyne. Of all its achievements only the name of its post during that terrible winter stands with those of Lexington and Concord, Bunker Hill, Trenton-Princeton, Saratoga, and Yorktown. Yet it was Washington's accurate estimate of the country-wide situation and the marching and fighting of his army throughout the summer and early fall of 1777 that made the victory at Saratoga possible. His masterly campaign of maneuver cleared New Jersey of the enemy without a battle. The heroic defense of the forts on the Delaware not only threatened Sir William Howe's army with starvation in Philadelphia but was an indirect cause of Sir Henry Clinton's fatal tardiness in going to the assistance of Burgoyne. The attack at Germantown, though it failed, did as much as Saratoga to convince the French King's ministers that in recognizing the independence of the United States of America they would not be going to war for a lost cause.

The heroism of Valley Forge itself, the drama of the conspiracy of Conway, Gates, Mifflin, and their collaborators to drive Washington from his position as commander in chief, and von Steuben's miracle of turning the half-disciplined American troops into an efficient and reliable army have combined to obscure both what those troops had already achieved and their effect on the strategic situation during that winter. The éclat of the French alliance has outshone their victorious campaign of the following summer. The endless and seemingly futile marches of the previous year had seasoned them to the fatigues and frustrations of war. Their resilient confidence in themselves and in their leader had kept the defeat at the Brandywine from becoming a debacle. It took the fog to beat them at Germantown. They were veterans when von Steuben took them in hand: all they needed was professional training. Their continuing presence at Valley Forge as an army in being—weak and on the verge of disintegration as it often was—had an effect on the outcome of the war that is almost unique in military history.

Closest to it, perhaps, is the part played by the British army in Portugal in the winter of 1810-11. But behind the impregnable lines of Torres Vedras, Wellington's troops lay well sheltered, well fed, and plentifully supplied through the unchallenged sea power of a nation which twenty years of war had accustomed to meet its army's every need, while in front of them the French under Marshal Masséna were reduced to starvation and despair by distance from their bases and the murderous activity of the Spanish and Portuguese guerrillas.

There was no such destitution among Washington's opponents. In Philadelphia they were snugly housed, adequately supplied, strongly entrenched, and numerically far superior to their adversaries. At Valley Forge, some twenty-five miles distant, the Americans were ill sheltered, half-clad, cold, hungry, and neglected by an ignorant, incapable, and jealous Congress. But so long as they remained there the British victories of the past autumn went for nothing, the possession of Philadelphia was valueless, and Sir William Howe's army was reduced to the situation of a beleaguered garrison. It might as well have been at New York, so slight was its effect on the conduct of the war.

Washington said afterward that if Howe had attacked the position at Valley Forge in the grim weeks of January and February, when there were neither enough troops to man the fortifications nor transport for a retreat, he would have won the war. In the past seventy-five years a number of critics who ought to have known better have sought to disparage Washington's ability as a general by dwelling on his adversary's lack of energy and enterprise. It is a good deal like saying that the young Bonaparte would have been less successful in Italy in 1796 had the Austrian generals opposed to him been less hidebound by their misconception of the military doctrine of Frederick the Great. When Washington took up his position at Valley Forge, it is unlikely that he anticipated the straits to which circumstances and Congress would reduce him. But he had not been campaigning against Sir William Howe for more than two years without learning Howe's shortcomings, and an able general's decisions are always influenced by what he knows of his opponent's character. It should not be forgotten, moreover, that when Howe was defending his conduct of the war before a committee of the House of Commons, his ablest subordinates supported him in maintaining that an attack on Valley Forge in midwinter was impracticable; that he lacked the facilities for making one.

The results of the twenty-one months of campaigning speak for themselves. The November of 1776 had seen Washington retreating with a defeated and diminishing army to the doubtful protection of the Delaware. The July of 1778 found him—"after two years of maneuvering and the strangest vicissitudes that perhaps ever attended any contest," as he himself put it—once more on the eastern bank of the Hudson. Under his command was an army that had lately pursued the British across New Jersey and beaten them in a pitched battle. A powerful French fleet lay off Sandy Hook to cooperate with him, and in New York the enemy were fortifying their last great base in the country in expectation of his attack. It was no fault of his, nor of his men, that the splendid promise of this situation was not realized.

In writing this book I have become deeply indebted to Mr. Andrew C. Imbrie of Princeton for allowing me to examine the Frazer family papers, which have been of great use to me, and for which I return my hearty thanks. My thanks are due also to Professor William Starr Myers, Professor Walter P. Hall, Professor Gilbert Chinard, and Professor Thomas J. Wertenbaker, all of Princeton University, and to Mr. Charles T. Cowenhoven, Jr., of Princeton, for many valuable suggestions and much kindly encouragement.

I am gratefully indebted to Professor Chinard for permission to quote from his *George Washington as the French Knew Him*; to the Henry E. Huntington Library and Art Gallery for permission to quote from *The American Journal of Ambrose Serle, Secretary to Lord Howe, 1776-1778*; and to Mr. Willard M. Wallace, who generously gave me permission to use in this book the maps of the Battle of Monmouth and Howe's Invasion of Pennsylvania which appear in his *Appeal to Arms, A Military History of the American Revolution*.

And again I thank warmly the officers and members of the staff of the Princeton University Library for their unfailing courtesy and helpfulness.

ALFRED HOYT BILL

Princeton, New Jersey.
November 27, 1951.

BOOK ONE
The Testing of the Ore

✫

CHAPTER I

☆

"Very Little Time to Do a Very Great Work In"

1

IT WAS LATE in the spring of 1777, the second spring since the April fighting at Lexington and Concord had started what was to become the War of Independence, the first spring since Independence had been formally declared. At Morristown, behind the rampart of hills that stretches across northern New Jersey from the Hudson River to the Delaware, the army under the command of General George Washington lay eagerly waiting to take the field at the first definite move of the British who were concentrating around New Brunswick on the plain some twenty miles to the southward.

General Henry Knox, its chief of artillery, called it "the most respectable body of Continental troops that America ever had" up to that time. Though its men were mostly recruits, large numbers of them had seen service in the earlier campaigns of the war, and most of them were now enlisted for a term of three years. But by professional military standards it was sadly wanting. Its equipment, though eked out with arms, powder, and blankets from surreptitiously friendly France, was barely adequate. Most of its regiments were new, had been but lately formed into brigades and divisions, and these had never acted together. Its total strength amounted to little more than eight thousand officers and men, and opposed to it was an army of British and Hessian veterans, magnificently equipped, that outnumbered it three to two. But the wonder was that there was any American army at all. Sir William Howe, the British commander in chief, had not expected there would be one.

3

After the early successes of the rebellious colonists—Ticonderoga surprised, Montreal captured, and Quebec all but stormed in 1775; the British compelled to evacuate Boston and repulsed in an amphibious attack on Charleston in the spring and summer of the following year—their record had been one of defeat and disaster. The autumn

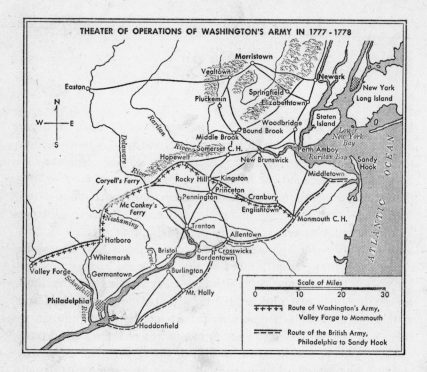

THEATER OF OPERATIONS OF WASHINGTON'S ARMY IN 1777 - 1778

of 1776 had seen Benedict Arnold's flotilla vanquished on Lake Champlain. Washington's Army had been defeated in the battle of Long Island. New York had been lost, Fort Washington stormed, Fort Lee evacuated, and the Hudson, by which New England might be isolated from the less insurgent states, was opened to enemy warships as far as the American forts in the Highlands above Peekskill.

By early December the British had overrun all of New Jersey as far as Bordentown, only twenty-five miles from Philadelphia, and with the enemy so close at hand, the Continental Congress had fled to the uncertain refuge of Baltimore. Only Sir William Howe's dilatory pursuit had enabled Washington to escape across the Delaware with the shattered remnants of his army. Washington had taken all the boats with him; but when the river froze hard enough to bear the weight of artillery, as it was soon bound to do, there seemed to be nothing to prevent the British from capturing "the rebel capital."

Washington had made good his retreat with only 3,000 men, and these were in the last stages of destitution. In the past twelve weeks he had lost 5,000 of his best troops, many guns, and invaluable stores of munitions and equipment. It was well known at British headquarters that the enlistments of nearly all his men would expire at the end of the year, that few of them would re-enlist, and that it would be several weeks before newly raised troops would join him. More significant still: as the British advanced across New Jersey, the inhabitants flocked to avail themselves of Howe's offer of pardon and peace to all who would renew their oaths of allegiance to King George.

Confident that cold, hunger, nakedness, and disease would dispose of Washington's army in the next few weeks and that the last embers of revolt would have ceased to glow by spring, Sir William decided that it was unnecessary to advance farther. He had little liking for winter campaigning, and he had never liked this war at any time. He had accepted the command in America only because he had hoped to bring about a peace with a minimum of fighting; he and his brother Richard, Admiral Earl Howe, who was in command of the British fleet in American waters, had been vested with the powers of peace commissioners. Now he ordered his troops into winter quarters, sent Sir Henry Clinton to capture Newport, and himself returned to the comforts and dissipations of New York.

Less than a fortnight later came that famous Christmas night when the American army crossed the Delaware. In the next nine days Washington had destroyed a Hessian brigade at Trenton and one of British troops at Princeton, led Cornwallis, Howe's second-in-command, on a wild-goose chase halfway across New Jersey and back again, and taken up a position at Morristown, on the British flank, so strong that Howe dared not attempt to drive him out of it.

The effect of this dramatic reversal had been enormous. At every court in Europe, from Madrid to Moscow, Washington's campaign was acknowledged to be a masterpiece of military skill. In Paris Benjamin Franklin, Arthur Lee, and Silas Deane, the American commissioners who had been sent to solicit the aid of France, no longer needed to minimize the disasters of the previous autumn. Instead they could point out that after two years of war all that Britain held in her North American colonies was New York and the island it stood upon, Long Island, Staten Island, Newport, and in recently conquered New Jersey the towns of New Brunswick and Amboy, where 10,000 British and Hessian troops were hemmed in by a population whom three weeks of British and Hessian brutality and plundering had turned from complacency to furious hatred. All New England, except Newport, was held by the patriots. At the strong fortress of Ticonderoga they barred the invasion route from Canada to Albany and the upper Hudson. Their forts in the Highlands closed the river against an advance from New York. Congress had returned to Philadelphia, and Washington in his fastness behind the Watchung Mountains was creating a new army.

In England, where the Government had exploited the capture of Newport as the culmination of a campaign that had practically brought the war to an end, the disillusionment was profound. Horace Walpole, who had lately thought that nothing but the armed intervention of France could save the Americans, commented dryly that the campaign in America had "lost much of its florid complexion, and General Washington is allowed by both sides not to be the worst general in the field."

Even Sir William Howe himself had written to Lord George Germain, the secretary of state for the colonies, with "much concern," that the enemy's successes had "thrown us further back than was at first apprehended, from the great encouragement it has given the rebels." But with what should have been a more accurate judgment of the situation than was possible in England, he had taken his reverses philosophically. At worst, he believed, a brisk campaign in the spring would recover all that had been lost, and take Philadelphia to boot. But he expected that lack of supplies and the bitter winter cold of the Jersey hills would soon force Washington to lead his ragged soldiers back once more across the Delaware, and that amid the hardships and discouragements of that retrograde movement his army would simply melt away—as it had seemed about to do in December.

These expectations had, in fact, come close to being realized. It had taken Washington the rest of the winter and most of the spring to prove them wrong.

2

In the brief radiance of the victories at Trenton and Princeton, Washington, seldom oversanguine, had thought that he might be able to drive the British out of New Jersey altogether. They were reported to be "in great consternation," sending their heavy baggage over to Staten Island. Their garrisons were driven out of Hackensack, Newark, and Elizabeth Town, and throughout the state the population had sprung to arms in the patriot cause. To hasten the British departure Washington sent orders to Generals Heath and Lincoln, who commanded the American troops in Westchester County, to threaten New York by a demonstration against the British outpost at Kingsbridge on the Harlem River. He retired to Morristown, intending to remain there only long enough to give his men a few days of much needed rest before renewing the offensive.

But no sooner had he reached Morristown than the Pennsylvania militia, which formed nearly half of his strength, began to go home. They had fought manfully, but they had served their term, and they had had enough of fighting for the present. Of the Continental troops, whom Washington had persuaded to remain with the colors for six weeks after their enlistments had expired, most would be taking their departure too soon to be of use in a new campaign, and very few new regiments marched in to take their places. Instead of being stirred to increased activity by the recent successes the country at large seemed to Washington to have sunk into inertia and apathy. Disaffection to the cause of Independence was reported to be prevalent in Pennsylvania, and even the Jersey people, though they missed few opportunities to avenge themselves upon the British garrisons for the injuries done them during the occupation, were greatly discouraged.

In the previous September Congress had authorized the creation of eighty-eight battalions of infantry to replace those whose enlistments were soon to expire. In the dark days of December they had authorized sixteen more, together with three regiments of artillery and 3,000 light horse. If the various states had at once set about raising these new organizations, Washington should have had 76,000 troops at his disposal by spring. But the fighting at Lexington and Bunker Hill had given the country a false confidence in the abilities of the militia, and people everywhere were suspicious of the plan for Continental regiments—organizations created, paid by, and directly under the authority of the Continental Congress—as a scheme to fasten a standing army on the infant United States. Even in ardently patriotic Massachusetts, late in the February of 1777, Abigail Adams wrote to her husband John, who was sitting in Congress at Philadelphia, that they were just beginning to talk about raising recruits for the new Continental regiments.

Each state, moreover, obsessed by its own peril and unable to realize that the safety of one could only be achieved through the success of all, was more interested in raising troops for its individual defense. Washington, disgusted with the inefficiency and expense resulting from the one-year enlistments of the past, had insisted that the new term must be for three years, and men hesitated to bind themselves for so long a time. Rather than do so they paid a fine or else enlisted in their state regiments, in which the terms were much shorter and they received a bounty much larger than the twenty dollars Congress had thought sufficient to attract volunteers to the Continental organizations. Continental recruiting suffered accordingly. The new levies that came in to Morristown to fill the ranks of existing regiments were poor material out of which to make soldiers. Some of them, General Nathanael Greene discovered, were actually convicts who had been purchased from their masters. "Oh, that Americans were spirited and resolute!" he exclaimed in a letter to his wife.

Reinforcements came in so slowly that at the end of January Washington began to fear that he would be left without any troops at all. The only regulars remaining at Morristown were 800 Continentals, due to go home by the middle of February, five Virginia regiments, and three other battalions, each of which the attrition of service had reduced to about one hundred men. Every officer who could be spared was sent off on recruiting duty and to collect stragglers, of whom there were many. But only the arrival of 700 Massachusetts militia made it possible for Washington to keep up an appearance of strength before an enemy double in numbers and apparently about to be strongly reinforced.

Morristown was an excellent position both strategically and tactically. Behind the barrier of the hills roads connected it with both the Delaware and the Hudson. A courier could arrive there with dispatches from Philadelphia by noon on the day after they were sent, and through Peekskill communications were open to Albany by river and by road to New England. Morristown itself was so placed as to be highly defensible and could be approached only by such rugged defiles that even militia could be counted upon to make an attempt to storm them extremely costly. But with so few troops of any sort to defend them Washington was convinced that only ignorance of his weakness could account for the enemy's not attacking him, and he begged Congress to send him every militiaman the states of Pennsylvania, Maryland, and Virginia could be persuaded to turn out for service until the new regiments should join him.

In mid-February his secret service, which was excellent, informed him that the British forces in New Jersey had been reinforced by a number of heavy pieces of artillery and several Hessian regiments from the garrison of Newport and that General Howe himself had come down to New Brunswick. This could only mean that the British were about to make a second advance upon Philadelphia. If they did so, Washington was powerless to stop them. He had only 4,000 men, and of those 1,000 were in the hospital and the New England militia would be going home in the middle of March. The New Jersey militia, he wrote to John Hancock on March 14, were so tired that they were beginning to abhor the service. Unless the new troops arrived soon, he continued with eloquent restraint, "we must before long experience some interesting and melancholy event."

Fortunately the enemy offensive did not materialize. Fortunately also, in the circumstances, few of the newly raised regiments put in an appearance at Morristown for several weeks to come. For Washington was finding it difficult to maintain even such troops as he had. The country was well wooded, and in the Loantaka Valley, some three miles from Morristown village green, the main body of the army established itself in huts of its own building, which were reasonably comfortable according to military living standards of the day. The inhabitants were ardent supporters of Independence, and the neighborhood was rich in provender and cattle. But the able and zealous commissary general, Joseph Trumbull, was detained at Philadelphia for the convenience of Congress, and rations were often scanty and sometimes entirely insufficient. There was so little coordination both in his department and in that of the quartermaster general that all over the country their subordinates were bidding against each other, while the soldiers went hungry and grew more ragged day by day.

In dire necessity Washington reluctantly made use of the dictatorial powers Congress had conferred upon him and sent out parties to impress supplies, but the militia frequently plundered what was collected and little of it reached the camp. An observer who reported that the roads about Morristown were filled with naked and half-starved soldiers was doubtless exaggerating. But Washington himself addressed a circular letter to the governors of all the states, begging for shoes, stockings, and shirts, want of which, he told them, had been the ruin of the old army. And on his birthday he wrote that the cry for provisions came to him from every quarter.

The discipline of the troops, which had never been of a high order, naturally deteriorated greatly under these conditions. A Tory historian of the war observed that in order to lighten the tedium of camp life Washington kept his men occupied by continually harassing the enemy, beating up their outposts, and cutting off convoys and foraging parties. Small actions of this kind were frequent. But the New Jersey militia, with their intimate knowledge of the country, were best suited to this work. The Continentals meanwhile, undernourished, half-clad, and bored to desperation, took to gambling, stealing, and fighting among themselves. The increase in swearing was deplorable, and their drinking was only slightly checked by the high prices of venders who, to Washington's deep disgust, swaggered among the huts in the uniforms of colonels and majors of the local militia.

A good many men deserted. In a detached force under the command of General Israel Putnam down at Princeton a whole company of artillery ran off when for several days the rum ration had been lacking and Putnam refused to issue all the arrears at once on the arrival of a fresh supply. Others absconded for less frivolous reasons. Some were led astray by British offers to pay as much as twenty dollars for a deserter's arms, which appeared in enemy newspapers and were reported in patriot journals. Many more, tempted by the large additional bounties some of the states offered in order to fill the ranks of the Continental regiments required of them, slipped away to re-enlist fraudulently as recruits. A man willing to risk a hundred lashes of the cat-o'-nine-tails could thus collect as much as eighty-six and two-thirds dollars in Massachusetts.

Want of money, the tardiness and irregularity of pay, was the soldiers' greatest cause of discontent. Washington's military chest was chronically all but empty; again and again he had to beg for even small amounts of the depreciated currency which was the best Congress could send him. The army's distress on this account, he wrote, was great and the injury done to the service almost inconceivable. The officers he sent out on recruiting duty often had to go without funds to pay the authorized bounties, and the recruiting of the regiments suffered accordingly.

Officers, too, became anxious to quit the service. Some of those on recruiting duty coolly sent in their resignations as soon as they reached their homes. The departure of such men, and of a good many others, could be regarded as good riddance. In the previous October Greene had written: "Our men are infinitely better than their officers." Owing their positions to election by their subordinates, too many of the captains and lieutenants, and even some of the colonels and majors, had no other qualification for their rank than their ability to get votes. Some had proved to be lacking in courage. Most of them remained serenely unconscious of their responsibility for the well-being of those under their command, or were utterly indifferent to it. A few quietly appropriated the pay of their companies, on the rare occasions when any pay at all was forthcoming.

But excellent officers also wished to resign: many of them for the very good reason that the shrunken purchasing power of their pay made it impossible for them to maintain themselves in the army even though they sent nothing home for the support of their families. Others, who had private means, had became infected, Washington believed, with "the universal listlessness" that he found everywhere confronting him. Even the gallant John Glover, whose regiment of Marblehead fishermen had saved the army from capture after the battle of Long Island, had to be persuaded to remain in the service, though he had been promoted to the rank of brigadier general.

"Can any resistance be expected of the people, when deserted by their leaders?" Washington wrote to him. Congress itself seemed incapable of the spirit and energy which the desperate state of affairs demanded. To Robert Morris Washington wrote: "Nor is it in my power to make Congress fully sensible of the real situation of our affairs, and that it is with difficulty, if I may use the expression, that I can, by every means in my power, keep the life and soul of this army together. In a word, when they are at a distance, they think it is but to say, *Presto begone*, and everything is done."

February came to an end; March began; and still the enemy remained quiescent. But the threat of their advance remained imminent; the troops with which to meet it still remained absent; and that nothing should be lacking to the sum of his difficulties, smallpox broke out in both camp and village, and Washington himself came down with a severe attack of quinsy.

3

Washington's illness was severe. On the night of March 7 the doctors resorted to the operation known as cupping, and for a couple of days his friends were anxious about his recovery. But he was in the prime of life—just past his forty-fifth birthday, endowed with a magnificient constitution, and possessed of physical strength which his youthful employment on the Virginia frontier had hardened to endure the extremes of privation, fatigue, and anxiety. So swift was his recovery that one looks in vain in his enormous correspondence for a gap in the dates that would indicate his being incapacitated for more than a day or two. Voluminous letters issued steadily from his headquarters. He was an adept at dictation, as it was practiced before the days of stenography, able to keep five amanuenses busy at once; and he dealt with almost every subject related to the conduct of the war.

He urged the making of maps, of which the army was deplorably lacking, though the British had excellent ones. He recommended a more lenient treatment of the Tories, whose loyalty to the Crown was being strengthened by persecution at the hands of their patriot neighbors and the militia. He was forced to haggle continually with General Howe about the exchange of prisoners, to protest repeatedly against the horrible conditions prevailing on the British prison ships, and at the same time strive to curb the barbarous reprisals inflicted by the Americans on their prisoners of war.

Probably no other man of his day could have coped successfully with the many-sided task that confronted him. Early training and a wide and varied experience of life had combined with unusual physical, mental, and moral qualities to fit him for it. It was no more than the truth that Robert Morris, the patriot financier, wrote to him at this very time in answer to one of Washington's rare confessions of discouragement: "Heaven has blessed you with a firmness of mind, steadiness of countenance, and patience in suffering, that give you an infinite advantage over other men." His tall, well-made form, fine bearing, and the grave imperturbability of his handsome features gave assurance to all who saw him.

As owner and manager of a great Virginia plantation, on which almost every article necessary to human existence was either grown or made, he had gained a practical knowledge that enabled him to deal intelligently with his soldiers' every need, from the making of garments to the butchering of a steer. At Mount Vernon he had been for many years responsible for the health of between two and three hundred human beings, and he met the threat of the smallpox outbreak with wisdom and moral courage based on long experience.

The disease was a deadly enemy of armies in winter quarters in those days: it had done more than the British to drive the Americans out of Canada the previous winter. Vaccination had not yet been discovered, and the only known protection against it was a filthy and sometimes dangerous inoculation. This put the patient to bed for several days with a form of the disease that was generally mild but resulted in death often enough to cause the treatment to be generally feared. Its use in Virginia had been prohibited by law, but Washington was a firm believer in its efficacy.

He ordered the whole army to be subjected to it and new troops to be inoculated at Philadelphia and other mobilization centers before joining his command. Most of the thousand men on the sick list when the British offensive first threatened were undergoing this treatment. The local inhabitants, of whom three died in each week of February in Morristown, supported these measures heartily. The congregations of the two churches in the village gave up their buildings to be used as hospitals and held their services out of doors when the weather permitted them to do so. The spread of the disease was soon checked, and it was eventually eradicated from the army.

The epidemic of desertion proved to be more stubborn. In order to make it useless for the culprits to return home Washington begged the governors of the various states for laws that would punish not only the offenders but any persons who harbored them. He counteracted the blandishments of the enemy with a finesse of which he was often capable, though it is seldom attributed to him. Knowing that he could count on the gossip of the latrines to spread the story, he caused it to be mentioned casually at his headquarters mess table that deserters who sold their arms to the British were seized and themselves sold as slaves to the East India Company. But to correct the basic cause of the trouble, the irregularity and often total lack of pay, he could do little beyond writing urgent letters to Congress; and by spring his need of men had become so great that he promised pardon to all who had deserted, even second offenders, if they would return to the colors before the middle of May.

Trained from boyhood to earn an arduous living, and an ardent lover of his own home, Washington could well understand the problems of his officers and men who were poor or in moderate circumstances, and he sympathized warmly with their longing to be back at their shops, their farms and their firesides. The very limitations of his military education were an advantage to him in the handling of these men and boys to whom soldiering was an avocation in the fullest sense of the word. His command of provincial troops in the French and Indian War had taught him not only their virtues and defects but the reasons behind their habitual casualness, their slovenliness and frequent unreliability. Horatio Gates and Charles Lee, trained in the British army from their youth and accustomed to the automatic obedience of hireling soldiers, were contemptuous and distrustful of American volunteers who expected to understand the reason for an order before they obeyed it and who often acted on their own responsibility. Washington saw in their critical intelligence and individual initiative qualities out of which could be made far more efficient soldiers than the most highly trained mercenaries.

He bore himself toward them accordingly, and many a man who cared little whether King George or the Continental Congress governed the country was bound to the colors by loyalty to a chief who shared equally in his hardships, sought the most dangerous places on the battlefield, and treated him as a reasonable being. Of the militia who served under his command he was equally understanding. He addressed them "very spiritedly and politely," one Jerseyman noted after they had made a number of successful raids on the British outposts and convoys in the neighborhood of New Brunswick. They went home to spread throughout the country the fame of his fine qualities and excellent ability, and he became a kind of personification of his country's cause. And although the regulars who felt his influence were few during these winter months, they were the nucleus of the army that was to assemble in the spring; and from these few it received the tone and spirit that carried it through the terrible ordeal of the year to come.

For his relations with the great—with governors, legislatures, and enemy generals—he was equally well equipped. The richest man in the thirteen colonies, he enjoyed the assurance and prestige of great wealth. He was under no obligation to Congress for his appointment as commander in chief. He had accepted the position only after much persuasion. He would take nothing for his services, except his expenses, and of these he kept a scrupulous account. His former membership in the Virginia House of Burgesses and in Congress enabled him to understand and make allowances for legislative vagaries and jealousies that continually hampered and sometimes ruined his best efforts. Believing deeply that the military must always be subservient to the civil authority, he rarely and only in cases of absolute necessity ignored or disobeyed orders from Congress, or made use of his dictatorial powers when a thing could be accomplished by means of the civil government. Even when Congress adopted, as it did in March of this year, a resolution that contained a thinly veiled censure for having accomplished so little this winter, he answered it with patient irony.

"Could I accomplish," he wrote to President Hancock, "the important objects so eagerly wished by Congress—'confining the enemy within their present quarters, preventing their getting supplies from the country, and totally subduing them before they are reinforced'— I should be happy indeed. But what prospect or hope can there be of my effecting so desirable a work at this time? The enclosed return, to which I solicit the most serious attention of Congress, comprehends the whole force I have in Jersey. It is but a handful, and bears no proportion, in the scale of numbers, to that of the enemy."

His wife arrived at Morristown in the week following the worst of his illness, and her brisk and cheerful presence doubtless helped him to keep his temper in such circumstances. General Greene wrote home that the commander in chief and his wife were evidently very fond of each other. In after years Martha Washington used to say with satisfaction that she usually heard the closing guns of every campaign and the opening ones of the next. She set to work at once to alleviate the austerity of the life he had been leading thus far by moving him into more commodious quarters than the two rooms above the bar in the Freeman's Tavern which had been serving him as bedroom and office.

"Lady Washington" to her contemporaries—since some sort of

title seemed to be required in those days by her husband's exalted position—had arrived in what was described as "a plain chariot." But her postilions rode in liveries of white and scarlet, and her reputation for great wealth aroused expectations of some pomp and ceremony among the notables of the neighborhood. They dressed in their very best for their first calls upon her, only to find her a quite simple and unpretentious person, "rather plump, but fresh and of an agreeable countenance," as one of them wrote of her, wearing a check apron over a plain brown dress, and with her hands busy at knitting a stocking for her husband. She had a pleasant way of referring to the commander in chief as "the old man," which doubtless lessened the awesome effect of his grave presence at social gatherings. It was not long before she had these new acquaintances organized in knitting and sewing clubs for the benefit of the soldiers, and she became the center of a cheerful society of far more sophistication and culture than might have been expected in those remote and rugged hills.

Morristown was what the wife of a Virginia colonel of light horse described as "a clever little village," which three church spires—it had but two—would have made "pretentious." There were about fifty dwellings, two excellent taverns, and several patriot families of wealth and distinction who had fled from New York and the enemy-occupied area of New Jersey had taken refuge there. Among these were the Elias Boudinots and John Morton, "the rebel banker." The wives of several of the general officers and regimental commanders joined their husbands as the winter wore away. The fine house of Major General William Alexander, who was always known as Lord Stirling because of his pretensions to a lapsed Scottish earldom, and whose brother-in-law was William Livingston, the patriot governor of New Jersey, was close by and filled with guests.

At Freeman's Tavern there was a commodious room for assemblies and other important occasions. Young Alexander Hamilton, whom Washington had lately taken from the command of a field battery to be one of his aides, presided at the headquarters dinner table and kept the conversation lively. Of evenings there were "tea drinking parties," since tea no longer paid a tax to the British Crown; and as spring advanced, Mrs. Washington rode with her husband through the burgeoning beauty of the woods and hills on "horseback parties" which the presence of Governor Livingston's three lovely daughters made popular with the General's aides.

Washington loved to ride and was devoted to his horses. Observers had noted with amusement that the first greetings between him and his wife were no sooner exchanged than he asked eagerly about the health and condition of his horses at Mount Vernon. He spent hours in the saddle almost every day, visiting the cantonments in the Loantaka Valley, the outposts and less distant detachments, and studying the terrain for miles around. He found time to attend Masonic meetings in the large room at Freeman's Tavern and on one occasion, it is said, received communion with the local Presbyterian congregation. But the pressure of his multitudinous cares and anxieties never slackened.

The slipshod method by which Congress attempted to deal with every branch of the government through committees compelled him to add to his work as commander in chief many of the functions of a secretary of war and chief of the general staff. Not only were soldiers lacking; there was a want of muskets even among the few troops at Morristown, and Washington greatly feared that there were not enough weapons in any of the states. The absence of any system of accountability had resulted in what he called "a scandalous loss, waste, and private appropriation of fire arms." When time-expired men went home, they simply shouldered their muskets and walked off with them. Most welcome was the news of the arrival of two ships from France—one of them at Philadelphia, the other at Portsmouth, New Hampshire—with a total of 23,000 muskets, a number of cannon, and other much needed equipment.

To speed up the production of other articles—cannon, cartridges, hatchets or tomahawks, and wagons for intrenching tools—Washington sent Nathanael Greene down to Philadelphia. Greene was ten years his junior and had been called "the learned blacksmith" because he always kept an open book beside him while he waited for the iron to heat in the family's Rhode Island foundry. He had led the Rhode Island troops to the siege of Boston in 1775 and had been in the fighting ever since. He was a thorough student of the art of war, understood the army's every need, and was the man to get what was wanting, if it was obtainable.

A shortage of blankets and tents presented another difficult problem, though the French ships brought a limited supply of the former. Of the latter, 1,600, enough to have sheltered 8,000 men, went up in smoke when Tryon, the Tory governor of New York, crossed Long Island Sound on a raid into Connecticut in April and destroyed the American military stores at Danbury. Other supplies and equipment were burned by a British force that caught the American garrison at Peekskill napping. Only by appropriating to the troops under his immediate command all the tentage he could lay his hands on was Washington able to equip them with even inadequate shelter for the approaching campaign.

4

But more perplexing than any material difficulty was one of wounded feelings among his officers. Seldom unmindful that they were by nature and training civilians who, like himself, had taken up arms for this war only, Washington treated their shortcomings, complaints, and grievances with a consideration and patience that were fairly monumental. To General Horatio Gates, who faced at Albany an increasing threat of invasion from Canada, he wrote courteously to explain his action regarding the tentage. The army assembling at Morristown, he pointed out, must be an army of maneuver, living in the field, whereas Gates's troops would be acting purely on the defensive and could shelter themselves in huts and barracks.

When General Heath made a laughable fiasco of the demonstration against the British post at Kingsbridge, Washington sent him an official letter expressing no more than mild regret and reserved for a private communication a severe rebuke in which he called Heath's management of the operation "farcical." He gave Heath a desired permission to go home, only asking him to make his absence as brief as he conveniently could, since other generals also wished to visit their homes before the opening of the campaign.

To Major General John Sullivan, who fancied himself slighted in

some obscure matter of an independent command, he replied with
an admonition as kindly as it was firm. Although only thirty-seven
years old this February, Sullivan had become a New Hampshire
lawyer of considerable wealth before the war. He was an excellent
officer: it was not his fault that he and his troops had been surrounded
and captured at the battle of Long Island. Returned to the American
army by a prompt exchange of prisoners, he had commanded the
right wing at Trenton with singular judgment and success. But
Washington now told him plainly that no other officer of rank in
the whole army had so often thought himself slighted and ill-used.
"Your ideas and mine respecting separate commands," the letter
continued, "have but little analogy. . . I have not time to dwell upon
a subject of this kind. But I shall quit it with an earnest exhortation
that you will not suffer yourself to be teased with evils, that exist only
in the imagination."

By the beginning of March, however, he was sympathizing earnestly
with the grievances of several of his other generals. He had asked
Congress to appoint three lieutenant generals, nine major generals,
and twenty-seven brigadiers. But down in Philadelphia John Adams
was not the only congressman so blind and deaf to the exigencies
of an efficient military establishment as to insist on the apportionment
of generalships to each state according to the number of troops it
furnished to the army. Adams would even have had the generals
elected annually after the manner of ancient Greece and Rome. The
list of appointments that Congress sent to the commander in chief
late in February contained no lieutenant generals at all, only five
major generals, and but ten brigadiers.

The consequence was that a number of officers who richly deserved
promotion were passed over and felt deeply hurt. John Stark, who
had served with distinction from Bunker Hill to Princeton, retired
to his New Hampshire farm—whence he emerged the following
August to lead the militia to victory at Bennington; and he was not
the only one who persisted in quitting the Continental service in
spite of Washington's dissuasion. Benedict Arnold, the hero of
Quebec and Lake Champlain and senior brigadier, was omitted from
the list of new major generals for the reason that Connecticut already

had its full quota of general officers, and he consented to withhold his resignation only upon Washington's pointing out to him how great would be the need of generals when the army was finally assembled. A later list of appointments rectified some of the injustices done by the first one, though by no means all of them. Arnold was promoted to major general's rank in recognition of his services during the raid on Danbury, but he remained, in spite of his protests, junior to some who had been below him in his old grade.

As far as it went, however, the list was well chosen. Of the major generals Thomas Mifflin had covered the retreat from Long Island, had been a tower of strength in the Princeton campaign, and was now acting as quartermaster general at Philadelphia. Arthur St. Clair, an Edinburgh Scot, had fought under Amherst at Ticonderoga in the French and Indian War, and in Canada and at Trenton and Princeton in this one. Adam Stephen, another Trenton veteran, had been lieutenant colonel in Washington's own regiment in the French and Indian War. Lord Stirling had seen service in the previous war, and at Long Island and in the campaign of the past winter. Benjamin Lincoln was new to the Continental service, but he had commanded the Massachusetts militia with marked ability last fall.

The new brigadiers were equally good. Their records included service in the French and Indian War, at the siege of Boston, and in the fighting of the past year. Notable among them were John Glover, Anthony Wayne, who was in command of a brigade of his fellow Pennsylvanians at Ticonderoga this winter, and the Reverend John Peter Muhlenberg, the gallant Lutheran pastor from Virginia. Muhlenberg was a newcomer to this theater of the war, but he had taken part in the defense of Charleston in 1776. He had led a wild life in his student days in Germany, where he had been sent to study for holy orders, had been expelled from the University of Halle, and had got his military training in the ranks of the army of the Prince of Anspach. He had preached his last sermon with his Geneva gown over his uniform and had told his congregation that there was a time to pray and a time to preach but now was the time to fight.

As spring advanced, however, the whole matter of promotions was complicated for the commander in chief by an influx of foreign

volunteers—French, German, and Polish officers—most of whom
Silas Deane, in his capacity of American Commissioner, had sent over
from Paris with recommendations for rank that were too often
based only on what the applicant thought himself entitled to. Accepted by Congress at their face value, these gentlemen arrived at
Morristown with expectations of being given the command of regiments, brigades, and even divisions, over the heads of American
officers who had raised the troops they commanded and had served
in the war from its beginning. Some of them proved to be officers of
character and ability, especially those of the artillery and engineers.
But even of the latter, two who held high rank in the French army
appeared to Washington, who was a competent judge of such matters,
to know nothing of engineering.

In February Washington had described himself as "laid under" by
the application of French officers for commissions. Near the end of
May he wrote Richard Henry Lee that he was "haunted and teased
to death by the importunity of some, and the dissatisfaction of
others," and he complained to Congress of the effrontery of mere
captains and lieutenants, "hungry adventurers," who had mysteriously
lost their papers, but who nevertheless expected field officers' commands, though they knew not a word of English. Congress, however,
was so impressed by the prestige of foreign military training that four
officers of the French army held commissions as American generals
by the time the campaign opened.

The performance of these gentlemen was the reverse of brillant.
De Fermoy, who had already exhibited doubtful courage in the
Princeton campaign, was to prove incompetent before the summer
was over. Deborre was to retire before the end of the year rather
than face a court of inquiry. Of Thomas Conway, Irish-born major
in the Regiment of Anjou, much more is to be told later, but little
good. The fourth, a certain Monsieur Ducoudray, caused trouble
from the day he landed in Boston, which he did with great éclat,
early in May of this year.

Although his rank in the French service had not been high,
Ducoudray had the covert backing of the French government and immediately caused it to be understood that Deane had promised

him the post of chief not only of the American artillery but also of the engineers, with rank superior to that of even such veteran major generals as Sullivan and Greene. The fat was in the fire at once, and in the highest quarters. As soon as Washington heard of the matter, he wrote both to Congress and to Richard Henry Lee to protest against entrusting so important a position to a foreigner and to warn them that Henry Knox, the present able and devoted chief of artillery, would undoubtedly resign if he were superseded.

The injustice of the thing cried to high heaven. Knox, though a Boston bookseller by trade and only twenty-seven years old on his next birthday, had been for years a thorough student of gunnery and military engineering. He had joined the army in its early days at Cambridge, had laid out the fortifications there, and had soon proved himself to be a born artilleryman. It was he who brought over the snow-clad Berkshires from captured Ticonderoga the guns that forced the British out of Boston. The *esprit de corps* and technical skill which the American gunners had demonstrated on every battlefield since then were his creation.

When he slipped out of Boston to join the "rebel" forces, his wife Lucy, child of Tory parents though she was, went with him, with his sword sewn into the lining of her petticoat. He wrote to her now that although he did not feel that he could resign while the country was in its present straits, he thought that this campaign would be his last; and he informed Congress that he intended to leave the service if he were displaced by Ducoudray. Greene and Sullivan also threatened to resign.

The response of Congress was a resolution rebuking all three. John Adams drafted it and, in a personal letter to Greene, advised him either to apologize or to leave the service. "The delicate point of honor," Adams wrote to him, "is one of the most putrid corruptions of absolute monarchy" and "must be bridled." Greene sent a dignified reply to Congress, ignored Adams's letter; and the warm friendship between the two came to an abrupt end. Knox refused to acknowledge that he had been guilty of any impropriety. And there, so far as the American generals were concerned, the matter was allowed to rest. Congress decided that Deane had exceeded his powers in the

Ducoudray appointment. Washington suggested that Ducoudray be mollified by high rank in another field of activity, and the office of Inspector General of Ordnance and Military Manufactory was created for him. He continued, however, to make a nuisance of himself until September, when a fractious horse, from which his *amour-propre* would not permit him to dismount, drowned him at a ferry on the Schuylkill.

The campaign had opened before the matter was settled, and there have been armies in which it would have been dangerous for the commander in chief to take the field with two of his ranking division commanders and his chief of artillery at odds with their government. But with Greene, Sullivan, and Knox the cause of Independence came a long way ahead of personal ambition; and to them Washington, rather than the collection of politicians at Philadelphia, was the representative of that cause. Throughout the whole affair they continued to discharge their duties with undiminished devotion. Knox returned from Massachusetts, where he had spent most of the winter establishing an arsenal at Springfield, as cheerful and optimistic as he seldom failed to be. He asked no better than to resume his post at the head of the artillery with the rank of brigadier general, which he had received in December.

After so many weeks of bickering and self-seeking, his return and that of Wayne, who was ordered down from Ticonderoga to take command of the new Pennsylvania Continental regiments, must have made a pleasant change for the harassed commander in chief. In spite of the best care that Wayne had been able to give them, hunger, pestilence, and the northern winter had reduced the 2,000 troops under his command there to 900. Himself he had sustained with frequent bottles of Bungundy and had kept up his spirits by reading *The Life of Tristram Shandy, Gent.,* though his surroundings, he wrote home, appeared to be "the last part of the world that God had made, and I have some ground to believe that it was finished in the dark."

The Ticonderoga winter had so damaged his wardrobe that he arrived at Morristown in a rusty reddish coat, faded black cravat, and a battered three-cornered hat that bore a sadly tarnished cockade.

But it was not long before he appeared, smart and immaculate, in lambskin breeches and a uniform coat of bright blue with red linings, the work of his Philadelphia tailor. He loved the "spit and polish" of soldiering, assigned a barber to every company of his command, promising punishment to any man who appeared on parade unshaven; and he complained bitterly to the Council of Pennsylvania when his new regiments arrived in hunting shirts already so ragged that they were, he wrote, despised both by themselves and by others.

He was noted for a certain "vaunting style," which was supposed to resemble that of the celebrated French Marshal Villars. He was reputed to be, after Washington, the wealthiest man in the country. But he sought promotion as little as Knox did. When the army finally took shape, he was placed in command of the equivalent of a division, a position that entitled him to the rank of major general. He was doing the work of three generals, he boasted. But he made no effort to be advanced beyond the grade of brigadier, which had recently been conferred upon him.

But the best of officers can accomplish nothing without soldiers to carry out their orders. Arms, equipment, tentage, and supplies are useless if there are no men to use them; and as the weeks of spring slipped by and the new troops continued to come in only by driblets, there must have been times when Washington asked himself whether all his preparations, negotiations, expedients, and improvisations were not mere acts of a mistaken faith. In April he was writing to his brother that the campaign would open without men on the American side unless they came in faster than he expected; to Patrick Henry that no troops had joined him from New England and but few from the southward; and to Hancock of "the langour and supineness that prevail everywhere."

5

It was past the middle of May before the new Continental regiments began to arrive at Morristown in any considerable numbers, though by that time they had been in existence for several weeks. They were held back, many of them, on absurd or frivolous pretexts.

It seemed next to impossible, Washington wrote in his exasperation, to make the officers of any state exert themselves to bring their men to the field, as if it did not matter whether they came at once or a month later.

These gentlemen, probably, and quite naturally, preferred their snug home quarters to the rickety huts and hardships of camp life in the Jersey hills and deferred their departure to the front as long as they could find a decent excuse. But higher authorities were not less to blame. Congress, following a pernicious practice of disposing of troops by issuing orders to them directly, not only without consulting the commander in chief but even without letting him know that it had done so, detained regiments at Philadelphia, where they were useless. Some of the state executives issued orders that Washington called "ridiculous and inconsistent." Even the able and usually broad-minded Governor Trumbull of Connecticut, made apprehensive by the raid on Danbury, would have held back two of his state's Continental regiments if Washington had not protested.

By the 20th of May, however, Knox was able to write to his wife: "Our forces come in pretty fast and are disciplining for war . . . well supplied with arms and ammunition of all kinds [but] increasing most rapidly in impiety." Disciplining they undoubtedly needed badly. Late in January Washington had warned Congress: "We have very little time to do a very great work in. The arranging, providing for, and disciplining of a hundred odd battalions is not to be accomplished in a day; nor is it to be done at all with any degree of propriety when we have once entered upon the active part of a campaign." But that was the task that now confronted him, even though the number of battalions was far from what he had hoped for.

Individually, however, the men were the makings of excellent soldiers, strong, healthy, in high spirits, and eager for battle. Nearly all of them were good shots with either musket or rifle, and many of them had been under fire on the battlefields of '75 and '76. Most of them had enlisted for three years, and their commander could now hope to introduce in the course of time a uniform system of discipline and training, for which there had been no opportunity in the past.

Equipment and supplies were adequate, if only barely so. The shortage of tents had not been entirely overcome, and there were just enough blankets to go around. The commissary department was still on a hand-to-mouth basis. There was an outbreak of what was known at the time and for a century after as "camp fever," which was believed to have been caused by a lack of fresh vegetables in the ration. This Greene proposed to cure by the daily administration to each man of a half-pint of vinegar mixed with molasses, rum, flour and water. But nobody went hungry, and neither the disease nor the remedy seriously affected the health of the troops as a whole.

The army's most serious want, however, was the fundamental one of numbers. The table of organization, to be sure, was impressive: forty-two regiments, which were grouped in five divisions of two brigades each. But officers and men together added up to only 8,378, although the meager ranks of too many of the battalions had been swelled by an infusion of short-term militiamen. And the cavalry were far too few. Shortly before the opening of the campaign they numbered only 180, not enough to furnish the necessary mounted sentinels and patrols, whereas the British had upwards of 700 with their forces in New Jersey. Cavalry was expensive everywhere and especially in America, where a horse that would have sold for ten pounds in England fetched forty.

But inadequate as his forces were, Washington's assembling of so many men under his immediate command subjected him to some criticism at the time and has been a target for several armchair strategists since then. As commander in chief, he was held to be responsible for the defense of every part of the country; appeals for protection against anticipated invasion or local raids came to him from many quarters; and his letters contain frequent and patient explanations of the first principle of strategy: namely, that the attempt to defend every point results in weakness everywhere, and that only in the concentration of force at the right time and place lies the possibility of success.

The greatest justifiable cause for anxiety was on the northern frontier. After defeating Arnold's flotilla on Lake Champlain in the previous autumn, Sir Guy Carleton, the governor of Canada, had

retired to winter quarters. But he was expected to resume his advance
with the return of warm weather, and it was reliably reported that
he had been reinforced by a large number of British regulars and
German auxiliaries. These were expected to move against Albany
by way of Lake Champlain under General John Burgoyne, while
a strong body of Tories and Indians pushed down the valley
of the Mohawk from Oswego with the same objective.

Washington, however, greatly doubted that the concentration of
enemy troops in Canada was more than a ruse to lure him into
weakening his own army by sending reinforcements to Major General
Philip Schuyler, who had lately relieved Gates in command at
Albany and was organizing the defense of that area. If Howe followed
the rules of sound strategy, as Washington naturally expected him
to do, he would bring the troops in Canada to New York by sea
and thus be able to take the field with an overwhelming superiority
of numbers. Howe's position at New York and in New Jersey gave
him what are known in military parlance as "interior lines," which
meant, in this case, that he could move directly against a variety
of objectives—once more across New Jersey against Philadelphia, or
up the Hudson to attack the forts at Peekskill, or across Long Island
Sound to Newport, which would afford him a base for an advance
against Boston—whereas Washington could oppose him only by
long and circuitous marches on the periphery of the theater of
operations. Howe's great fleet of transports, moreover, with the warships of his brother to escort them, could land his army at any point
on the coast before Washington could learn of his whereabouts.

But if the invasion from Canada turned out to be genuine—
supposing even that the fortress at Ticonderoga failed to bring it to
a halt—Washington was convinced that it would not penetrate very
far, if it were resolutely opposed by the troops that Schuyler would
have at his disposal. In Braddock's expedition he had seen an army
of British regulars utterly defeated by a feeble opposing force in a
wilderness similar to the Lake George country. But with Burgoyne
pushing toward Albany, Howe must certainly advance up the Hudson
to take Schuyler's forces in the rear; in that event Washington had
need of as large an army as possible to support the Peekskill forts

in stopping him; and in any event, as Washington pointed out, there was no use in guarding frontiers if the enemy were already ranging the interior of the country.

He sent Knox, Greene, and Arnold to Peekskill to see to the strengthening of Fort Montgomery, the building of galleys, and the closing of the channel with a great boom and chain against the passage of enemy warships. He strengthened Schuyler's forces by sending to Albany many of the Continental regiments that had been raised in New England and New York. But several of these he held at Peekskill, whence they could be moved quickly to Morristown or up the Hudson as circumstances might require. His own command he formed chiefly of regiments from New Jersey, Pennsylvania, Delaware, Maryland, and Virginia, kept them busy at drill and target practice, and waited for the enemy to move. The British position and superior numbers now forbade any such daring attempt to seize the initiative as their dispersal had favored in December.

By the grace of God, working once more through his highly imperfect servant, Sir William Howe, the enemy had remained inactive throughout the spring. Save for a quick thrust at General Lincoln's advance post at Bound Brook, some sixteen miles to the south of Morristown, in April, and as swift a withdrawal, they had made no movement of importance. But it was known at American headquarters that some reinforcements from England had arrived at New York, and additional troops from Newport at Amboy, and that for some weeks New York and Staten Island had been humming with preparations for an offensive.

In early May the evacuation of the sick and wounded, camp women, and other noncombatants from New Brunswick and Amboy was only one of the indications that Howe was about to open the campaign. But in what direction, and whether by land or sea, remained uncertain. Spies reported that seventy transports lay ready to embark troops in New York harbor, that in the horse transports the stalls were being lined with sheepskins as if for a sea voyage, and that flatboats suitable for landing craft in an amphibious operation had been under construction for several weeks. On the other hand, the arrival from England of a pontoon train, which might have ensured the capture of Philadelphia if it had been available at the Delaware in December, indicated an advance by land. In that case the objective must certainly be Philadelphia.

Patriot secret agents in New York gave warning that four spies—a captain, a lieutenant, and two sergeants of the British service—were operating in the Morristown area, disguised as countrymen; and Washington told Greene to be on the lookout for "a suspicious person met with at Bullion's tavern." Still further to confirm the conclusion that Philadelphia would be the enemy's goal, a British force under the command of Major General Sir James Grant advanced to Bound Brook for the second time on May 26 and attempted to feel out the American position there. In the skirmish that resulted a cannon ball took the head off the British general's horse. He was badly bruised by the fall of the animal, and his coat was plastered with mud—a fact that Wayne noted with satisfaction, since this was the Grant who had boasted in Parliament two years before that he could march from one end of the American continent to the other with five thousand men.

Two days later Washington broke up his camp at Morristown and led his army southward to the Middlebrook Valley, a little to the north of Bound Brook and only about ten miles northwest of New Brunswick. Thence he could both threaten the flank of any British advance on Philadelphia and easily march back through Morristown to Peekskill if Howe should move up the Hudson. Tactically his position was so strong, with the Raritan River in his front and deep ravines covering his flanks, that Howe might well hesitate to attack him; and strategically it was such that if Howe ignored his presence and pushed on, he would be leaving an unbeaten army in his rear. On the last day of May Greene wrote jubilantly to Sullivan, with whose division of 1,600 men Washington had extended his right as far as Princeton: "The Philistines are upon thee, Samson!" Sullivan drew back into the Sourland Hills. But nothing happened for almost another fortnight.

Washington was well content to await Sir William Howe's convenience. Every day now his forces grew stronger: the New Jersey militia turned out in large numbers; the Rhode Island regiments were hastening from Peekskill to join him; and down on the Delaware, where he had placed Benedict Arnold in command, the Pennsylvania militia were rallying enthusiastically to the defense of the river crossings if that should become necessary.

It was the 11th of June when the British finally advanced. But when they did so, they came not down the direct route to Philadelphia through Princeton and Trenton but straight westward on the road through Middlebush and Somerset Court House that led to the Delaware at Coryell's Ferry (the present Lambertville): almost under Washington's nose, with the right flank of their long column wide open, as if daring him to fall upon it.

☆

A Military Game of Chess

1

WASHINGTON'S SATISFACTION in General Howe's dilatory conduct of the war was far from being shared by the British and Hessian troops in New Jersey. They had passed what a Hessian chaplain described as "a disturbed and hateful winter" and had been spoiling for a fight for weeks. Ever since mid-January the American forces had held a line that ran from Princeton northward through Bound Brook and thence eastward to Woodbridge, which was but three miles from Perth Amboy; and within that area the angry and enterprising New Jersey militia, with occasional stiffening by detachments of Washington's small force of regulars at Morristown, had subjected them to every form of fatigue, discomfort, privation, and danger.

At neither Perth Amboy nor New Brunswick was one of their men safe if he strayed beyond the line of sentinels. They strengthened their positions with redoubts and entrenchments. But false alarms frequently kept them up all night, and so continual were the attacks that the outposts had to be doubled at daybreak. It was found necessary to turn out a whole brigade, even of the Guards, to cover one flank of a foraging expedition: the Americans were so numerous and so skillful in firing and falling back from thicket to thicket and reversing the operation as soon as their opponents began to retire. They knew very well what they were about, observed Lord Percy. He had suffered severely from just such tactics at Lexington and had recently gone back to England in disgust at Howe's method of carrying on the war.

Feeling became bitter on both sides, the fighting savage. In support of a protest against the behavior of the British Washington sent in to their outposts the body of a young American which had been brutally slashed and mangled. The outpost commander refused to receive it and returned it with the explanation that he was not the coroner.

The British garrisons found themselves, as a disgusted Tory historian of the war phrased it, "in a manner beleaguered." Their horses died from want of forage. Food became scanty. Even officers' messes were reduced to eating the army ration of salt meat and ammunition bread, whose badness was so notorious that the King himself deplored it. Food, fodder, and even fuel had to be sent from New York, and the ships that brought it up the Raritan passed under the fire of musketry and, on one occasion, of cannon from the banks.

Housing in the two little New Jersey towns was utterly inadequate to shelter the sudden influx of ten thousand soldiers. Barracks had to be improvised out of barns and sheds. When seven thousand more troops arrived from Newport and elsewhere for Howe's abortive offensive in February, many of them had to be bunked on board ships anchored in the river; and what with crowded quarters, bad weather, and the want of fresh food, many fell sick.

In February Howe had come down to New Brunswick intending to drive Washington out of his mountain fastness and destroy the nucleus of the army he was endeavoring to gather there. But the miserable condition of the British horses and reports of the great natural strength of the American position at Morristown caused him to decide to wait for the season of green fodder, settled weather, dry roads, and reinforcements from England: a decision that was probably confirmed by a short, sharp fight between his escort and about a thousand "rebels" on his way back to New York. A good many of his officers, however, felt that a successful attack on Washington's position, strong though it might be, would have been less costly than the steady attrition of sniping, ambush, and disease to which their troops were continually subjected.

At New Brunswick they strove to lighten the tedium of existence by formal calls, supper parties, and dances that were rather dim imitations of the British-Tory gaiety in New York that winter. The young ladies of the neighborhood, whatever their politics, were not so set in their opinions as to scorn the allurements of partners in scarlet and gold. But Colonel Harcourt of the Dragoons observed that England had not two disinterested friends in the town. The hard lot of the royal troops in New Jersey became a subject of conversation in London drawing rooms. King George himself did what he could to cheer them by sending his formal thanks to Colonel Mawhood for the stubborn fight that officer had put up at Princeton, and to Harcourt for making a prisoner of Charles Lee, formerly of the British army, who had become a major general in the American service. Evidently the fiasco of the recent campaign had made His Majesty grateful for small favors.

In New York Mr. Ambrose Serle, secretary to Admiral Earl Howe, saw "a happy appearance of the speedy termination of the war" in exaggerated stories of Washington's illness. On the word of a maid-servant who had come through the lines it was gossiped about that the American commander in chief had become "agitated in his countenance and incoherent in his speech . . . his eyes sunk and dejected . . . frequently caught in tears about the house . . . constantly dejected and unhappy." But a young British deputy adjutant general was more impressed by the fact that merely in covering a foraging expedition Mawhood's brigade had lost one officer and five men killed and sixty-five wounded.

Early in April Lord Cornwallis, who had assumed command of the British troops in New Jersey, became thoroughly out of patience with the harassment of his outposts and struck the first of those blows at Lincoln's post at Bound Brook that have already been mentioned. He surprised and routed the American detachment there and breakfasted at the house where Lincoln had dined the night before. But he accomplished little else except the capture of Lincoln's papers, from which he learned that the Americans were singularly well informed about the British dispositions.

Of this incident and the raid on Danbury, which took place about the same time, Horace Walpole expressed an opinion of Howe's inactivity that was held by a large part of the British public. "Cornwallis," he wrote to his friend Mann, "has gained a puny advantage and Governor Tryon has burnt a magazine." In America the disappointed Tories sneered bitterly at Sir William's amorous diversions, at his gunning and his gambling. But he continued to enjoy his life in New York for another couple of months, confident of the favor of his sovereign, who had rewarded his services of the past year by making him a Knight Commander of the Bath and receiving his wife at St. James's "most graciously," according to the newspapers.

Howe was nearing his forty-eighth birthday, he was growing fat, and he was by nature self-indulgent. In Boston he had picked up a charming mistress, a Mrs. Josiah Loring, who had accompanied him to Halifax and rejoined him in New York, where she queened it in the ballroom of the City Tavern this winter and shared his pleasure in playing for hundred-guinea stakes. But he knew very well what he intended to do in the approaching summer's campaign, was confident as to the time it would take to accomplish it, and made as sure as possible that every means necessary to that end should be at his disposal.

By the end of May he had assembled in the New Brunswick-Amboy area a field army of 11,000 troops as excellent as his most experienced officers, both British and German, had ever seen; the Hessians, though annoyingly slow on the march and too heavily clad for the American summer, made a splendid appearance. Their riflemen, Jägers in their own tongue, whom the British called chasseurs, were notably smart in boots and green uniforms. The British soldiers, in marked contrast to their scantily clad opponents, each had an extra shirt, an extra pair of shoes and stockings, and extra heels and soles in their knapsacks. Warm weather had made it possible to relieve the crowded quarters by placing many of the troops under canvas. Their health was now excellent; spring fodder had restored to fine condition the horses of the dragoons, the artillery, and the baggage train; and strict orders had been issued to keep down the number of the baggage wagons, which had seriously impeded operations in the campaign of the previous year.

On June 11 the army finally took the road. But the orders about the wagons had not been obeyed. The train comprised more than a thousand vehicles, and the march was correspondingly slow. At the end of the second day the advance guard had reached a point only

three miles west of Somerset Court House (the present Millstone)
and but thirteen miles from New Brunswick. The rest of the column
stretched back through the hamlet of Middlebush for several miles,
presenting, as Howe intended it to do, a tempting opportunity for
Washington to sweep down upon it from his position at Middlebrook.

The lure, however, was too obvious to mislead a commander of
Washington's prudence and perspicacity. He persisted in remaining
where he was, and Howe found himself, as Washington had foreseen,
on the horns of a dilemma. He must either attack the American
position at Middlebrook, which his senior officer of engineers reported to be naturally so strong and so well fortified that an attempt
to storm it would be disastrous, or else make a mortifying retirement.
He dared not push on to the well-guarded crossings of the Delaware
while Washington's growing army remained undefeated in his rear.

For six days Howe pondered the problem, though he was compelled to concentrate his forces at Middlebush while he did so, and,
to the derision of the Americans, fortify his camp. For Daniel
Morgan's frontier riflemen and parties of New Jersey farmers on
horseback cut up his outposts by night and ambushed his convoys
by day. On the 19th he pocketed his pride and retired, not only
to New Brunswick but on to Amboy, where he began ferrying his
troops over to Staten Island.

Knox gloated that the movement had cost the British about a
hundred men killed, wounded, and captured. But Washington,
though he sent Greene forward with three brigades in pursuit of the
enemy, followed cautiously with the main body of his army. Greene
cleared the Hessians out of the redoubts at New Brunswick with a
single charge and might have captured the whole of the British rear
guard if delay and loss of orders to Sullivan's division and a brigade
under Maxwell had not prevented their cooperation. Pressing forward on Greene's left, Stirling's division had all but reached Staten
Island Sound when suddenly Howe turned about, and the pursuers
became the pursued.

At the head of troops who were furious at having to show their
backs without a fight to adversaries whom they despised, Cornwallis

fell upon Stirling's division and routed it, capturing three of its guns. Through summer heat so terrific that several of the British flankers went mad and fired on their own troops, Howe pushed northward with his whole army as far as Westfield, as if he intended to seize the mountain passes through which ran the American communications to Peekskill. He hoped that to prevent this maneuver Washington would attack him where he stood. But Washington had marched back to Middlebrook and remained there, confident that Howe would never involve his army in country where the Americans would have every opportunity for the kind of fighting they liked best; and on June 27 nothing remained for Howe to do but retire once more.

This time he moved his entire army to Staten Island, abandoning to the patriot forces the whole of New Jersey except the post at Paulus Hook, where Jersey City now stands. "Never was an army more chagrined than by this retreat," wrote a British observer. The soldiers relieved their frustration by plundering and cruelties which their officers appear to have made no effort to restrain. To force a respectable woman of middle age to reveal the hiding place of her valuables they hung her up by the heels for so long that she died a few minutes after being cut down. A young Englishman reported that all the country houses between New Brunswick and Amboy were left in flames. The smoke of their burning could be seen from New York.

The Tory inhabitants, many of whom retreated with the army, were furious at the evacuation of their colony and the pillage and destruction that accompanied it. Including the hurried abandonment of the Trenton-Princeton country in January, this was the third time that a powerful British force had been expelled from the American mainland.

Howe's reputation suffered even among his soldiers, though he was generally popular among them and had thanked them handsomely in general orders for their exertions. A rumor went about that he had refused to listen to guides who had offered to show him a route by which the American position at Middlebrook could have been outflanked and taken. Mr. Serle, who had lately quoted from a

French author on the difference between a general and a great man, thought that the troops were dejected. He himself felt mortified and, two days after Washington had celebrated the first birthday of the American nation by hoisting Betsy Ross's new flag over the camp at Middlebrook, he deplored the rebels' thanksgivings "for driving us out of the Jerseys."

Sir William explained afterward that the principal object of his recent maneuvers had been to tempt Washington into giving battle, and that he had always had another plan in mind if that should fail. Some weeks back he had written to Lord George Germain that owing to his lack of reinforcements—he had asked for 15,000 and received only 2,900—he no longer hoped to end the war this year but did expect to be in possession of New York, the Jerseys, and Pennsylvania by the conclusion of the summer's campaign. Since March he had been considering a movement by which all this, and possibly a good deal more, might be accomplished. The idea had originated in a scheme—"Mr. Lee's plan" Howe labeled it—which had been submitted to him by the egregious Charles Lee, for whose capture in December the King had thanked Colonel Harcourt.

Before coming to America Lee had been a lieutenant colonel in the British army, and on the ground that his resignation of his commission had never been accepted, it had been intended to send him back to England to be tried as a deserter. Only Washington's threat of severe reprisals on British officers who were held prisoner by the Americans had prevented this from being done. But meanwhile the wretched Lee, in terror for his skin, had sought to placate his captors by offering a plan for the subjugation of the colonies, on the success of which, he stated, he would stake his life.

In six closely written foolscap pages he proposed that Howe, with 14,000 men, should clear New Jersey of the rebels and capture Philadelphia, and that at the same time a seaborne force of 4,000 should seize Norfolk and Annapolis. By this method Maryland could be easily occupied; the "German districts" in Pennsylvania would follow Maryland into the loyalist fold; Virginia would thus be cut off from sending troops to Washington; and the whole rebel confederacy, with its capital and the center of its territory in the hands of the British, would simply collapse.

Howe had not enough troops to carry out this plan, but he believed that by reducing the garrisons of New York and Newport to the numbers absolutely essential for holding those places he could assemble a force sufficient for the capture of Philadelphia by a sea-borne expedition. Then, if Lee should prove to be right about the latent loyalty to the Crown in Maryland and the Pennsylvania Germans' indifference to the patriot cause, the rest might follow.

Most of his general officers, to be sure, opposed the plan: Sir Henry Clinton, whom he called from Newport to command after his departure, was much against it. They felt strongly that Burgoyne's advance from Canada should be assisted by an advance up the Hudson. But Lord Cornwallis and Sir James Grant favored it. Howe, although he was commander in chief in the rebellious colonies, had never been consulted about the Canadian expedition; Burgoyne, on leave in London during the past winter, had gone over Howe's head to persuade the King and the Government to authorize it. Howe had never received any positive orders to cooperate with it and had written to Sir Guy Carleton in April that he did not intend to do so. On July 15, moreover, came the news that Burgoyne had captured Ticonderoga, and with nothing more formidable than a few raw Continental regiments and the New England and New York militia to oppose him, it seemed unlikely that Burgoyne would need any help from Howe. But if help should be needed, Howe thought that he would probably be able to capture Philadelphia and return in time to give it.

He had begun to put his troops aboard the transports as soon as he returned to New York, and the embarkation had gone steadily forward. The pontoon train and the flatboats were taken on board. There were six vessels for the engineering department alone. The field artillery had 300 rounds per gun and a reserve of between 5,000 and 6,000 rounds. Eight camp women were taken along for every hundred men, and certain persons described as "ammunition wives" accompanied some of the officers. For the march after landing, five wagons were provided for each battalion, ten for each corps of light infantry and grenadiers. Each field and staff officer and each captain was allowed to take one horse.

On July 23 all was ready, and the transports, escorted by the warships under the command of Sir William's brother, put to sea. It was a magnificent armada—two hundred and eleven sail, as Washington's spies counted them, with swallowtail pennons flying from the mastheads of the ships of corps commanders and the principals of departments. But with the wisdom of its setting forth unfriendly observers on both sides of the Atlantic were not favorably impressed. For although its destination was kept secret, Philadelphia was generally believed to be its objective. Horace Walpole wrote of it caustically: "It is hoped and thence supposed that General Howe is gone to take some place, or beat some army that is more practicable than disobliging Washington . . . France sits by and laughs . . . and winks at Franklin." But at least it had the merit of mystifying Washington.

2

The eight weeks that followed Howe's retirement in the early days of that July were for Washington a period of such grinding anxiety as few army commanders have ever been called upon to endure. Unable to believe that the British high command would sacrifice to a large extent their advantage of interior lines by invading the country concentrically, he continued until the middle of June to expect that the fine British and Hessian regiments in Canada would be sent to New York by sea. A fortnight later he reinforced Schuyler by sending to Albany four Massachusetts regiments that were at Peekskill. But although he knew that Howe had moved his whole force to Staten Island and had begun to embark them on board his transports, he remained in some doubt as to the genuineness of the threat from Canada until the 7th of July.

On learning, however, that Burgoyne was actually advancing up Lake Champlain, he thought it hardly possible that Howe's embarkation could have any other purpose than to cooperate with that movement by an attempt to capture the forts in the Hudson Highlands. He ordered Sullivan's division to Peekskill and sent Stirling's after it a few days later. But he still hesitated to move his whole army to the Hudson. Howe's destination might possibly be Philadelphia after all: the British transports were reported to have taken in provisions and water for a voyage of three or four weeks duration.

To warn him of a sudden appearance of the British fleet at the Capes of the Delaware, he had arranged signal fires on the hills between Princeton and Morristown. The better to watch the situation nearer at hand, he kept his headquarters constantly on the move between Morristown and the passes west of the Hudson, one night sleeping in the only bed in a log cabin, with his staff on the floor around him. "Our situation," he wrote to Hancock, "is truly delicate and embarrassing."

The news of the fall of Ticonderoga, which reached him five days before Howe received it, shocked and amazed him. "Unaccountable," he called it, and "among the most unfortunate" things that could have happened. Behind those ramparts nineteen years earlier Montcalm had repulsed a British army of 15,000 men, inflicting upon it a loss of 2,000. Now the place had been neither stormed nor reduced by siege but simply evacuated, and by St. Clair, who had proved his mettle in the Princeton campaign. The reports appear to have said nothing of the British guns hauled to the summit of Mount Defiance, where young John Trumbull had pointed out the previous summer that they might be planted with disastrous effect.

Only a storm that made the roads impassable prevented Washington from moving to Peekskill with his whole army on receiving this news, so certain was he that Howe would shortly attack the defenses there. The boats at Albany were summoned to take Glover's brigade up the river; Nixon's had already been dispatched. Additional supplies of powder and lead followed, and Arnold was sent north to take command of the Massachusetts and Connecticut militia, who were backward in turning out under Schuyler's leadership.

Always at his best in the face of disaster, Washington wrote to Schuyler: "We should never despair. Our situation has been unpromising before and has changed for the better; so, I trust, it will again. If new difficulties arise, we must only put forth new exertions. Though our affairs for some days past have worn a dark and gloomy aspect, I yet look forward to a fortunate and happy change."

But Howe's actions continued to be, as Washington described them, "puzzling and embarrassing beyond measure," and his intelligence service did little to lessen his uncertainty. According to information from various sources the British transports would be at one time standing up toward the Hudson, a little while later going up Long Island Sound, and in another hour leaving Sandy Hook. Not until July 24 came the definite information that Howe's great fleet had actually put to sea, leaving behind it the general belief that the Delaware Capes were its destination and Philadelphia its objective.

Next day a letter from Howe to Burgoyne, promising an attack on Boston, was found on a captured enemy messenger. But the man's capture had been too obviously prearranged to deceive, and five days later four of Washington's five divisions were at Trenton and at Howell's and Coryell's ferries farther up the Delaware ready to cross into Pennsylvania. Sullivan's, however, he held at Morristown, for he still found Howe's abandonment of Burgoyne so "unaccountable," he wrote Hancock, "that I cannot help casting my eyes continually behind me."

This letter hardly had time to reach its destination when a report came in to headquarters that the British fleet had been sighted off the Delaware Capes. Orders were immediately given for an advance toward Philadelphia, and Washington himself rode through the city and down the Delaware to Chester, only to learn that the enemy ships had disappeared to the eastward. Was Howe's whole voyage then only an elaborate ruse to lure the American army into Pennsylvania and, before it could march back, seize the Hudson forts by a *coup de main* or strike at Boston? Back across the Delaware went the American baggage. But army headquarters were established at Germantown, for marching and countermarching in the extreme heat of the past five days had so exhausted the troops that by August 5 they had to be given a rest.

Under the burning sun, it is recorded, a most horrible smell pervaded the camp at Germantown, as it did all army camps in such weather until the introduction of modern military sanitation. Young Lieutenant McMichael of the Pennsylvania Continentals, who kept his diary in verse, wrote at the Cross Roads ten days later:

> Since we came here for to encamp,
>   Our mornings have been very damp,
> But at noon day excessive warm
>   And like to do us all great harm.

But the campaign thus far had been of the kind that seasons raw troops both physically and mentally better than camps of instruction or combat. From the apparently purposeless tramping back and forth on the same old roads, the long, inexplicable halts, and the disappointed hopes of action they were learning the hardest part of soldiering—the "hurry up and wait." John Laurens wrote to his father, who was soon to succeed John Hancock as president of the Continental Congress, that in their bivouacs in the pleasant Pennsylvania countryside the men were recuperating as well as strong drink and women would permit.

"A brigade of young ladies"—or so a contemporary account describes them—invaded the camp in three columns, and the occasion must have been a lively one. They were entertained with a double bowl of sangaree, a beverage composed of wine, brandy, and lime juice, sweetened and spiced. But discipline was tightened up a few days later. There was a review of the whole army, and the men were required to turn out for it with their hair dressed and powdered.

They must have looked with keen interest at an unfamiliar figure in the party that followed the commander in chief down their lines that day: a broad-shouldered young man of more than middle height, with red hair, pointed nose, receding chin, and flashing hazel eyes. He was the Marquis de Lafayette. Not yet quite twenty years old, he had slipped out of France disguised as a courier in order to elude the *lettre de cachet* his relatives had begged from King Louis to prevent his going to fight in America, and had arrived in South Carolina early in June.

With him had come the Baron de Kalb and eleven other French officers. But by the time they reached Philadelphia Congress had had more than its fill of foreign adventurers. De Kalb's mission, which was to further a scheme for giving the French Comte de Broglie supreme command of the American forces, was anything but a recommendation; they were sharply snubbed, and all but Lafayette and his aides and de Kalb went home. De Kalb was a shrewd, fifty-six-year-old veteran of the Seven Years' War; he had previously spent several months in the colonies, collecting political and military information for the Duc de Choiseul; he spoke English with some fluency, and it did not take him long to realize that nobody could successfully replace Washington as commander in chief. But he offered his services to Congress, and in November was made a major general and given the command of a division.

Lafayette soon made it clear that, for his part, he wished to serve only as a volunteer at first, and without pay. With no higher rank in the French army than that of captain on the retired list, he came to learn, he said, not to teach. Congress was charmed by his modesty and his sincere enthusiasm for the American cause and gave him the complimentary rank of major general, without command. Washington, who met him for the first time early in this August, appears to have taken to him instantly and invited him to join his headquarters. Hamilton's fluent French helped out the Marquis's sparse and halting English, and there began between the young French aristocrat and the middle-aged Virginia planter that firm friendship which lasted until Washington's death.

Almost a week went by and still there was no news of the British fleet. Where "the scourge of God and enemy of mankind" had gone on "this strange coasting voyage" nobody could guess, John Adams wrote from Philadelphia on August 11 to his Abigail in Boston, where the rumor that Boston was Howe's objective had thrown the city into something close to panic. But on that very day, just as Washington had decided to march back to the Hudson, a report came in that Howe's ships had been sighted sixteen leagues to the south of the Delaware Capes. This might mean that Howe intended to attack Charleston. If that were so, it would be useless to follow him, for by sea he could reach Charleston, capture it, and be back at the mouth of the Delaware before the American army could tramp the weary miles to South Carolina. Washington shifted his camp to the Cross Roads in Bucks County and again, on the 19th, to Neshaminy Bridge, where, one day's march nearer Peekskill and still only twenty miles north of Philadelphia, he waited once more for intelligence of the enemy's movements.

In the northern theater of the war, he was informed, there was a widespread fear of the Indians who accompanied Burgoyne's army, and he sent Morgan's riflemen to deal with them. But in general things seemed to be going better in that area. Horatio Gates had superseded Schuyler in command at Albany. St. Clair and the Ticonderoga garrison had, at least, escaped capture; the force of Tories and Indians which had been advancing to cooperate with Burgoyne by way of the Mohawk Valley had been brought to a stand by Fort Schuyler; and Washington felt confident that if the Americans fought with skill and determination, Burgoyne would soon find it difficult either to advance or retreat.

But about the defenses of the Hudson, the keystone of the defense of the entire country, Washington continued to be anxious. On the 11th he had written to Putnam, whom he had left in command at Peekskill, though he does not seem to have felt quite confident of the old man's fitness for the post, urging him to collect all the troops he could find. For it was unlikely, he pointed out, that Sir Henry Clinton had been left at New York merely to hold the city. And on the 21st, since he was still without news of Howe's whereabouts, he decided to march back to the Hudson with his whole army. He could only remain idle where he was, he explained to Congress, but in the Peekskill area he would be in a position to support Gates or to attack New York, as circumstances might determine.

Orders went out to start the army northward on the morrow. But next morning—once more just in the nick of time—came the intelligence so long desired: the British fleet had been sighted far up Chesapeake Bay. Howe's route, as Washington observed, had certainly been a strange one. But that his objective was Philadelphia now became unmistakable. He had only to sail up the Elk River at the head of the bay to land his troops within twenty miles of the Pennsylvania line.

Sullivan's division was immediately called in from Morristown. Nash's brigade and Proctor's artillery—that excellent battery of the Princeton campaign, which had now grown to be a regiment—were ordered from Trenton to Chester; and on the 23rd orders went out for the army to march southward through Philadelphia on the following day. It would be a Sunday; the route would follow the principal streets, down Front and up Chestnut; and the display of

armed strength, Washington thought, would have a desirable effect
upon "the disaffected," of whom there were many in the city.

They came down the Old York Road: the infantry divisions of
Greene, Stephen, Lincoln, and Stirling, with Bland's and Baylor's
light horse leading them, each brigade accompanied by its guns, and
the artillery train in the center. There were some forty cannon in all.
The light horse of Sheldon and Mailand brought up the rear. They
marched twelve abreast, but they took two hours to pass. Everything
had been done that could be done to make their appearance impressive. The camp women were strictly forbidden to march with the
column. They, and the camp kettles, which were usually carried by
the men, went with the baggage train, which was sent around the
city. To prevent straggling the commander in chief had promised
thirty-nine lashes to any soldier who left the ranks. There was a sprig
of green in every hat; the arms were clean and shining, the horses in
excellent condition, and over every regiment floated the new national
colors, the Stars and Stripes.

The smart Philadelphia City Troop, who had won their spurs
twice over between Trenton and Princeton last December and
January, formed Washington's escort. But there was no denying that
the clothing of the troops in general left much to be desired. It
varied from faded uniforms of different cuts and colors to fringed
brown hunting shirts. Some of the men were in civilian garb, and
the shoes of almost all were worn and broken. Their hats were cocked
in various ways. Their carriage and step were poor, although orders
had prescribed that the fifes and drums of each brigade were to be
massed in its center and were to play in such a cadence that the men
could keep step to it, not dancing along or disregarding it as, the
orders observed, had been too often the case. Lafayette thought that
"despite their nakedness, [they] made a fine appearance." They had
been cheered the previous day by the news that up in Vermont the
New England militia under John Stark had destroyed a force of 600
of Burgoyne's Hessians at Bennington, and all hearts were high with
anticipation of a battle after the long weeks of marching and waiting.

John Adams watched them march past and thought them "pretty
well clothed" and "tolerably disciplined" but having "not quite the

air of soldiers." He seems to have liked better Nash's North Carolina brigade, which marched through the city next day, with its band and baggage wagons, and Proctor's artillery, whose train was equipped with traveling forges. Knox, who had got leave to join Greene in a trip to Bethlehem "to purchase some things for my dear, dear Lucy," as he wrote to his wife next day, missed the parade. But on his return he observed that the army's excellent appearance and marching had astonished the Tories and made them very downcast.

Whatever the shortcomings of the American troops, marching— that is to say, the covering of distance on the road—was not one of them. Long ago Sir William Howe had discovered that they could outmarch the best of his British troops and leave the heavily equipped Hessians far behind them. The day after the parade through Philadelphia Washington reported to Congress that Greene's and Stephen's divisions were near Wilmington, twenty-five miles down the Delaware, and that those of Stirling and Lincoln were following them closely.

He added that the militia were turning out promptly. Five hundred of them under arms at Chester and Marcus Hook had been ordered to an assembly point. General Armstrong, the commander of the Pennsylvania militia, was directed to forward to the army all troops of that sort that were in Philadelphia and to send out light parties to collect all available vehicles and horses in the vicinity of the British landing place, since these would be invaluable to the invader. The enemy were already ashore on the banks of the Elk River, at Cecil Court House and Elk Ferry, and a large quantity of supplies for the American army had been accumulated at Head of Elk only five or six miles farther up the river. Most of these, including a large quantity of salt, that essential to the provisioning of an army in those days, Washington succeeded in hurrying away to safety. But 7,000 bushels of grain were lost through the lack of teams and wagons.

As for himself, Washington told Congress, he was setting out next day to study the terrain between him and the enemy. Two days later he reported that he had seen the British camp from a distance, but that only a few tents were visible, and he had not been able to esti- mate or to learn how many of their troops had landed. He had some

Delaware militia watching them, however, and 900 Pennsylvania militia were marching on the same mission. But for a succession of violent storms that had greatly injured both arms and ammunition, he would already have moved a part of his army in that direction. As soon as this damage was repaired he marched westward some five or six miles from Wilmington and took up a strong position on Red Clay Creek, where he barred the direct road to Philadelphia. There he waited once more for Howe to advance and attack him.

3

Since the first voyage of Columbus probably few men have been more pleased to feel solid ground beneath their feet than were the officers and soldiers of Sir William Howe's expedition when they landed on the banks of the Elk River that late-August day in 1777. After an auspicious start, head winds, tumbling seas, and fogs had made the progress of the fleet intolerably slow. It was a week before Cape May was sighted. Seasickness was general, and collisions so numerous that already five of the six ships of the engineering department had been damaged. As the expedition continued to sail southward, offshore storms, accompanied by violent rains, put a sloop on her beam-ends and blew into the maintops a swarm of crickets that chirped nostalgically in the ensuing stillness.

Though the ships were supposed to have been well supplied for a month at sea, two days of dead calm made it necessary to ration the water, which in another week began to stink. Food ran low, and officers rowed from ship to ship to borrow it. A party of wretched civilian carpenters would have mutinied but for the threat of stopping their rum. In the horse ships there was a want of fodder. On August 12 the west wind brought the heartening scent of pines. But no sooner was Cape Henry rounded and a course set up Chesapeake Bay than the heat became tropical on deck and unendurable below. Coats and even waistcoats were a burden. It was worse, wrote homesick Mr. Serle in the flagship, than Guinea or the West Indies: the nights, if possible, worse than the days. But to attempt to sleep on deck was to be drenched by thunderstorms of incredible violence. The lightning damaged several ships and killed a number of men and horses. By the 20th, twenty-eight days out from Sandy Hook, the shortage of water had become so great that a number of horses had to be dropped overboard as an act of mercy. Meanwhile rebel smoke signals on the shores of the bay sent northward the news of the expedition's progress.

Three days later, however, the armed schooner of Captain John Montrésor, senior officer of engineers, took Admiral Earl Howe and his brother the General to look for suitable landing places on the banks of the Elk River. The stream was thick with shoals, but the Admiral was possessed of the driving energy that was so lacking in his brother. He brought the transports up the tortuous channel without mishap and took charge of the disembarkation in person. A half-hour after the anchors were dropped next day, the flat-bottomed boats, with thirty men in each of them, were landing the troops, with sixty rounds of ammunition per man, and by nightfall everybody and everything, except the baggage and the camp equipage, was ashore.

The failure to land the tents was unfortunate. For on the following day the hot weather broke in a deluge of rain that lasted for thirty-six hours. The soldiers, who had no shelter but huts of brush and leaves, were drenched to the skin, their ammunition ruined. The Guards alone lost 16,000 rounds. And when the storm was over, the roads were mere rivers of mud in which even the medium 12-pounders all but bogged down. Pleasant weather returned on the 30th, and Howe ordered the army to advance. But although an extra day's ration of rum was issued, the order had to be canceled, so weakened by the hardships of the voyage were both horses and men.

The latter found a treacherous refreshment in the green apples and corn in which the country abounded, helping themselves from nearby orchards and gardens when they received, as they usually did, a cold welcome from the owners. The inhabitants were far from flocking in with loud cries of "God save the King," as "Mr. Lee's plan" had implied that they would. The Quakers among them remained quietly on their farms and went about their regular business; most of the others had fled, taking their livestock, wagons, and even their furniture with them. On landing, Howe had issued a proclamation promising protection and fair treatment to all who would renew their oaths of allegiance to King George. But his promises in this respect had been too often broken in the past; reports of the behavior of both British and Hessians in New Jersey were too recent to be disregarded; and from the day of disembarkation on the banks of the Elk the conduct of the invaders only went to confirm their truth.

Howe had issued strict orders against plundering. But the strength of the British army had been too rapidly increased for discipline to be maintained at the old standard. Whole new companies had been added to existing regiments; so unpopular was the war in England that it had been necessary to fill the ranks with jailbirds and the sweepings of the streets; and there was a shortage of company officers to control them. As for the Hessians, they had been given to understand that plunder was their privilege.

The provost marshal was instructed to execute plunderers on the spot. The first day ashore he hanged two and flogged five others severely—a thing that ought to have been done a year ago, thought Mr. Serle. Knapsacks were searched for loot. But forty-seven grenadiers and light infantrymen were captured by the enemy in the very act of pillage, and Serle continued to be "mortified" by the behavior of the British troops. The Hessians he considered "more infamous than any . . . a dirty cowardly set of contemptible miscreants." A British officer wrote home of "scenes of iniquity and horror," and that "the return of this army to England is to be dreaded by peaceable inhabitants."

The disappointing behavior of the people, the condition of his troops, their want of fresh food, and the lack of transport gave Howe plenty of time to consider the position in which he had placed himself. After traveling four hundred miles and squandering a month of priceless campaigning weather, he had arrived at a spot that was ten miles farther from his objective than he had been in December and as far from it as he had been at New Brunswick. He was only fifteen miles from New Castle on the Delaware, where, but thirty miles from Philadelphia, he might have landed at the end of July and

saved the long and exhausting detour by way of the Chesapeake.
And once more Washington stood between him and his goal.

A week went by before the British foragers collected enough for

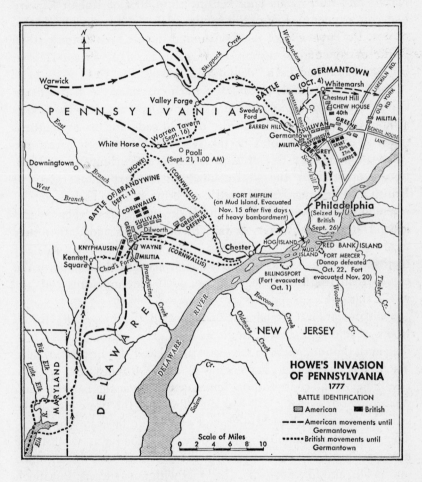

an issue of two days' fresh provisions. On the next day (September
3) the army began to advance. But it covered only ten miles and
then had to halt for a day while the wagons went back, loaded with
officers' baggage and other superfluous impedimenta, to bring up
supplies. The troops had suffered continual annoyance from "armed

bands of rebels constantly skulking about," wrote Major Stephen Kemble, deputy adjutant general. On August 30 Henry Lee of the American light horse, who was to earn the name of "Light Horse Harry" and thirty years later became the father of Robert Edward Lee, commander in chief of the Armies of the Southern Confederacy, captured twenty-eight of the British; and the next day Captain John André of lamentable memory recorded in his diary that a Hessian baggage guard had been "demolished."

Sorely missing Morgan and the riflemen whom he had sent to Gates, Washington had created a corps of light infantry by picking a hundred of the best shots from each brigade and had sent them under the command of General William Maxwell to harass the enemy. On the first day of Howe's advance five hundred of these troops, assisted by the Philadelphia City Troop, ambushed the British advance guard and forced it to bring three guns into action, whereupon they retired. Captain André wrote that they "fled," leaving arms and blankets behind them, and he added that they were reported to be "full of liquor." But Washington believed that their superior marksmanship had probably accounted for more of the enemy than the forty killed and wounded the Americans had lost in the skirmish.

Such operations, though they so affected the nerves of Howe's troops that one day some of them fired on a patrol of their own dragoons, do not appear to have greatly delayed the British advance. There was no enterprising enemy at hand, for instance, to take advantage of the confusion on September 9, when the baggage train was strung out over roads so bad and blind that the two wings of the army lost touch with each other and came close to losing their way. The difficulty of supplying the troops with food was what made progress slow. Communication with the fleet had been discontinued on the 6th, and foraging parties had met with poor success. But much rebel cattle had been rounded up on the 8th, and on that day the leading elements of the column had reached a point some eight miles southwest of Wilmington and only two or three miles from the position on Red Clay Creek where Washington awaited their attack.

The British advance guard, however, had orders not to attack but merely to hold Washington's attention while the main body of their army swung northward over the ten miles to Kennett Square, where they would be on his right flank and almost as close to Philadelphia as he was.

4

If strategy were not the handmaid of statecraft, and often even of politics, Washington might be severely criticized for risking his army in defense of Philadelphia. Howe did not believe that he would do it. Neither did Sir Henry Clinton, Mr. Serle thought it would be foolish. All summer John Adams had viewed with equanimity the prospect of the city's falling into the hands of the enemy. When he heard of the British landing in the Chesapeake, he felt that Congress itself could not have planned a better move for the defeat of Burgoyne. Philadelphia, he wrote to his wife, would be a dead weight on the enemy, as it had been on Washington, for it would require Howe's entire army to hold it. As late as August 29 he believed that the best policy would be to lure Howe into what would prove to be a snare, and he expected that Washington would then take up a position similar to that at Morristown, and with the same paralyzing effect.

But a week later both Congress and the people were demanding bloody action in defense of their capital. Adams himself, though he admitted that Washington's prudent course was perhaps the right one, professed himself weary of "so much insipidity." Even Nathanael Greene, able strategist as he was, wrote that Philadelphia had become "the American Diana" and must be preserved, the threat of Burgoyne in the North notwithstanding; and Washington, now more confident than ever that Burgoyne would come to grief without Howe's cooperation, yielded to the general clamor.

He sent General John Cadwalader down the eastern shore of the bay, General William Smallwood down the western, to raise the militia, who turned out willingly but were sadly lacking in weapons. To embarrass and delay the enemy's advance he did everything in his power. If the panic-stricken inhabitants had not taken every available horse and wagon to carry off their most valued possessions to places of safety, he would have saved the whole of the supplies at Head of Elk.

But he was most seriously handicapped by the want of means to get information of the enemy's movements. His cavalry were not only few but, excepting Henry Lee's troop, without aggressive and skillful leaders. On one occasion they failed even to find the British column, though its whereabouts had been correctly reported to them. And for such missions the newly organized corps of light infantry proved a poor substitute for Morgan's frontiersmen. So Washington did much of his own scouting. He loved the thrill of danger and sought it as daringly as if he had not known that capture would probably mean for him the scaffold at Tyburn and death by hanging, drawing, and quartering. On one of these excursions, when Greene and Lafayette had ridden with him, he was caught in a downpour of rain and took shelter for the night in a farmhouse not far from the British outposts. The situation closely resembled the one in which Charles Lee had been taken prisoner in December—there were plenty of Tories in the neighborhood who might have betrayed Washington's presence to the enemy; and Greene was so anxious that he did not sleep a wink.

Howe's attempt to deceive him as to the change of direction of the British advance on September 8 was so far successful that he waited throughout that day for them to attack him. But by nightfall he had guessed what Howe was about: that the troops in front of him were intended only to keep him where he was while the British main body marched past his right and by swiftly crossing Brandywine Creek and gaining the heights on its northern side placed itself between him and Philadelphia. At two o'clock on the following morning the American army tramped away northward through the warm, dusty darkness over the twelve miles that separated it from the crossings of the Brandywine and by evening was bivouacked on the hills that commanded Chad's Ford, once more blocking the British advance.

The position was naturally a strong one. The banks of the creek were in most places high and steep. At the ford that gave the locality its name the slopes were more gentle, and these the Americans for-

tified with entrenchments and three batteries of artillery. The crossings immediately to the north and south of it they blocked with
felled trees. And thanks to the deliberation with which Howe assembled his troops at Kennett Square they had the whole of the 10th,
the day after their arrival, in which to do this work. It was early on
the 11th when the American light infantry, scouting through the
heavy ground mist of the sultry morning, sent back word that they
had encountered the advance guard of a strong enemy column
moving toward the creek.

The American troops formed in the positions already assigned
to them, and Washington rode down their lines amid cheering so
hearty that it gave Lafayette a feeling of confidence in those ill-dis-
ciplined and half-trained boys and men who had so lately been
clerks and farmers. But there were only 11,000 of them, including
the militia; the line they had to hold was four miles long; and
15,000 of the best troops of Great Britain and Germany were marching against them. The quotas of all the states had continued to be
what Washington described to his brother as shamefully deficient.
As for the support of the local population, which would have sprung
to arms automatically at the approach of the enemy in New England or New Jersey, Greene, whose bed of dusty straw had given
him an attack of asthma and spoiled his sleep that night, observed
that these people had a poor stomach for fighting.

Sullivan held the right of the line with his own division and those
of Stephen and Stirling. Armstrong and the Pennsylvania militia
occupied a position on the left, which the nature of the ground
made almost unassailable. In the center, Greene, in command
of his own division, two other brigades, and Wayne's four brigades
of Pennsylvanians, covered Chad's Ford itself and the front to the
north and south of it, which was most accessible to attack.

In front of Greene, on the far side of the creek, stood the light
troops under Maxwell. They had orders to do their utmost to delay
and disorganize the approaching enemy, and they went at their
task with a will. Twice they drove back the 300 Hessians of the
advance guard in disorder. It took the main body to drive them
across the creek. This force, composed mostly of Hessians, num-

bered about 5,000, and it was stiffened by two British regiments and a numerous artillery. The Hessian General Knyphausen was in command. Arrived within range of Greene's position, he unlimbered his guns, opened fire, and proceeded deliberately to make his dispositions for an assault.

From a position behind Greene's troops Washington watched this demonstration with a divided mind. He had received word of a strong British column two or three miles to the westward, marching northward on a road that ran roughly parallel to the right of his line, and he had sent Sullivan orders to cross the fords in his front and attack it in flank. But no sooner had those orders gone out than word came in from Sullivan that no such column could be found. The few light horse that were with Sullivan that day did nothing to clarify the situation. Of their commander Henry Lee wrote afterward that although he had all the attributes of a patriotic gentleman, he was not cut out for the intelligence service.

Some little time later, however, old Thomas Cheney, a local squire, galloped up to Washington with his horse in a lather. He reported a strong enemy column in the act of turning Sullivan's right flank above the point where the two forks of the Brandywine united. He had seen it, had risked the fire of its advance patrols to bring news of it. He drew a map in the dust to explain the situation and offered to remain a hostage for the truth of what he told. "I have this day's work at heart as e'er a blood of you!" he exclaimed. But there were many Tories in the neighborhood, and this fiery old man might well be one of them who was willing to serve his King at the risk of his life by giving false information to the rebels. Washington continued to doubt him until, past midday, a message from Sullivan told of the appearance of two British brigades a couple of miles from his right rear, and a long column of dust behind them.

Washington at once sent Sullivan orders to swing the three divisions under his command across the path of this new threat. But it was too late. Owing to a clumsy system of maneuver and lack of training the Americans were notoriously slow in changing front, and this weakness was now aggravated by a silly squabble for the post of honor on the right of the line between two of the brigade commanders. Sullivan's troops were still in some confusion, not all of them arrived at their new positions, when the British fell upon them with a force that outnumbered them two to one.

Having spent the previous day in collecting information and arranging for the battle, Howe had ridden out at four o'clock this morning at the head of a column 10,000 strong, which was under the immediate command of Cornwallis. Composed chiefly of British troops, its mission was to cross the forks of the Brandywine some three miles north of the American position and come down upon the right flank and rear of Washington's army while Knyphausen's 5,000 kept their attention fixed on their front. It promised to be Long Island over again, with Sullivan again the victim, as he had been that day just a little over a year ago. And again, as at Long Island, Sullivan was taken off his guard.

The way was long, some fifteen miles by the winding roads, and through a strange and difficult country. The day was sultry, and the morning fog held the dust down on the sweating column and made breathing difficult. But it favored concealment. So confident was Cornwallis that his march was undetected that he ordered a halt for dinner. There would still be plenty of time to roll up the whole American line and drive it routed from the field before dark. Or there should have been, if Washington's army had been the army of the previous year.

It was four o'clock in the afternoon when, about a mile and a half in the rear of the right of Sullivan's former position, the British column encountered his half-formed divisions and deployed for attack to the strains of the Grenadiers' March—Guards on the right, grenadiers in the center, and light infantry and Jägers on the left. The Guards and grenadiers charged without firing a shot, and the Americans in front of them fell back, but fighting stubbornly from wood to wood and only after being shelled by the British artillery. Two of Sullivan's brigades, however, broke under the light infantry attack, and the others soon followed them. Stirling's division, with both flanks thus exposed, retreated in disorder, though their officers and Lafayette, sword in hand and on foot, with the blood from a bullet wound running out of his boot, strove to rally them. They had been fighting for an hour and a half, and many of them had fired their last cartridges.

At the sound of the firing to the northward Washington galloped toward it cross-country, guided by an unwilling old inhabitant whom he had mounted on the horse of one of his aides. "Press along, old man! Press along!" he exhorted. He had ordered Greene's division to go to Sullivan's assistance, and the tough Virginia brigades of Weeden and Muhlenberg covered the four-mile route to their new position in forty-five minutes.

Now, however, Knyphausen could see large bodies of the Americans in his front streaming off to the northeast and attacked in earnest. Greene's move to support Sullivan had left a long gap in the line to the north of Chad's Ford, and the smoke of Knyphausen's cannon hid his charging troops from the gunners in the American batteries. Wayne's brigades fought hard for the low ground where they stood. Knox's artillerymen, he wrote to his wife two days after the battle, did him great honor. Many of them stuck by their guns even after their infantry supports were gone and they were surrounded.

But British troops headed Knyphausen's attack, and they were not to be denied. Fourth and Fifth Foot, 71st Glasgow Highlanders, and 21st Fusiliers, they stormed over the entrenchments and took the guns, the future Lord Harris, who had been wounded some days before, riding bareback among them on the nag of the chaise in which he had insisted on continuing to advance with the army. Wayne's men fell back, fighting obstinately for every pasture fence and garden wall until the Guards, who had lost contact with Sullivan's troops among the woods and thickets but had kept their direction, emerged upon their rear and drove them from the field.

Meanwhile, too late to restore Sullivan's battle line, Greene's division, together with some of the more resolute members of the routed regiments, had been guided by Colonel Pickering, the adjutant general, to a defile three miles to the northeast of Chad's Ford. There, in accordance with Washington's orders, they took up a position to resist Cornwallis's farther advance. Still panting from their run, they opened their ranks to let the last of the fugitives pass through, closed them again, and, when the British grenadiers came tearing through the trees and scrub, flushed with victory and without an idea that they had anything capable of organized resistance in front of them, halted them with a murderous fire.

So heedless had been the grenadiers' advance that they were nearly surrounded when the Jägers came to their rescue. The British Fourth Brigade, which had been all but destroyed at the battle of Princeton, joined them. Cornwallis rode up, and for an hour and a half he and Greene, who were to match skill and valor in the South a few years later, shot it out at fifty paces as the twilight deepened. Under the general's eye the British charged repeatedly and were as often driven back by the heaviest fire of the entire battle. So fierce was the fighting that two of the Hessian captains earned their sovereign's order *Pour La Vertu Militaire*, the first of their comparatively humble rank to be so distinguished. Muhlenberg, the fighting parson, who was everywhere along his line on a big white horse, directing and encouraging his men, was recognized by the troops from Anspach, with whom he had served after being expelled from the university, and they recalled his wild youth with loud shouts of *"Hier kommt Teufel Piet!"*

Behind this redoubtable defense the broken regiments and routed troops of the rest of the army made their weary way over the fifteen miles to Chester, whither the heavy baggage had been sent the day before. When darkness fell, Greene withdrew his brigades in good order. The British were quite willing to call it a day, and there was no pursuit. At Chester at midnight Washington showed no signs of discouragement at the outcome of the battle. This new army of his had demonstrated that it could not only march and withstand the strain of a campaign of maneuver but could fight and fight well when given only half a chance. Yielding to self-indulgence, as he rarely did, he remarked to his staff: "Congress must be written to, gentlemen, and one of you must do it," and proceeded to go to bed.

Colonel Harrison, his secretary, handed the task along to Picker-

ing, who wrote for Washington's signature that he was sorry to
have been obliged to leave the enemy masters of the field and went
on to explain that this had been due to faulty information about
Cornwallis's flanking movement. The baggage was safe, he added,
but the enemy had captured seven or eight of the guns, and most
of the blankets, which were on the men's packs, were probably
lost also. He reported, however, that the troops were in excellent
spirits. On being roused from sleep to sign this letter Washington
put in a still more cheerful note. He hoped, he wrote, for "a more
fortunate result . . . another day."

Considering the numbers engaged, the battle had been the greatest, and Knox considered it the most severe action, of the war thus
far. There had been a larger force of British infantry on the field
than had fought at Dettingen in 1743 under the command of King
George II himself. And the casualties were the most numerous. The
British killed and wounded amounted to 600. The American losses
came close to 1,000, of whom one third were prisoners, and so many
of these had wounds that Howe wrote to Washington for the loan
of American surgeons to help in taking care of them, a request that
was immediately granted. The captured American guns, which had
been taken with their teams and ammunition wagons, were actually
eleven in number: a howitzer, five fine brass pieces fresh from France,
three of American make, and two of the highly prized battalion guns
that were trophies of the victory over the Hessians at Trenton.

Washington's letter awakened John Hancock in Philadelphia at
four in the morning of the 12th, and he had Congress assembled two
hours later to hear it read. All in all, the members were well pleased
by its contents and manifested what was rare with them, an intelligent comprehension of a military situation. Though the battle had
ended in defeat, the statement that the troops were in good spirits
proved that there had been no debacle like the retreat from New
York just a year ago. In a warm tide of appreciation they voted the
army thirty hogsheads of rum as a reward for its gallantry.

★

"Victories . . . Not Real Advantages"

1

WASHINGTON SPENT THE WHOLE next day at Chester, resting his troops and reorganizing them. They needed it. But by academic principles the delay was risky. If Howe had pressed on eastward to Derby through the night after the battle, it has been pointed out, he would have placed himself between Washington and Philadelphia and might either have taken the city without further serious fighting or pinned the defeated American army against the Delaware and destroyed it. But there was fatigue and confusion among the British forces also, as Washington was well aware. They had been marching and fighting since before dawn of the previous day, and darkness had caught them dispersed over some sixteen square miles of hills and valleys, small farms, woods, and thickets. Sir William Howe was not the man to collect them, reform and drive them through the night across the twenty miles of unknown and intricate country that lay between Chad's Ford and Derby, and Washington had not been fighting him for a year and a half without taking an accurate measure of his adversary's weaknesses. Howe also devoted the day after the battle to rest and reorganization and on the following day permitted Washington to march unmolested to Philadelphia.

Passing through the city, the American army encamped once more at Germantown. There it was in a position either to return to Philadelphia and defend the line of the lower Schuylkill or cover the fords of the upper river if the British attempted to cross above. But Howe moved slowly westward, as if to seize the American bases of supply at Reading and Lancaster, and by the 15th Washington was again west of the Schuylkill, this time determined to fight on the offensive. Next day the two armies met at Warren Tavern on the Lancaster road, twenty miles west of Philadelphia. Only the scouting of Count Casimir Pulaski, the celebrated Polish exile who had lately joined the Americans, prevented them from colliding without warning with the British advance guard. But before battle could be joined a storm of equinoctial violence overwhelmed both forces and kept up for two days. In vain did the American soldiers cover with their coats their poorly tanned leather cartridge pouches. Their ammunition, a total of 400,000 rounds, was ruined—"a terrible blow for us," even the usually cheerful Knox confessed.

With no reserve of ammunition closer at hand than Potts Grove, thirty-five miles from Philadelphia, Washington could only retire once more across the Schuylkill. From that place he hoped to dispute the British crossings of the river at Fatland and Swedes fords a few miles below. But even his retirement took him four days: so great had now become his want of provisions; and the condition of his men was deplorable. In the past ten days they had often gone hungry. Night marches had been numerous. The fords they had to cross were breast-deep, evoking, as Greene observed, "the national evil, curses." They had been drenched night and day by torrential rains, for their tents had been sent off with the heavy baggage before the battle at the Brandywine and they had not seen them since. Most of the men, as Washington had guessed, had discarded and lost their blankets in the battle, and four months of campaigning had reduced their clothes and shoes to tatters.

A thousand of them were barefoot, Washington wrote to Congress in a letter asking that shoes and blankets be sent him from Lancaster. Since there were neither blankets nor clothes in the public magazines, he sent Hamilton to Philadelphia to collect them from the inhabitants. It was a painful task, he admitted, and he advised delicacy and discretion in its performance; but it had to be done if the troops were to go on fighting in the cold and stormy autumn weather. A week later he wrote to Hancock to urge the cooperation of the Honorable Board of War in collecting a sufficient supply of shoes and stockings.

But men were what he needed most. His losses at the Brandywine had run close to 10 per cent of his regular troops. He ordered the Virginia militia assembled at Fredericktown in Maryland to join him as soon as they could be armed, sent Putnam a peremptory demand for 2,500 troops to be forwarded to him as quickly as possible, and asked Gates to return Morgan's riflemen the moment he could spare them. Until reinforcements arrived he could only remain where he was, with no hope of doing more than inflict some loss on the British when they crossed the river. And even for this he lacked the necessary intelligence. The local inhabitants were Tories to a man and would tell him nothing of the enemy's movements.

Meanwhile the British had been leading no life of ease. Though far better clothed and equipped than their opponents, they, too, had been chilled by the bitter northwest winds and drenched by rains that flooded the lowlands and turned the roads into quagmires. They, too, were without tents; their orders were to cover themselves in the best manner they could; and only the lucky were able to crowd into the few houses and barns that were available. Fever and ague became prevalent among them. Supplies ran so short that the issue of a little soap was noted in an officer's diary. Although they were among a population generally loyal to the King, the troops continued to plunder in spite of a standard penalty of five hundred lashes and the hanging of two flagrant offenders, and sniping and small ambuscades were a continual annoyance. It was something for the record when a day's march drew no hostile fire.

But British foraging parties scoured the country at will and brought in a hundred and fifty badly needed horses. On the 18th the Guards and the light infantry pushed up to the Schuylkill at Valley Forge, where they captured 4,000 barrels of flour and a large quantity of horseshoes, tomahawks, camp kettles, entrenching tools, and other equipment, which Washington had been powerless either to defend or remove, though they were invaluable to the American cause. Three days later the British rear guard surprised Wayne's brigades at Paoli and narrowly missed destroying them.

Wayne had been left at Paoli to keep the British under observation. An ardent believer in the offensive, he had decided on the night of the 20th to attack Howe's rear guard, which lay not far away. His home was close by, and he knew the country well. But that was a game that two could play at. The neighboring Tories had given Howe's headquarters full information as to Wayne's position, and at two o'clock in the morning of the 21st a British force led by Sir Charles Grey, later Earl of Howick, fell upon him with a ferocity that caused the affair to go down in American schoolbooks as the Paoli Massacre. Grey, like Wayne, was a great believer in the bayonet. To make sure that his men should rely on it alone, he had the flints knocked out of the locks of his soldiers' muskets before they attacked and was known as No-flint Grey ever after. The British claimed to have killed or wounded three hundred Americans that night. They captured eight of Wayne's provision wagons, and Wayne was lucky to succeed in rejoining Washington by a circuitous route without losing any of his guns.

Howe, who had been keeping Washington puzzled for the past few days by a variety of maneuvers, feinted upriver in the direction of the American right flank on the 22nd and that night, leaving his campfires burning as Washington had done at Trenton in January, crossed the Schuylkill at Fatland and Swedes fords without being interfered with and headed for Philadelphia. A bright moon lighted his crossing, and behind him the sky was red with the flames of the greater part of the village of Valley Forge, which his troops had set on fire.

To defend so long a fordable river was, as Knox observed, impracticable—there were fourteen fords in the thirty-five miles between Potts Grove and Philadelphia. Washington, with an army almost barefoot and desperately short of provisions, could not even pursue the enemy. Wayne had not yet been able to rejoin him; and on the 25th Cornwallis, with the leading elements of the British army, marched into Philadelphia.

Washington moved forward to Skippack Creek, about twenty miles from Germantown, and halted. Until reinforcements arrived he dared advance no farther.

2

In Philadelphia news of the defeat at the Brandywine caused a repetition of those scenes of panic and flight that had occurred when the British army reached Trenton the previous December. Gone were the gay and confident days of the spring and summer, when the streets were brilliant with parading light horse, cosmopolitan with the presence of French, German, and Polish soldiers of fortune, and the hanging of a British spy became a public festival. War contracts had made business boom. Fresh issues of Continental currency had sent prices skyward, and Tories were carted out of town for refusing to accept it. Although John Adams had called the city a mass of cowardice and Quakerism, the first anniversary of the Declaration of Independence had been celebrated with a public banquet and the smashing of Quaker windows, and Adams had written home that the country's affairs were "in fine prosperous train."

Now the footways in front of the houses of prominent Whigs were cluttered with chests of plate and piles of handsome furniture to be loaded into wagons bound for the refuge of Lancaster and York. Coaches and wagons crammed with fugitives filled the roads leading northward. Near nightfall Washington's marching regiments would meet whole families seeking shelter in a state so miserable that the soldiers, forgetful of their own wretchedness, pitied them. Six wagon-loads of Quakers were deported—their uniform, decent gray clothing diversified by the red coat of a Tory fencing master who was sent to share their exile. The church bells were carted off lest the British cast their metal into cannon. Window weights had already been collected and sent to be melted into bullets.

"If Howe comes here," Adams had written to his wife in August, "I shall run away, I suppose, with the rest. We are too brittle ware, you know, to stand the dashing of balls and bombs." The Congressmen postponed their departure, however, until the news of Wayne's defeat at Paoli destroyed their last hope that Washington might prevent the capture of the city. Then, prudently choosing the safe route up the New Jersey bank of the Delaware, they departed to rendezvous at Lancaster.

So great was the exodus that when Corwallis marched in at the head of 3,000 grenadiers and Hessians on the morning of September 25, something between a sixth and a third of the population had departed. He had wisely decided to make his entry that of a liberator rather than a conqueror. Joseph Galloway and other leading Tory citizens who had rushed off to join Howe at Trenton in December, expecting his immediate advance upon the city, rode with the British commander at the head of the column. The troops marched with colors cased. When they halted, the grenadiers' band played "God Save the King"; the tall soldiers shook hands with the children in the crowd; and for the time being the terrific aspect of the "Green Coats," as the Hessians were called, was mitigated by decent behavior.

On the arrival of the news that the British had crossed the Schuylkill the population—men, women, and children—had thronged Philadelphia's moonlit streets as if it had been a market day. A Tory-led rabble celebrated the British entry with a torchlight procession out to Germantown and back, and this time it was not the Quakers' windows that were broken. But keen British observers noted that the crowd of some thousands that acclaimed Cornwallis's troops was composed mostly of women and children, the rest being chiefly riffraff and Quakers.

There was some fear that the city would be burned in obedience to a two-year-old Downing Street order to destroy every town where seditious governing bodies had held their sessions. But the British promptly went to work to make themselves comfortable and secure. They seized the boats at the Schuylkill ferries, searched the city for others, for scows, and for arms, and found a considerable number that had been hidden. Since there was an American flotilla of gunboats and row-galleys on the Delaware that might easily bombard the city, they were in such haste to build batteries along the waterfront that they offered wages as high as eight shillings a day for men to work on them, but found few takers.

Cornwallis's troops went into billets in the city. The rest of Howe's army occupied Germantown and pitched their tents on a line that stretched for about two miles and a quarter from the point where Wissahickon Creek enters the Schuylkill along School House Lane to the Germantown market place, with the light infantry in an advance position at Mount Airy two miles to the front. Howe himself found comfortable quarters at Stenton, a fine country house in rear of the right of the line.

Sir William was well pleased with the results of his campaign. Though but few of the Pennsylvania people had taken up arms for their King, they had been most helpful with information about the enemy and had denied it to the rebels. So confident was Howe of the completeness of his conquest that he proclaimed an end of the "indulgences" he had offered on landing at Head of Elk. In the thirty-two days since then he had beaten Washington in a pitched battle, maneuvered the exhausted Americans into a position where their opposition was negligible, and had taken the rebel capital. The 17th Foot had taken Wilmington on the day after the battle at Chad's Ford, and his brother's fleet was well on its way around from the Chesapeake to the Delaware.

The progress of Admiral Earl Howe's ships up the river might, of course, be somewhat difficult. The Americans had blocked the channel at Billingsport, some eight or ten miles below Philadelphia, and at Red Bank, two miles farther up the river, with what they called chevaux-de-frise—arrangements of transverse beams bolted together and strongly pointed with iron, which rose close to the surface of the water—and these were guarded, the one by a fort on the New Jersey shore, the other by two forts: Mifflin on Mud Island and Mercer on the Jersey mainland.

Until these barriers were destroyed satisfactory communication with the supply ships would be impossible. Meanwhile, however, Howe had at hand enough ammunition to go on with, and he felt no doubt of being able to provision his troops from the surrounding country. Trusting in reports of his intelligence service that Washington was still fifteen or twenty miles from his outposts, he sent a force three thousand strong down and across the Delaware to capture the fort at Billingsport. He scouted the story of certain deserters that the Americans had been celebrating a victory over Burgoyne, and he gave no credence whatever to rumors that reached his headquarters on October 3 to the effect that Washington was about to attack him.

But at daybreak next morning he was aroused from sleep by the sound of firing so heavy that his transit from bed to saddle was a brief one. As he galloped toward the front, through a fog that made it impossible to see for more than a hundred yards, the noise grew louder and more intense. Then disordered parties of light infantry began to stream past him. He halted them, blasted them with his scorn:

"For shame, Light Infantry! I never saw you retreat before. Form! Form! It's only a scouting party."

To the satisfaction of the retreating soldiers a salvo of enemy grapeshot gave him his answer. It brought down upon him a shower of twigs and splinters from the tall chestnut tree under which he had pulled up his horse, and a moment later the van of a strong American column loomed out of the fog ahead. A rattle of small-arms fire far to the left told that the Jägers were fighting for the heights above the Wissahickon. From the farther end of the village street came the crackle of musketry punctuated by the thud of cannon shots. Immediately in front of him, to the right and left of the market house, Knyphausen's Hessians, the Guards, and the brigades of No-flint Grey, Grant, and Agnew were barely holding their ground against a foe who shouted: "Have at the blood hounds! Avenge Wayne's affair!" and charged across the buckwheat fields with the bayonet and a fury they had never shown before. On the right flank, which lacked the support of any natural obstacle, the enemy were already among the British tents.

Unless they were stopped Howe would have to retreat, perhaps even evacuate Philadelphia, and he had no fresh troops at hand with which to stop them. Cornwallis had 3,000 men in Philadelphia, but that was five miles away. It would take him at least an hour to reach the battlefield by forced marching, and by the present look of things he would arrive too late to save the day.

3

Howe's intelligence as to the distance of the American army from his outposts on October 3 had erred only by understatement. Some five miles beyond Skippack Creek, it was actually about twenty-five miles away. Four days earlier, moreover, Washington had been able to report to Congress nothing more encouraging than the arrival of some Maryland militia, his expectation of a few Continentals and eight or nine hundred militiamen from New Jersey, and his intention of moving forward four or five miles that day to reconnoiter with a view of attacking the enemy when further reinforcements joined him.

By the 3rd, however, the troops from Peekskill had brought the number of his Continentals up to 8,000, and he had 3,000 militia. The men were in high spirits, undiscouraged by the loss of Philadelphia and cheered by the news that on the 19th Gates's army had inflicted a severe defeat on Burgoyne at Freeman's Farm. Washington celebrated the event by a salute of thirteen guns and wrote to Governor Trumbull that he had hopes of putting affairs in Pennsylvania in a more flourishing condition.

On learning that Howe had detached 3,000 men on the Billingsport expedition, he resolved on a night march and a surprise attack on the British at Germantown at daybreak. If it were successful, he might even drive the British out of Philadelphia. Two days' cooked provisions were made ready, and the customary American battle allowance of forty rounds per man issued to the infantry. The plan of attack was essentially the same as the one that had worked so well at Trenton last Christmas: two columns advancing by parallel routes to deliver simultaneous assaults; and the commanders of two were the same as in that phenomenally successful action.

Again Greene led the left, which was composed of his own division, Stephen's, and the brigade from Peekskill under McDougal. Sullivan's division and Wayne's Pennsylvania brigades formed the other main column, with Sullivan in command. The brigades of Nash and Maxwell, under the command of Stirling, followed Sullivan's troops and formed the reserve. Still farther to the right Armstrong at the head of the Pennsylvania militia had orders to engage the Jägers on the heights above the Wissahickon. Smallwood and Forman, with the Maryland and New Jersey militia, were to push forward on Greene's left. There were about 10,000 men in all, and forty guns. The troops moved out of their bivouacs at about seven in the evening of October 3. As at Trenton every officer was distinguished by a piece of white paper in his hat.

But it is one thing to synchronize the movements of 2,500 men in a night march of only six hours and deliver simultaneous attacks on a front but little more than a half-mile in breadth—which was the problem at Trenton—and quite another to do the same with four times that number, marching more than three times as far in the dark and attacking on a front six times as broad. Greene's route, which led him against the enemy's highly vulnerable right by way of the Limekiln road, was far longer than Sullivan's, and his march was delayed by his guide, who at one point lost his way. The rising sun was striving vainly to break through the heavy fog that shrouded his column, and he was still three-quarters of an hour's march from his objective, when brisk firing broke out about a mile and a half to his right.

Sullivan's column, advancing directly upon Germantown by the Reading road, had reached Mount Airy, and Conway's brigade, which was in the van, was driving the British light infantry helter-skelter before it. The rest of Sullivan's leading troops swept after them across the fields and down the single mile-long street of Germantown. But about halfway down the length of the street Colonel Musgrave and six weak companies of the British 40th Foot threw themselves into the strong stone house of Chief Justice Chew, whom the patriots had deported for his stubborn loyalty to the Crown, and when Sullivan's leading elements had rushed past, opened a heavy fire from the shuttered windows on those that followed.

Washington, who was riding with Sullivan, halted and hesitated. It was neither the first nor the last time that he acted as if he were acutely conscious of his lack of a professional military education. He consulted the generals who happened to be near by. Should the advance continue, leaving this enemy strong point behind it, or must the column be halted and the house stormed? Knox cited the old adage against leaving an enemy castle untaken in one's rear; nobody seems to have suggested leaving a corps to observe and contain its garrison and going on with the rest. The house was surrounded, field guns brought up and unlimbered.

But their round shot only rebounded from the thick stone walls and smashed the marble statues in the surrounding gardens. An officer who ran forward to demand surrender was shot down, the white handkerchief on his sword point unseen through the fog and powder smoke. The guns blew in the great front door, but the defenders barricaded it with furniture and repulsed the assault that followed with a hail of musket balls. A French officer, the Chevalier Duplessis-Mauduit, got over a window sill only to find himself without followers, and was lucky to escape with his life. Young John Laurens made a gallant attempt to set the house on fire by hurling blazing brands through a basement window, but without success.

Meanwhile various regiments, already confused by the fog, moved in the direction of the firing. Soon three thousand troops, almost a third of Washington's entire army, were milling uselessly around this scene of minor combat. One of Stephen's brigades blundered into one of Wayne's. Each took the other for the enemy, opened fire, and retreated. The whole attack lost both in drive and in the time essential to exploiting the surprise.

As the snarl around the house gradually untangled and the superfluous troops followed those that had already gone forward, they ran into stubborn resistance. Down the village street and between and behind the houses the British fought for every doorway, garden wall and orchard close. In the fields they set fire to the flax stubble and unmown hay, and the smoke added to the confusion the fog had already created among the attacking troops. Officers became separated from their men. Organizations were broken up. Their various elements lost touch with each other and fired into each other as Wayne's and Stephen's brigades had done. Lieutenant McMichael, who had fought at Long Island and Chad's Ford, wrote of it in his diary:

> I then said I had seen another battle o'er,
> And it exceeded all I ever saw before.

Nevertheless the attack pressed on. For two hours, Knox wrote home three days later, the Americans appeared to have victory in their grasp. They could hardly have failed to win if the brigades of the fiery Wayne had struck simultaneously with those of Greene as planned. In Sir Henry Clinton's opinion there was no telling what might have happened if Washington had left a corps of observation at the Chew house and pushed the main attack with all possible vigor. Some of Sullivan's division were fighting among the enemy's standing tents, and Greene was nearly a mile inside the British lines when the tide of battle turned.

Suddenly, inexplicably, confidence gave place to uncertainty. As the heavy firing around the Chew house kept up, the men in front grew nervous lest the army was being attacked in the rear. Many, moreover, had begun to run short of ammunition. Five or six soldiers would be seen together, carrying a single wounded man from the field. Some of Sullivan's men, mistaking the appearance of Greene's on their left for a counterattack on their flank, beat a retreat. Others began to give way. And now Cornwallis, with his 3,000 grenadiers and Hessians, arrived from Philadelphia at the double.

Thus reinforced, the British ceased to retire. They counterattacked vigorously, and all along the line the Americans fell back before them. Greene, far out in front as he was, saw his troops in danger of being surrounded. His "Tall Virginians," indeed, the 9th Virginia Continentals, were captured in their entirety. But the rest fought their way clear and even saved all their guns, though one of these had been dismounted and had to be loaded on a wagon. In the thick of the melee musket balls cut off a lock of Greene's hair and the queue of one of his aides. The British General Agnew and two British colonels fell, mortally wounded.

As the fighting rolled back toward the Chew house, Wayne's horse went down, twice wounded, pinning him beneath it, but his men pulled him clear of the menacing British bayonets. Though his left hand was wounded and his left foot bruised by a cannon ball, Wayne formed his rear guard in line and repulsed his pursuers. Since the Jägers' position on the heights above the Wissahickon had proved too strong for the Pennsylvania militia, the American right flank would now have lain wide open. But Nash's brigade from the reserve defended it with a stubbornness that cost its commander a mortal wound.

Again the light horse, though now led by Count Pulaski, failed to make good. Ordered to cover the retreat, some of them rode over one of their own divisions. But the infantry everywhere retired in good order. As they streamed past Washington, they replied to his protests and adjurations to turn and fight by showing him the emptiness of their cartridge pouches. In spite of their lack of ammunition, however, their rear guards stood so firm that the British dragoons balked at charging them.

Although bitterly disappointed, Washington accepted the outcome of the battle with the equanimity, good judgment, and energy that always characterized him in defeat. He organized the retreat promptly and with such skill that although Cornwallis kept up the pursuit for five miles, he did not venture to attack. Thomas Paine, who acted as one of Greene's aides from time to time, wrote of the retreat that "nobody hurried," the soldiers appearing to be "only sensible of disappointment, not of defeat"; and that the enemy "kept a civil distance behind," halting three-quarters of a mile away when any part of the American army halted.

By nine o'clock that night the Americans were again in their bivouacs in the neighborhood of Skippack Creek. In the twenty-six hours since leaving them they had marched forty-five miles and fought from daybreak till noon, and were well content to rest for a while upon their laurels. And from generals to rear-rank privates they were satisfied that they had genuine laurels to rest upon. Had they not, among other feats, withstood three successive British bayonet charges, a thing hitherto unheard of in this war?

Wayne, now three times defeated in as many weeks, called the day of Germantown "a glorious day." Knox pointed out in a letter to his wife that it was the first time the Americans had attacked the British main body. His men were spoiling for another fight, he told her, and he added proudly that whereas most nations yielded after one or two defeats, "America rises after a defeat." Greene lectured his men for retreating without orders but thanked them for their gallant behavior. Washington reported to Congress that the outcome of the battle had been "rather unfortunate than injurious," the enemy having gained no advantage by it; that the troops were not in the least dispirited, and the younger ones had profited by the experience.

Judged by cold facts, the battle was, of course, an American defeat. They had attacked and been repulsed with heavy loss—673 killed and wounded, and 400 missing, of whom almost all were prisoners.

Howe reported less than a hundred of his men killed and somewhat more than 400 wounded. But people who came out from Philadelphia in the next few days told—probably with some exaggeration—of two hundred wagonloads of British wounded going into Philadelphia. Again Howe asked for the loan of American army surgeons to help in caring for the American wounded who had been left on the field; and Dr. Foulke of the Philadelphia Medical College astonished the British surgeons by performing in twenty minutes amputations that took them twice as long. Once more André recorded that many of the American prisoners were drunk; but if so, it was to good purpose, for their defeat was owing rather to fog, confusion, and want of ammunition than to the enemy.

That the Americans had attacked at all and, on being repulsed, had retired in good order deeply impressed observers in Europe, old Frederick the Great in particular. Politically Germantown was an American victory hardly less potent than the surrender of Burgoyne in influencing France to come openly to the aid of the United States. Nothing, Count de Vergennes, the French minister of foreign affairs, told the American Commissioners, had impressed him so much as General Washington's attacking Howe's army: that to bring an army raised within a year to that point promised everything. But for the time being Washington could only remain where he was, resting his troops and reorganizing them while he once more waited for reinforcements. He had lost upwards of a thousand men in the battle, and the New Jersey militia had become so uneasy about the situation in their home state that he let them return to it.

4

That the British victory at Germantown was a singularly barren one became unmistakable in the next few weeks. The surprise attack on the morning of October 4 left their troops so apprehensive that parts of their line were turned out on false alarms three times in the week following, in spite of a threat of severe punishment for sentinels who were responsible for them. Howe was opposed on principle to field fortifications as injurious to morale, but he now set his men to making fascines for the construction of redoubts.

The batteries on the water front routed an attack by the gunboats and row-galleys of the American flotilla, in which the fine frigate *Delaware* was captured. Her crew ran her ashore and deserted her in a manner that Washington found difficult to understand and Knox called "scandalous." But parties of rebels were continually firing across the Schuylkill, and small outpost and patrol actions, in which the honors were not unequal, were frequent. When headquarters sent dispatches to England, it took a whole regiment to escort the messenger to his ship, though the vessel lay no farther down river than the mouth of Darby Creek.

It was considered advisable to defend the floating bridge that had been thrown across the Schuylkill at the end of Center Street by the construction of a *tête-de-pont*. A high tide combined with a freshet and the cutting of a dam by the Americans upstream to sweep the bridge away, and it had to be laboriously rebuilt. On the Jersey shore guerrilla bands were so active and numerous that only foraging expeditions of great strength could be safely sent across the Delaware. For these Howe could hardly spare the men, and the feeding of his army, to say nothing of the civilian population of the city, became a serious problem.

By October 4 some of the British ships had completed the roundabout voyage from Elk River and arrived at Chester. At Washington's orders the garrison had evacuated the fort at Billingsport, and Admiral Earl Howe's sailors had weighed up and destroyed the chevaux-de-frise at that point. But so long as the American forts prevented their clearing the channel at Mud Island the fleet could not come up to Philadelphia, and the transport of supplies from the ships to the city was a task almost as dangerous as it was difficult. Only on very dark nights could convoys of boats from the fleet slip up the shallow Tinicum Channel between Mud Island and Province Island close to the Pennsylvania shore and thence into the Schuylkill without drawing a heavy fire from Fort Mifflin. But land transport was next to impossible. It took 3,000 men to give adequate protection to the wagon trains on the long fifteen miles between Chester and Philadelphia.

By the end of October, according to Captain Montrésor, the senior officer of engineers, the British in Philadelphia were an army without provisions or rum, with scarcely any ammunition, no clothing, no money, and lacking the siege guns necessary to destroy the enemy forts. Fuel, too, was scarce. The troops were put on half-rations. On a visit to the city early in November Mr. Serle saw neither meat nor fowl, and very few fresh vegetables, and he sensed an atmosphere of discouragement throughout the army.

Late in October had come rumors that Washington's troops were celebrating a no less incredible event than the surrender of Burgoyne and his whole army at Saratoga. Serle had put it down as one of those imaginary victories which, he thought, the rebel leaders often celebrated to keep up the spirits of the deluded people. But presently Howe admitted its truth in General Orders. Of the campaign in Pennsylvania Serle wrote to Lord Dartmouth that the victories had yielded no real advantages and—prudently in a time when nobody's letters were safe from examination—added in Latin that the campaign had been lost by delay.

A reinforcement of 4,000 Hessians from New York brought news that was equally depressing. It was said that if these troops had not been drawn from what Clinton had called "the damned starved defensive" Howe had assigned to him, he would have been able to capture Albany and save Burgoyne. Their departure to Philadelphia had filled New York itself with fears of being attacked. One officer in Philadelphia was so discouraged by all this that he wrote to his brother in New York, advising him to send his family back to England. And two recent failures to capture the Delaware forts by a *coup de main* had done nothing to raise the spirits of the soldiers.

Of the defenses of the Delaware which placed Howe's army in so difficult a situation, Fort Mifflin on Great Mud Island stood in the middle of the river and Fort Mercer on the heights at Red Bank on the Jersey shore. The guns of the former covered the channel and the four tiers of chevaux-de-frise that blocked it. The latter, a little more than a mile distant, was so placed that its fire could contribute to the defense of the channel and at the same time prevent effective bombardment of Fort Mercer from the rear. Both fortifications were unfinished, however, for Washington had been unable to spare the men to work on them. Baron d'Arendt, an experienced foreign officer, whom Washington had lately placed in command of Fort Mifflin, thought it the worst fortification he had ever seen.

It was a sprawling arrangement of earthworks, palisades, and wooden blockhouses. But it possessed one lofty redoubt strongly built of stone, and when some of the British warships attacked it on October 6, it withstood a whole day's bombardment, which was all that their supply of ammunition could afford at that time. Field artillery was planted on Carpenter's and Province Islands, just across the Tinicum Channel. But their fire proved equally ineffectual. Army and city grew hungrier day by day, and British headquarters decided that the quickest way to capture Fort Mifflin was to take Fort Mercer and turn its guns on Fort Mifflin's rear.

Colonel von Donop asked the privilege of making the attack: his Hessians had long been anxious to clear their record of the stain their comrades had placed upon it in the Christmas battle at Trenton. His request was granted, though with a stinging rebuff when he asked for a stronger artillery support than had been assigned to him. With three battalions of grenadiers and a strong regiment of ordinary infantry—2,000 men in all, and all of them Hessians—he was ferried across the Delaware to Gloucester Point on October 21, spent the night at Haddonfield, and advanced on Fort Mercer next morning.

Only 400 men of two Rhode Island regiments held the fort, and it had been designed for a much larger garrison. On the advice of his engineer officer, the Chevalier Duplessis-Mauduit, who had behaved so gallantly in the Chew house fighting, Colonel Christopher Greene, the commander, had dismantled and abandoned the outer line of defenses and concentrated his force in the small pentagonal redoubt that formed the center of the works. Reminded in a dispatch from Washington that all the British hopes of remaining in Philadelphia depended on their capturing the forts on the Delaware, Colonel Greene hoisted his flag on a tall hickory tree that stood within his lines; and when Donop sent in a demand for surrender, which was accompanied by a threat of "no quarter" if it were refused, he rejected it scornfully. Then he walked along the rampart, cautioning his men to hold their fire until the enemy were close at hand, and reminded them to aim low and to sight on the broad white belts that distinguished the Hessian uniform.

Woods covered the Hessian advance to within four hundred yards of the fort. Across the open ground they charged, their officers, sword in hand, leading them on foot. They swarmed over the deserted outer works and, confident of victory, rushed at the central redoubt. Forty minutes later four hundred of them lay dead or wounded, while the rest, excepting a considerable number who preferred capture to being shot in the back in flight, ran helter-skelter for the woods. They left three of their colonels and a score of other officers killed or wounded in the works. Donop himself was mortally hurt and taken prisoner. "I am in your hands: avenge yourselves," he replied stoically, when his captors reminded him of his threat of "no quarter." Washington ordered that he should be given every possible attention, but his case was hopeless, and he died, as he himself said, the victim of his own ambition and his sovereign's avarice.

While the attack was in progress on Fort Mercer, the British warships seized the opportunity to bombard Fort Mifflin. They, too, were beaten off with heavy loss. H.M.S. *Augusta*, 64-gun ship of the line, ran aground, took fire, and blew up. The 18-gun cruiser *Merlin* also grounded and, under a hail of American shot and shell, had to be set on fire and abandoned by her crew.

If Sir William Howe wished to avoid the ignominy of evacuating Philadelphia and retiring to his ships, the only course now left open to him was to reduce Fort Mifflin by a formal siege. Reluctantly Captain Montrésor, who had designed the fort for the government of Pennsylvania when he was senior engineer officer in the colonies some years before, began the work with the construction of siege batteries on Carpenter's and Province Islands. It was a task of great difficulty. Washington had foreseen this situation and had ordered Province Island to be inundated in September. The weather turned foul, and rains and floods deepened the mud that already prevailed there. November brought cold like the depth of winter, a howling northwest wind, and ice a half-inch thick. The guns of the fort prevented all work except at night. Cold and hard labor killed many of the horses, for pasture was poor and grain hard to get. To supply the army's lack of siege guns, 32-pounders from the warships had to be brought by boat up the Tinicum Channel and mounted under cover of darkness. It was the 10th of November when the bombardment of the fort began in earnest.

The events of the next six days constitute one of the most brilliant, and probably least generally known, feats of arms in American military history. All day long and every day, and all night long as well, five land batteries of heavy howitzers added their fire to that of the four 32-pounders, six 24-pounders, and a 13-inch mortar, which had been brought up from the fleet. They played upon the fort at a range of only six hundred yards. Four 64-gun ships of the line, and two of 40 guns each, anchored and cannonaded it at nine hundred yards, while smaller vessels swept in to fire from the shallower waters between the fort and Fort Mercer. The bombardment, said a Hessian officer, was like a constant thunderstorm.

The garrison—300 Maryland troops and 150 Pennsylvanians from Washington's army—replied with equal fury. Their fire drove the crew of a great British floating battery from its guns and forced them to jump overboard. They sent thirty-four cannon shot through H.M.S. *Isis* from side to side. But they had no weight of metal to compare with their enemy's. The palisades were demolished, barracks set ablaze, and the nights were made hideous by enemy fire, fear of an attack by boatloads of troops under cover of the darkness, and the grim necessity of repairing so far as possible the damage wrought during the day.

To help with this work militia were brought over each night from the Jersey shore—they could not abide the place by day. But neither fascines nor enough tools were sent with them, and little could be accomplished with the watery soil of the island. Each night, also, reinforcements had to be sent in, for the total casualties of the garrison amounted to two hundred and fifty or, according to the British, four hundred. Baron d'Arendt had fallen sick, and Colonel Samuel Smith, who succeeded to the command, was wounded and had to be evacuated. Captain Lee, who commanded the artillery, was killed. Major Fleury, the French engineer officer, though he stuck to his post, was twice wounded.

The deep mud afforded one advantage. The enemy shells buried themselves in it, their fuses were extinguished, and they failed to burst. But gun after gun was smashed or dismounted by the solid shot. More and more men could do little but cower under the thick stone walls of the redoubt. By the 15th only two guns could be fired; and at eleven that morning a ship with twenty 24-pounders, and another with three, anchored so close in that sailors in their tops could toss hand grenades into the fort. At that short range their marines shot down any defender who showed himself. Their heavy guns raked the fortifications from end to end. The last cannon in the fort were dismounted, and that night what was left of the garrison slipped away across the river to Fort Mercer, leaving their flag flying.

They had defended the place, wrote Serle, with a spirit they had shown nowhere else to an equal degree during the war. And he added that a more dismal picture of ruin than the place presented could scarcely be conceived. Howe thanked his troops in General Orders for their "great exertions and indefatigable zeal throughout that very laborious operation." But he neglected to mention Montrésor in his dispatches home, which sadly disgruntled that devoted officer, who had spent nine days in the Province Island swamps and kept on his feet only by dosing himself with tartar emetic.

The fall of Fort Mifflin brought the defense of the Delaware to a speedy end. Two days later Cornwallis, with 5,500 men, crossed the river at Chester and advanced up the left bank against Fort Mercer. General Nathanael Greene, at the head of a strong force from Washington's army, was marching to join in its defense. But of this Colonel Greene had not been informed. He evacuated the fort on November 20, and Duplessis-Mauduit saw to the removal of the guns and stores and blew up the magazine.

Upon orders from Washington, Commodore Hazelwood, the commander of the flotilla, proceeded to dismantle a part of his vessels at Bordentown and destroy the rest. At four o'clock of a moonlit November morning Philadelphia was treated to a pyrotechnical display at which Montrésor and other Britishers gloated that it was costing the rebels a cool half-million sterling. Seventeen sloops, brigs, and floating batteries drifted past the city on the rising tide, their sails, spars, and rigging aflame, their guns and magazines exploding in the heat of their blazing hulls.

The flotilla had made a mixed record. Disheartened by the capture of Philadelphia, where many of the men had their homes, the crews had shirked action until the battle at Germantown revived their spirit. Since then, though short of ammunition, they had fought bravely in defense of the chevaux-de-frise; their flanking fire had contributed to the ruin of Donop's assault on Fort Mercer; and lack of numbers rather than good will had prevented Hazelwood from supplying guard boats to protect Fort Mifflin from the threat of night attacks. To Hazelwood, as well as to Colonel Smith and Colonel Greene, Congress voted presentation swords—which the resolution specified were to be "elegant"—in recognition of their services.

But the sad fact remained that the river was now open; that the golden opportunity to force the enemy out of Philadelphia had been lost. No sooner had Fort Mercer been evacuated than Admiral Howe's sailors broke through the last of the chevaux-de-frise, and a day or two later British supply ships dropped anchor off Philadelphia's waterfront with the food and munitions so badly needed there. Quite a number of people—some of them well intentioned and some otherwise—began to ask why, in the seven weeks since Germantown, Washington had done so little to aid a defense which, if vigorously supported, would have compelled Howe's army to retreat ignominiously to their ships. According to patriot propaganda Washington had sixty thousand men. With such numbers, why had he not simply blockaded the British line between the Schuylkill and the Delaware, contained the bridgehead on the Schuylkill, and fallen upon the rear of the batteries on Province Island?

The answer was that instead of the sixty thousand men imputed to him he actually had but little more than ten thousand, that more than a fourth of these were militia, and that all of them were so lacking in everything, from food and ammunition to blankets and shoes, that he was barely able to keep the field at all. But that answer could not be made public lest the enemy learn of his weakness; and the consequences of this general misunderstanding of his situation

came close to being more disastrous to the cause of Independence
than the greatest defeat could have been.

<h1 style="text-align:center">5</h1>

Three days after the battle at Germantown Washington had
reported to Congress from the far side of Skippack Creek that he
intended to remain where he was until he received reinforcements.
When these should have arrived, he added with prudent vagueness,
he would "act according to circumstances." Meanwhile he was busy
with the tightening of discipline and details of administration, which
in the past month of march and battle had been sadly neglected.

It was high time. There was an epidemic of stealing among the
troops: officers' swords simply disappeared, and handsome pistols
vanished even out of the holsters on the saddles of horses tied in
front of headquarters. The commander in chief, it was stated in
General Orders, found a deplorable waste in the drawing and cook-
ing of rations, valuable hides spoiled by carelessness in the butchering
of cattle, and he observed "with grief and amazement" the condition
to which carelessness had reduced both weapons and equipment. The
soldiers were set to cleaning their arms and greasing their cartridge
pouches and were promised severe punishments if they neglected
them in future. The brigades were drilled daily in changing from
column into line and back again to correct the inefficiency in those
maneuvers, which had contributed to the defeat at the Brandywine.

After lingering for several days in agony General Nash died of the
wound he had received in covering the army's retreat, and he and
others who had suffered a similar fate were buried with military
honors. Courts of inquiry and courts-martial were convened for the
examination and trial of officers and men accused of cowardice and
other misconduct in the recent actions and ran their dreary course
through several weeks to come. Wayne, who had been roughly
handled by a court of inquiry for his defeat at Paoli, demanded a
trial by court-martial and was exonerated.

Sullivan also was tried. Congress, angry with him for allowing his
flank to be turned at the Brandywine, had asked Washington to relieve him of his command; he was already under charges of mis-

managing a small affair on Staten Island in the past summer. But Washington had replied that Sullivan could not be spared; that when the expected reinforcements arrived, there would still be need of six more major generals and eleven more brigadiers than were at present with the army. And a court-martial now cleared Sullivan of all charges against him.

The Frenchman Deborre, who had been generally unsatisfactory and had a way of trying civilians by court-martial and hanging them, quit the service rather than face an inquiry into his conduct at the Brandywine. Maxwell, though his troops had fought so gallantly in front of Chad's Ford, was charged with being "disguised in liquor" that day and "a little elevated" on two other occasions. He was triumphantly acquitted. Major General Stephen, however, was convicted of being intoxicated at the Germantown battle and was sentenced to dismissal from the service.

But among his many cares and distractions Washington found time to keep his relations with the enemy on the high plane of courtesy that was demanded by an age in which war was still regarded as the business of gentlemen. On October 7 a flag of truce carried to the British headquarters in Philadelphia the following note:

"General Washington's compliments to General Howe—does himself the pleasure to return to him a dog, which accidentally fell into his hands, and, by the inscription on the collar, appears to belong to General Howe."

On October 18 the army received the glorious news of the surrender of Burgoyne. "Let every face brighten and every heart expand," ran Washington's Order of the Day. There was a salute of thirteen guns, a *feu de joie* of blank cartridges was fired by every brigade and corps in the army, and the chaplains were instructed to deliver short discourses suited to the joyful occasion. The glad tidings were doubly welcome, for three days earlier had come word that Sir Henry Clinton had sailed up the Hudson from New York, captured the forts at Peekskill, and gone on as far as Poughkeepsie with the evident intention of extricating Burgoyne from his difficult situation.

The bad news had not shaken Washington's conviction that Clinton would not advance to Albany and that in any event his movement came too late to save Burgoyne. The forts on the Delaware continued to be his chief concern. But he must have more men, and his men must have ammunition and food, shoes, blankets, and clothing before he could march to support them. He complained bitterly to Thomas Wharton, President of Pennsylvania, that although it was the richest and most populous state of the thirteen, Pennsylvania had only twelve hundred militia in the field and its Continental regiments were never more than one-third full—a sad contrast to the zeal of New Jersey and New York. But his complaint bore little fruit.

Upon receiving the news of Saratoga, he sent Hamilton to Albany to tell Gates that he must have reinforcements from Gates's army, and that with them he could probably reduce Howe to Burgoyne's position. But all Gates sent him was Morgan's riflemen, and they arrived barefoot from their fighting in the North. Once more Washington was reduced to offering pardon to all deserters who would return to the colors, and he warned Congress on October 24 that unless shoes and blankets were provided within a few days, two-thirds of his troops would be unfit for service. To Henry Laurens, who had just succeeded John Hancock as President of Congress, he wrote a week later that so far the want of ammunition and shoes had prevented his taking the offensive, but now there must be clothes for the army if the campaign was to go on.

Anticipating the criticism that would follow upon the news of the evacuation of Fort Mifflin, he sent Congress a painstaking explanation of the course which circumstances and legislative negligence, jealousy, and ineptitude had compelled him to take. Only by crossing the Schuylkill with his whole army, marching past Philadelphia, and attacking the British works on Province Island in the rear could Fort Mifflin have been relieved. But by doing that he would have left the American supply depots at Easton, Bethlehem, and Allentown open to an enemy raid from Philadelphia. It would also have left Fort Mercer without the possibility of support should the British make a second attempt to capture it. And anxious lest the

reputation of his troops should suffer, he added that if the compara-
tive strength of the opposing armies were considered together with
the abstract of clothing now wanting for his men, the wonder would
be how they kept the field at all in tents at that season of the year.

The best he could do was to advance cautiously toward Philadelphia, marching sometimes not more than five miles in a single
move, with the faint hope that his approach might lessen the enemy
pressure on the forts. The 2nd of November found him encamped at
Whitemarsh, whence he could see across the hills to the southward
the smoke of the British outpost fires in front of Germantown. There
he remained, though the enemy guns were soon battering Fort
Mifflin into ruins. It was as far as he dared to go.

When he learned, however, that upon the fall of Fort Mifflin
Cornwallis had started up the river to attack Fort Mercer, he sent
Greene, with more than one-third of the troops at Whitemarsh, to
strengthen its defense. Greene marched with all possible speed.
Crossing the Delaware at Burlington, he covered thirty-five miles in
a single day. But Fort Mercer had been evacuated on the very day
of Greene's departure from Whitemarsh, the British had turned to
foraging, and Greene could do no more than harass them as they
fell back to the ships which had been sent up the river to take them
back to Philadelphia. For Conwallis refused to fight, although Greene
pressed so closely upon his retirement that the British warships had
to use their guns to cover the embarkation.

On receipt of an urgent note from Washington stating that Howe
was probably planning to attack the American main army, Greene
hurried back to Whitemarsh to find that a few hot headed generals
had been urging the commander in chief to hazard everything in an
attack on Philadelphia. Washington at this time had only about 8,000
Continentals and 2,700 militia, and of the latter nearly 2,000 from
Virginia and Maryland would soon be going home. Howe had
certainly not less than 10,000 men available for the defense of the
city. But Wayne argued that even if the attack should fail, the army
would be no worse off than if it continued to remain inactive.

At a council of war, however, eleven of the generals voted against
attacking. Among them were Sullivan, Knox, and de Kalb, who had

been given the command of a division the day before, and their opinion was supported by General Duportail, late captain of engineers in the French service, who had lately joined the army and had made a thorough study of the fortifications Howe had been building. Greene got back too late for the council, but he agreed with the majority, holding that Philadelphia could now be taken only by a siege, and for a siege the army lacked not only sufficient numbers but siege guns and ammunition.

The British system, as Captain André noted in his diary on November 21, had now become totally defensive. The light troops had been drawn in to a line of fortifications that stretched from the Schuylkill to the Delaware on the heights just north of Callowhill Street. The redoubts had been armed with field guns, and the intervals between the works were filled with abatis—felled trees piled with their branches toward the enemy and sharply pointed, which answered the same purpose that barbed wire does in fortification today.

Nor were these defenses superfluous. For the next two weeks André was recording the activities of American scouts and light horse, who annoyed the outposts and pickets continually, and flying parties that infested the roads leading into the city and had to be cleared out by the Guards' light infantry. Whatever the shortcomings of the American cavalry, this sort of fighting seems to have suited them exactly. In more than one encounter they worsted patrols of British light dragoons and grenadiers and took a number of prisoners. On one occasion they had the impudence to charge on no less a personage than General Grey when he was riding only a short distance beyond the line of sentinels. By way of reprisal the British had been able to do little more than burn some of the houses in front of their lines and commit, as Washington described it, "the most wanton spoil in many others." But by the beginning of December the restoration of Howe's service of supply enabled him to take the field once more. On the 4th he marched out with horse, foot, and guns, and from Chestnut Hill his troops could see the American lines stretching away for about three miles to the eastward of Whitemarsh church.

The movement was intended to be a surprise. But Washington had been expecting it for a fortnight and had kept his men busy in preparing for it. And Mrs. Lydia Darrah, in whose Philadelphia home Captain André was billeted, had listened at the keyhole to a late nocturnal staff conference in her dining room and had contrived to furnish Washington with the final details. For three days Howe probed along the American line for a spot weak enough to justify an assault. But everywhere the heights bristled with abatis, with Knox's guns and the American infantry ranged behind it. For although their numbers were too few for an offensive, they were adequate for the defense of this position, and the spirit and discipline of the men were excellent. Lieutenant Alexander Graydon, who had recently rejoined the army after several months as a prisoner of war, thought it better than he had ever seen it in the past. In front of it and on its flanks Morgan's riflemen and the Pennsylvania and Maryland militia made the enemy's reconnaissance difficult and dangerous, and between the British rear and Philadelphia the country sputtered so continually with guerrilla action that it took three regiments to bring up their supply train in safety.

Three weeks earlier Howe had written home asking to be relieved of his command, since, he stated in his letter, the government had denied him the support his task required. It would have been gratifying, of course, if he could have followed this request with a report of a decisive victory. But Sir William had led the slaughterous attack on Bunker Hill, which cost the British a thousand casualties out of the thirty-five hundred men who were engaged in it; and at Whitemarsh, as at Middlebush and elsewhere, the ghosts of that Pyrrhic victory appear to have risen up to daunt him. Most of the other officers, according to André, also considered that Washington's position was too strong to be attacked, and that, if an attack should succeed, the Americans could make a successful retirement. So on December 7 the British marched ingloriously back to Philadelphia. Strong detachments of American light troops followed them and pressed them so closely that the Jägers, who formed their rear guard, had to deploy on every hilltop and open fire with their battalion guns to check the pursuit.

The rest of Washington's army returned jubilantly to their bivouacs and a double ration of rum. The tense situation of the past four days had deprived them of even that essential of the soldier's life of the time. For four nights they had lain out on the bare hilltops without so much as the slight shelter of the huts of sticks and brush they had learned to substitute for tents when their cautious commander sent away the heavy baggage to a place of safety. They had lacked kettles it which to cook their stringy beef, the very salt with which to season it, and their water had come from a brook made dirty and muddy, as one of them wrote of it, "by the dippin' and washin' " of the whole army.

Even before the tents were sent away, life at Whitemarsh had been hard. Early in November Lieutenant McMichael had written:

> The weather now began to cover with snow
> The Earth; likewise the wind N. W. did blow.

The storms that delayed the construction of the siege batteries on Province Island flooded the ground at Whitemarsh so that Thomas Paine could not make his way from one part of the camp to another. The soldiers can have felt no regrets when, three days after the British retirement, they were marched off westward to cross the Schuylkill at Mattson's Ford, where Norristown now stands.

Once more the predominance of Tory sentiment in the neighborhood resulted in a lack of information about the enemy. No sooner was the American advance guard across the Schuylkill on this westward march than it ran head on into a force of four thousand British troops out foraging under the command of Cornwallis and after a brisk skirmish was driven back across the river. Cornwallis, his mission accomplished, returned to Philadelphia. But it was three o'clock in the following morning before Washington's troops had succeeded in crossing the stream. For some of them there was a fragile bridge of rafts, for the rest a series of wagons so shakily connected by fence rails that the men had to go over it in single file. They bivouacked for the rest of that night in a defile known as the Gulph—a dreary place, on which Surgeon Albigense Waldo, evidently with a line from Milton running in his head, commented:

"Not an improper name, neither." They were without tents, blankets, and even rum, and it was snowing hard.

For a week they lay at the Gulph, short of food, and with but a single day of fine weather. Many men reported sick, though presently the baggage train came up and tents were pitched for the first time in weeks. But even when a cold northwest wind began to drive a heavy rain before it, Waldo noted "an alacrity and contentment unexpected among such young troops." Generally among them it was: "Good morning, Brother Soldier; how are you?" which was answered with sardonic cheerfulness by: "All wet, I thank'ee. Hope you are so." Given plenty of food and rum, these men, Waldo believed, "would storm Tophet."

It was well that such a spirit prevailed. For near the end of this ordeal by rain, cold, and snow the commander in chief made it plain that further hardships must be endured before any greater degree of comfort could be expected.

BOOK TWO

The Tempering of the Steel

CHAPTER IV

★

☆

Winter of Discontent

1

General Orders.

Headquarters at the Gulph   December 17, 1777
Parole Warwick. Countersigns Woodbridge, Winchester.

THE COMMANDER IN CHIEF, with the highest satisfaction, expresses his
thanks to the Officers and Soldiers for the fortitude and patience with
which they have sustained the fatigues of the Campaign. Although in
some instances we unfortunately failed, yet upon the whole Heaven hath
smiled upon our arms and crowned them with signal success; and we
may upon the best Grounds conclude that by a Spirited continuance of
the Measures necessary for our defense we shall finally obtain the end of
our Warfare, Independence, Liberty, and Peace. These are blessings
worth contending for at every hazard. But we hazard nothing. The power
of America alone, duly exerted, would have nothing to dread from the
forces of Britain. Yet we stand not wholly upon our own Ground. France
yields us every aid we ask, and there are reasons to believe the Period
is not very far distant, when she will take a more active part, by declaring
War against the British Crown. Every motive therefore irresistibly urges
us, nay commands us, to a firm and manly perseverance in Opposition to
our cruel oppressors, to slight Difficulties, endure hardships, and contemn
every Danger . . .

The General ardently wished, the order went on to explain, that
he could lead his troops to the best of winter quarters. But to retire
to the interior of the state would not only add to the distress of
hundreds of refugees who had crowded into the towns to the westward; it would leave a vast territory open to the devastations of the
enemy. The army must therefore take up a position in the immediate
neighborhood, where it could both protect many firm friends and
prevent the enemy from drawing supplies from the rich country

near by. The troops would have to build cabins in which to house themselves, but in these, the order assured them, they would live warm and dry and be "compact against surprise."

Thus did Washington announce to his stormbound army in its dreary camp west of the Schuylkill that any dreams they may have cherished of snug billets at Lancaster, Reading, or Allentown had gone glimmering. Only with veteran soldiers could he have prudently been thus confidential. And veterans seasoned by one of the most arduous campaigns in American military history his men had now become. For the past six months they had kept the field, marching hundreds of weary and often fruitless miles in summer's heat and dust and the mud and frost of autumn. Twice they had outfaced one and one-half times their number of troops as fine as Great Britain had ever assembled. Three times, counting Paoli, they had fought and suffered defeat with unshaken courage and unbroken spirit. Even now, shivering in tents and huddled around smoky campfires, hungry, ragged, many of them barefoot, they would have responded eagerly to an order to attack the well-equipped, victorious, and numerically superior enemy that lay within a few hours' march of them.

It was no mere form of words when the order went on to tell them that their commander "persuades himself that the Officers and Soldiers, with one heart and one mind, will Resolve to surmount every difficulty with Fortitude and patience becoming their profession and the Sacred Cause in which they are engaged." And they could hear with equal confidence his promise that he would share in every hardship and inconvenience. He had not seen his own baggage for more than two weeks, as they well knew.

But perhaps they listened somewhat ironically to the rest of the order, which provided for the observance on the morrow of the day set apart by the Honorable Congress for public Thanksgiving and praise, when the chaplains would perform divine service at which all officers and soldiers were exhorted to attend. In their present circumstances they may well have asked themselves what they had to be thankful for. After the services, however, the usual lean boiled beef gave place to roast pork for dinner, at least in some of the messes.

Next morning they marched the eight miles northwestward to Valley Forge and faced the scene whose name their hardships in the next three months were to make a synonym for misery and indomitable endurance. As they halted in front of it, weary, hungry, and cold, that bleak December afternoon, its aspect must have been the reverse of encouraging. Before them a densely wooded slope some two miles in breadth rose gradually to a ridge that terminated at its

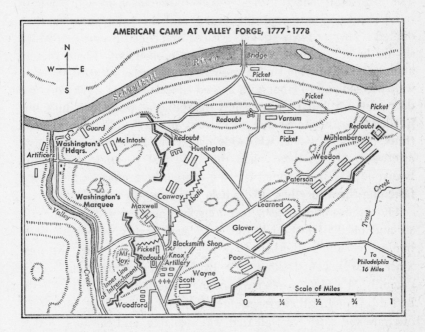

western end in a commanding eminence called by the misleading name of Mount Joy. On its western side Mount Joy fell abruptly to the Valley Creek, which wound northward for about a mile and there emptied into the Schuylkill, forming a natural protection for the right flank of the position. A concave curve of the Schuylkill itself, which at this point flowed generally eastward, covered the rear and the left flank. From where they halted, the troops could not see the village. It lay behind Mount Joy on the low ground at the junction of the creek and the river. But the army had passed close to it in the fall—Hamilton and Henry Lee had narrowly escaped capture in a skirmish there. Many of the soldiers had seen it, and they knew it to be no cheerful rural center like Morristown, but only a hamlet; and of that the greater part had been reduced to blackened ruins by British official incendiarism or the wanton carelessness of British soldiers in September.

Orders had already been issued for the building of the cabins. The men were divided into parties of twelve, each of which was to build its own. Tools were distributed, and the commander in chief offered a prize of twelve dollars for the best-constructed cabin which should be the soonest completed in each regiment. There was an abundance of suitable timber growing on the site. Most of the men were accustomed to labor with ax and shovel. Storms and bitter cold delayed them, but they were less miserable at work than huddling in their tents, where, as one man noted, it was "colder than one can think." Thomas Paine, who rode over from Lancaster, wrote of it afterward: "I was there when the army first began to build huts. Everyone was busy; some carrying logs, others mud, and the rest fastening them together. The whole was raised in a few days."

The cabins were sixteen feet long by fourteen wide, with walls six and one-half feet high, and into each corner were built three bunks, one above another. Clay filled the gaps between the logs. Since boards were lacking—the British had destroyed the village sawmill—Washington offered a prize of one hundred dollars for the best substitute for them for roofing. But sapling poles and a covering of straw and earth were all that was available, and the roofs leaked dismally after a few hours of rain or thaw.

Split oaken slabs formed the doors. Oiled paper, when it could be come by, filled the windows. Some of the cabins sported stone chimneys, but most of the groups contented themselves with chimneys and fireplaces built of wood and lined with eighteen inches of clay. The officers' cabins stood in line behind those of their men and differed little from them. There was one for each general, one for his staff. The field officers of each regiment shared one, each regimental staff another. The commissioned officers of every two companies were quartered together. The noncommissioned officers bunked with the privates.

By New Year's Day, less than two weeks after the army had arrived on the ground, Surgeon Waldo recorded that the camp began to look like a spacious city. Well it might, for, quartered in units of twelve, and with the additional buildings for officers and hospitals, the troops must have required close to a thousand cabins. They stretched in a double line along the entire crest of the ridge from the Schuylkill to the southern slope of Mount Joy, housing nine brigades, with Knox's artillery a little in rear of the right of the line. The other five brigades were located from one-half to three-quarters of a mile farther to the rear, on the northern slope of the ridge and near the Schuylkill.

"We are all going into log huts—a sweet life after a most fatiguing campaign," Greene grumbled in a letter to his wife. One lance corporal, however, told his brother that the huts were very comfortable, and Waldo, who had added a stone chimney to his and bought a bearskin to lie on, said the same of them. In contrast to the brushwood shelters, frigid tents, and the many nights under the open sky they doubtless seemed so. But there was not enough straw for bedding to go around, and to keep from freezing many men who had lost their blankets were forced to sit up all night around the fires, where, wrote Waldo, "cold and smoke make us fret."

When de Kalb saw the place, he said that only a speculator or one of Washington's ill-wishers could have suggested wintering in such a wilderness. But he doubtless judged it by the standards of Europe, where, in the vocabulary of the time, it would have been described as "savage." It had been selected after much discussion and against the opinion of the majority of the officers: they had favored quarters along the Lancaster-Reading line. The ardent Wayne, however, had argued that a position no farther away from the enemy than Wilmington or in cantonments about twenty miles from Philadelphia was essential if the army was to maintain its reputation, and the reasoning outlined in Washington's order of December 17 had prevailed.

All things considered, the position was well chosen. The nature of the ground was admirably adapted to defense, and there was an abundance of wood and water. With outposts sixteen miles from Germantown, it was sufficiently distant from the enemy to be safe from surprise and at the same time close enough to Philadelphia to protect a considerable area of rich country from foraging expeditions, unless these were made in great strength; and for this purpose a bridge was soon built across the Schuylkill to make the territory east of the river readily accessible. At Valley Forge the army covered Reading and Lancaster from an enemy offensive, and with adequate supplies of food and clothing from those well-stocked bases, which were only forty or fifty miles away, there was good reason to anticipate a healthful and fairly comfortable winter for the troops, and one in which their position would exert a continual and embarrassing pressure on the enemy.

But from the first days at Valley Forge, food and clothing, the essentials to these ends, had been wanting. Throughout the autumn there had been times when the army—"clogged and retarded," as Washington complained to Richard Henry Lee, for want of bread and meat—could not march; days when the commissary had not even a single barrel of flour to issue; and it had been necessary to keep scores of men in the hospitals because they were too nearly naked to endure the life of the bivouacs. Now, three days after the arrival at Valley Forge, Washington informed Congress grimly that unless it set to work with vigor to improve the service of supply the army must dissolve. It was no overstatement of the situation. That very night two brigades refused to march against a British foraging expedition unless they were given food, and an open mutiny was narrowly averted.

With nerves rasped by the humiliation of having to report so shameful an occurrence, Washington tore off a scorching letter to President Laurens. All he could do to meet the emergency, he wrote, was to send out parties to collect enough food to satisfy the soldiers' immediate and pressing want. "But will this answer?" he demanded. "No, sir; three or four days of bad weather would prove our destruction. What then is to become of this army?" There was only one commissary in camp, and he had "not a single hoof of any kind to slaughter and not more than twenty-five barrels of flour!"

2

Through the frosty murk of the January dawn came the roll of drums. Along the two-mile double line of log cabins slab doors creaked on their wooden hinges and pinched faces looked out at the inhospitable day. In tattered garments that could no longer be called uniforms men stepped gingerly out upon the frozen mixture of snow, mud, and ice in feet swathed in strips of blanket or shod with clumsy rawhide sandals. Their bare flesh showed filthy and blue with cold or black with neglected frostbite through rents in stockings and leggings and at the ragged knees and elbows of breeches, coats, and hunting shirts. Under battered hats and knitted nightcaps their eyes, cavernous with hunger, many of them bright or dull with fever, looked out above hollow cheeks. The hands with which they grasped their rusty muskets were red and knotted with chilblains and rheumatism. From the open doors behind them came the reek of dead wood smoke, the smell of pent-up sleep, and the stench of foul straw, dirty clothes, and unwashed bodies.

"No bread, no soldier!" The cry arose, plaintive but with that sardonic parody of self-pity that seems always to have been characteristic of the American in arms. It was taken up, embellished, and ran down the line of quarters of the nine brigades that stretched from the bank of the Schuylkill to the steep escarpment where Mount Joy dropped to the Valley Creek. "No bread, no meat, no soldier!" To the northwest, half a mile away, the three brigades of the second line echoed it, and the brigade by the river made reply. The headquarters guard down by the burnt-out ruins of the village heard it. So did the commander in chief.

The daily ration was supposed to consist of one and one-half pounds of flour or bread, one pound of meat or fish, or three-quarters of a pound of pork, and a gill of whisky or spirits; or else a half-pound of pork or bacon, a half pint of peas or beans, and a gill of whisky or spirits. But on December 21, when Varnum's brigade had tasted no meat for forty-eight hours and no bread for a still longer time, Waldo recorded his thanks to Providence for a little mutton. Thanks to the foraging parties that Washington had sent out, there was mutton and grog on Christmas Day, and Waldo and his hut-mates finished the year with a good drink and thankful hearts. But it was January 7, nearly three weeks after the army's arrival at Valley Forge, before it became possible to issue a four days' supply of fresh provisions, and such occasions continued to be rare.

For days together it was "Firecake and water, sir," for breakfast, and for dinner "Water and firecake." Some of Sullivan's men, who were camped near the river, varied this diet with a soup of clams. Some indomitable humorists were discovered by a curious officer boiling a stone in their camp kettle. "They say there's strength in a stone, if you can get it out," they explained solemnly. Greene, who seems to have fancied himself as a dietitian, recommended what he called a "firmity" of wheat and sugar as a substitute for meat. But often there was nothing to eat but frozen potatoes.

The weeks went by, but food became no more plentiful. In the middle of February Washington was constrained to beg Governor Clinton of New York for help in a shortage of supplies that amounted to little less than famine. All the available supplies in New Jersey, Pennsylvania, Maryland, and Delaware, he told him, could not support the army for more than another month, and a terrible crisis must ensue unless all the states turned in to help avert it. To the President of Pennsylvania he described the sufferings of his troops as beyond all description. Two or three times, he wrote to John Cadwalader in March, they had been days together without provisions and once for six days without meat.

Waldo, no sentimentalist, wrote into his diary a vivid vignette of these weeks: "Here comes a bowl of beef soup full of dead leaves and dirt. There come a soldier. His bare feet are seen through his worn-out shoes—his legs nearly naked from the tattered remains of an only pair of stockings—his Breeches are not sufficient to cover his nakedness—his Shirt hanging in Strings—his hair disheveled—his face meagre."

The want of clothing, shoes, and blankets was as great as that of food, and its consequences hardly less menacing. Two days before Christmas Washington reported to Congress that 2,898 of his men, more than one-third of his strength on paper, were useless owing to their lack of garments, footgear, and covering against the cold at night. Wayne calculated that nine out of ten deaths and desertions were due as much to the men's nakedness as to the scanty and poor food. Washington had offered a prize of ten dollars for the best rawhide substitute for shoes, but with so little success that sentinels were seen standing in their hats to keep their bandaged feet out of the snow—and this although a man's hut-mates would club their clothing so that he might be as warmly clad as they could make him when he went on guard duty.

Wayne, though he had the advantage of being in his own state and appealed repeatedly to the Pennsylvania Council, had to endure the mortification of seeing his sergeants, fifers, and drummers appear on parade in tatters. As late as the end of March he was begging for linen overalls, shirts, shoes, gaiters, and black stocks for three thousand men, adding that if thread were sent with the linen, the overalls could be made in camp. This was done, and all the tailors in the army were excused from other duties until the garments were finished. Twelve hundred of the shirts were turned out at Lancaster, every patriotic family in the town taking a hand in their manufacture.

The destitution of the officers very nearly equaled that of the men. Their personal baggage had been sent to Bethlehem with the rest of the train before the battle at the Brandywine. It had been returned to them much the worse for the carelessness of guards and the plundering of hangers-on; and with their continually depreciating pay many of them were unable to replace their losses. Surgeon Waldo spent a stormy day learning from a regimental adjutant the trick of mending socks so that the darns looked like knitting. John Laurens, who was by no means poor, got down to his last pair of breeches. Foreigners who had lately joined the army were amazed by the sight of officers mounting guard in old dressing gowns or blankets worn cloakwise.

On the 1st of February General Orders announced the arrival of some clothes from Virginia. Gentlemen, it was stated, might now furnish themselves with comfortable clothing. But the rare shipments of clothing from Lancaster continued to be deplorably inadequate. One sufficient for six hundred men had to be distributed among the neediest individuals in fourteen regiments. Another lot could not be issued at all because the garments had been sent without buttons. When a more considerable supply reached the camp on February 23, it came none too soon. The returns for that month showed 3,989 men too scantily clad and ill shod to be fit for duty and, out of the entire Continental army's paper strength of less than 18,000, only 5,012 effective rank and file.

Among troops so roughly housed, scantily clad, and close to starvation, many fell sick, and their condition became dreadful. Two hospital cabins had been built behind each brigade. The limited supply of boards and shingles had been devoted to roofing them. To purify the fetid air of the quarters it was ordered that the powder of a cartridge or else pitch or tar should be burned each day. Inoculations against smallpox were begun, and the recipients were dosed with a mixture of calomel, jalap, niter elixir, vitriol, Peruvian bark, and Virginia snakeroot.

The itch spread throughout the army. Nostalgia, the subtle forerunner of melancholia, became increasingly prevalent. The hospital cabins were soon filled to overflowing with sufferers whose maladies ranged from pneumonia to fingers, feet, and legs so badly frostbitten that they had to be amputated. On Christmas Eve, Waldo had recorded that, thanks to mutton and grog and "no piddling pills," few had died. But the invalids' diet generally consisted of little more than Indian meal and rice. There was either a shortage or a complete lack of hospital stores. A field officer was detailed to be always on duty at the hospitals. But he could do nothing to remedy the want of straw, and the sick continued to lie on the bare poles of their bunks, often with no covering but their ragged garments.

The severest cases—if they seemed likely to survive the fifty-mile journey by wagon—were shipped off to the base hospital at Bethlehem. In that little Moravian community of five hundred inhabitants Washington had established the General Hospital of the Continental Army in December, 1776. Knox had written of the town, when he visited it in the following July: "This singularly happy place where all the inhabitants seem to vie with each other in humility and brotherly kindness." They had continued to do so in September and October, when the wounded from the Brandywine and Germantown came in by the cartload; and they did not change their ways this winter, though the town grew steadily more crowded with soldiers suffering from dysentery, pulmonary diseases, and those eighteenth-century terrors, jail fever and putrid fever. When the Hostel for Single Brethren, with a capacity of two hundred and fifty beds, was crammed with seven hundred and fifty patients who lay only two feet apart on straw that perforce was never changed, they opened their houses to later comers. But in spite of their best efforts the mortality was shocking. Out of forty patients belonging to one Virginia regiment only three survived.

Dr. Benjamin Rush, the physician general of the army's medical department, resigned, partly in disgust at a situation which he lacked the authority to correct, but partly, it would seem, to pursue a professional vendetta against Dr. William Shippen, Jr., the director general. Disapproving of the organization which Congress had fixed upon the Department, Rush had accepted his position reluctantly. But he had done his full duty thus far. Often in the field, he had attended the wounded after the battle at Princeton and had worked among them so self-forgetfully at the Brandywine that he narrowly escaped capture. A pioneer in military sanitation, he had published at Lancaster in the past year his *Directions for Preserving the Health of Soldiers*, and before he resigned he gave Washington the benefit of a scathing criticism of the military hospitals.

The number of patients was in itself enough to condemn the American system, he maintained. There were five thousand of them as against one thousand British, although, he went on with notable unfairness, the British had been exposed to the same hardships as the Americans in the recent campaign. But he told no more than the truth when he said that in the hospitals the sick and wounded were crammed by twenties into rooms only large enough for six or eight well men and were allowed to lie there in shirts and under blankets that they had been wearing and using for the past four or five months. Thus they caught fevers, if they did not have them when they were admitted, and nine out of every ten fever cases ended in death. Discipline was worse than lax among them, since there were no guards to enforce it. The patients dirtied their quarters and fought among themselves. They strolled outside at will, sold their clothes and blankets for rum, and bullied and plundered the local inhabitants.

Greene had heard something of the same sort about the hospitals in New Jersey when he was at Mount Holly in November. He charged it to the negligence of the surgeons. Washington complained that patients' clothing and equipment were stolen by hospital personnel—a charge not unheard of in more recent wars—with the result that men who were cured could not return to their regiments. But it was too much to expect from physicians fresh from civil practice and totally inexperienced in military methods that they should be able to administer successfully the hastily improvised and inadequate organizations of which they were put in charge. Neither Rush nor any other critic, moreover, told where clean clothes and blankets, fresh straw, sufficient medicines, and men for hospital guards were to be found to supply those deficiencies. For Washington the mere policing and sanitation of the camp at Valley Forge was a task of unending difficulty.

Commenting on conditions in the rebel army, the Tory *New York Gazette and Daily Mercury* jeered that the Continental Congress need never lack rags for its paper money: their army could furnish plenty; and as for livestock, the soldiers had an abundant supply on their backs. And the maddening thing about the whole situation was that it was entirely unnecessary. Actually there was enough of everything, if only it could be delivered where it was needed. Abroad, in France and the French West Indies, large quantities of clothing were held up by the squabbles of rival agents. At home legislative stupidity and departmental confusion and red tape caused exasperating delays.

When Wayne drew upon his large private means to the amount of £4,500 to furnish new clothing for his men, the clothier general refused to issue the garments because he regarded the transaction as "irregular." Scanning the list of shoes and clothing that had been issued to their troops since the beginning of the previous year, the Council of the State of Pennsylvania owlishly opined that the soldiers must have been selling their clothes to the sutlers for liquor; and deliveries of shoes and garments in store at Lancaster were held up because the Council neglected to pass the order for their issue.

Confusion reigned in the supply departments. Against Washington's advice, Congress had made the subordinates in the Commissary Department directly responsible to one of its committees instead of to their chief, and Joseph Trumbull, the devoted and able commissary general, had resigned in despair. Major General Mifflin, the quartermaster general, had left army headquarters in a huff the previous summer upon Washington's refusal to march to Philadelphia when Mifflin thought he ought to do so, and in the six months since his departure Washington had received no assistance from him. In November Mifflin had quit as quartermaster general, retaining, however, his major general's rank, without pay. But in spite of Washington's urging Congress had neglected to appoint a successor to that vital post.

The transportation of supplies was a part, and a most important part, of the Quartermaster Department's functions, and the want of wagons and horses was chiefly responsible for the army's severest needs. Contractors demanded forty-five shillings a day for a wagon with a driver and four horses. But Congress would pay only thirty shillings, and the risk of being fined for absence from state militia duty made men unwilling to serve as drivers. Many of those who did so were inefficient or unreliable. Without supervision, they would lighten their loads by draining the brine from the casks of salt meat, and the meat would spoil in transit. They spilled the flour and other perishable goods or spoiled them by unloading them in the wet when their wagons bogged down. Or they simply quit on the job, dumped their loads on the roadside and drove off, leaving food, clothes, shoes, blankets, and tools to be stolen or ruined by the weather.

Bad roads, deep snows, and floods on the Susquehanna delayed or stalled the cargoes of the more faithful drivers. Nor was the army able to help itself in this respect. For when food for the men was lacking, grain and hay for the horses was nonexistent, and snow covered the pastures. Washington sent the light horse to winter quarters at Trenton, where the New Jersey farms could be drawn upon for the subsistence of their animals. At Valley Forge the horses of the artillery and the train died of hunger by the hundreds. Twice a week fatigue parties had to be charged with burying them. "Could the poor horses tell their tale," wrote Washington, with the Virginian's innate love of the creatures, "it would be in a strain still more lamentable [than the men's], as numbers have actually died of pure want." When Elias Boudinot joined headquarters in pursuance of his duties as commissioner for the exchange of prisoners, the nearest farm where his horses could be fed was eighteen miles away.

3

On February 17 John Laurens wrote to his father that hunger had brought the troops to the verge of mutiny. But no mutiny occurred. In the three long months of want and nakedness there was no general disobedience of orders, actual or constructive, among the troops in the continental service, excepting the refusal of those two brigades to march against the enemy in December unless they were given supplies for the expedition. The danger of it, however, always darkened the horizon. March was nearing its end before Washington could write: "Contrary to my expectations, we have been able to keep the soldiers from mutiny or dispersion, although, in the single article of provisions, they have encountered enough to occasion one or the other." De Kalb said that no European army would have endured such hardships.

The troops had remained obedient. Half-famished though they were, they had not scattered over the country in search of food. But of military discipline in the usually accepted meaning of that term little was to be seen among them by a superficial observer. For drills and ceremonies, even when snow, rain, or bitter cold did not prevent them, there was hardly time or strength after the fatigue duties required by the daily struggle for the mere essentials of existence. And from such work many had to be excused because they were too scantily clad to face the weather. These were kept busy in a laboratory, molding bullets and making cartridges, for which the paper, seized for that purpose, was the unbound leaves of *The Martyr Book* of the Pennsylvania German Theosophic Society at Ephrata. A blacksmith shop was built, and men were kept busy indoors there at the making of spontoons. For it had been observed in action that captains and lieutenants armed with muskets or rifles became absorbed in using their firearms instead of directing their men. So they were now to be equipped with the steel-headed half-pike which was carried by officers of their grades in most of the armies of that day. The rest of the soldiers, more fortunate in the matter of clothing, were occupied with an endless routine of hewing wood, drawing water, clearing brush, hauling provisions when these were to be issued, burying dead horses, and the digging and filling of latrines.

Sanitation, that essential to the existence of an army in a permanent camp, was a continual problem. Most of the troops came from small towns or thinly settled districts where sanitary precautions could be safely neglected; the frequent changes of location during the recent campaign had made them comparatively unimportant; and it now became necessary to inculcate their very rudiments among the soldiers. From January until far into the spring the headquarters orderly book is sprinkled with reiterated orders, exhortations, and reproaches on the subject of dead horses left unburied, and the prevalence about the huts of "much filth and nastiness," which was revealed by every thaw. When the line officers were slack, as they generally were in the enforcement of these regulations, division and brigade commissaries were charged with the task, and no plea of ignorance was accepted as an excuse for failure to observe them. But even the promise of severe punishment failed to induce country boys to make the frigid journey to the latrines on winter nights, and in at least one brigade the sentinels were instructed to fire on any man "easing himself elsewhere than at ye vaults."

These circumstances and the continual alternation of freezing cold with thaw and rain placed the sources of water supply in frequent danger of contamination. With the approach of mild weather wells had to be cleaned out and barrels sunk in the springs. It was discovered that the keeping of the huts in weatherproof condition could not safely be left to their exhausted and often sickly occupants. A regular system of inspections had to be established, with special attention to leaky roofs, not only in the hospitals but in all other quarters.

Under the pressure of such conditions the administration of the camp would have been a herculean task even with officers of wide experience and a professional military education. But although the previous winter at Morristown had winnowed their number of the least desirable, all too many of those in the lower grades, excellent fighters and combat commanders though they had proved themselves to be, still added indifference and negligence to their ignorance of their duties and responsibilities.

They knew little of guard duty and were careless in its perform-ance. Many of the captains were utterly casual about company roll calls. Some kept no roll calls at all. Many took to drinking, messing, and sleeping with their men. It was particularly difficult to make young ensigns who had old friends in the ranks understand the necessity of maintaining the proper distance between officers and enlisted men. Others did not hesitate to desert their grim huts and take up more comfortable quarters when they could find them. They shared largely, too, in the army's besetting sin of straggling and going absent without leave, against which Washington had always to be on the alert. After the retreat from Germantown he had to send the light horse to scour the country for miles to the northward of Pen-nebecker Mill to round up men who, be it understood, had no intention of deserting but, like the Confederate soldiers eighty-five years later, could not see the sense of hanging around a camp when there was no fighting in prospect and their farms needed them.

Just across the Schuylkill lay a pleasant country abounding in provender in spite of the foraging of both armies during the past autumn. Once over the bridge at the northeastern angle of the camp a soldier, or an officer, could lead a far more cheerful life than among the stump-studded snowfields, smoky huts, and endless fatigues of Valley Forge. Many were quick to do so, with the result that a far worse thing than straggling soon followed. On the day after Christmas a General Order announced the commander in chief's grief and indignation at the outrages and robberies committed by soldiers on the other side of the river. Unwarrantable in enemy country, they were, in the army's own country, not only in the highest degree base and cruel but injurious to the cause, he told his men. He cracked down on granting furloughs, restricted to field officers the right to issue passes for leaving the camp, and threatened to punish severely any man caught outside the guard line without a permit.

The better to deal with these and other offenses enough animals were drawn from the army's dwindling herd to mount the provost marshal's guard on horseback. Its men were armed and equipped like light dragoons, and four of their number were appointed executioners. Their prisoners were kept in tents until everybody else had a hut to sleep in and suffered so severely from cold and exposure that a court-martial excused from further punishment a man convicted of a minor offense. Trials were held daily to relieve others from such hardships. But in general the sentences were characterized by all the brutality customary in the civil as well as the military courts of the day.

The cases were numerous and ranged all the way from petty larceny to one of sodomy. Those of desertion, attempted or actual, were the most frequent, although a good many deserters got safely away to the British lines. It was notable, however, that most of those who succeeded in doing that were "old-country men," i.e., not native Americans. One hundred lashes was the usual penalty for those who were caught. But one man, who had deserted three times, was sentenced to fifty lashes on each of two successive days and to have his back "well washed with salt and water" after the second infliction. Another third offender, who had forged a discharge and re-enlisted, was given three hundred. A woman convicted of laying a plot for desertion to the enemy was sentenced to a hundred lashes and drumming out of camp. And two men—one for repeated desertions, the other for deserting when on guard duty and taking two prisoners with him—were hanged on the Grand Parade in the presence of detachments from all the brigades in the camp.

For other offenses the convicted man was sometimes sentenced to run the gantlet of his comrades, while a soldier with a fixed bayonet at the culprit's breast backed slowly before him lest he escape a good beating by actually running. But a surgeon was required to be present at all punishments to see that the recipient did not receive more stripes than he could bear, and the commander in chief disapproved as illegal a sentence of five hundred lashes and ordered a new trial. In the militia offenses were dealt with less formally. Down at the Gulph a militia regiment on outpost duty persisted in giving trouble by nightly false alarms. Colonel Aaron Burr was sent down to stop this nuisance, found an incipient mutiny on his hands, and quelled it by slashing off the leader's arm with his sword.

A few officers were brought to trial on such serious charges as cowardice in the face of the enemy. Convicted, they were cashiered. More were tried for playing with cards and dice, amusements which Washington had forbidden at Morristown in the spring as a vice so pernicious that it would never escape his severest punishment, since it had been the ruin of many a promising young officer. A commissary, found guilty of theft, was mounted on a bareback horse, facing the animal's tail, with his hands tied behind him, and drummed out of camp by the massed drummers of his division. A captain was cashiered for stealing a hat, and his name and crime were ordered to be published in the newspapers of every state, particularly in those of his own. A lieutenant who had combined "infamously stealing" with "association with a private" was sentenced to have his sword broken over his head on the Grand Parade at guard mounting. But a colonel, who had, to be sure, an excellent record, was let off with a reprimand, though he had been absent without leave for between two and three months.

The most frequent charges against the commissioned personnel involved "behavior unbecoming an officer and a gentleman." This ranged from drinking, messing, and sleeping with enlisted men to challenging and striking a fellow officer. With the hardship and monotony of camp life, nerves grew raw. Quarrels between officers came more and more frequently before the courts, and on charges so frivolous and ill-sustained that near the beginning of spring a General Order stated that they seemed to the commander in chief to be more owing to personal dislike and private animosity than to a desire to promote the good of the service. They gave him, the order continued, "sensible pain," for he wished the officers of his army "to consider themselves as a band of Brothers, cemented by the Justice of the Common Cause," and not to "add Papers to the Public files which may hereafter reflect disgrace upon themselves and the army."

But the slackers, the deserters, and the malefactors were relatively few. The vast majority, officers and men alike, did their duty as patiently, laboriously, and faithfully as famished and frostbitten bodies and bored and anxious minds would permit. No force of military police, however efficient, no courts-martial, however just and punctual, could have saved the army from anarchy and dissolution if this had not been so. A Congressional committee reported of the troops that their sufferings were equaled only by their patience and fortitude, and went on to tell how, since horses were wanting, the men yoked themselves to little carriages of their own making and carried wood and provisions on their backs.

When they had been for a week without meat and for a number of days without bread, they came to their superior officers like humble petitioners for special favors, as Greene described it in a letter home, and stated respectfully that they could not remain longer in camp without food and clothing. Greene and some other officers took up a collection to relieve their immediate needs. And all this was only ten days (February 26) after John Laurens had warned his father of the imminence of mutiny.

· Given half a chance, there was even gaiety among the cabins, though Lafayette described them as "no gayer than a dungeon," and the commander in chief was alert for every opportunity to encourage it. On January 3 pleasant anticipations were aroused by the announcement that Congress had rewarded their soldierlike patience, fidelity, and zeal in taking post in a country destitute of houses by voting them an extra month's pay. When a ship from France arrived at Portsmouth, New Hampshire, with a cargo of guns, mortars, muskets, entrenching tools, powder, and cannon balls, General Orders spread the cheerful news. And there was a special satisfaction in some of the shipments of clothing, which had been intended for the enemy.

Throughout the winter British supply ships bound for Philadelphia were forced ashore by the ice in the lower Delaware and captured by the troops of Smallwood's division, which was stationed at Wilmington. Others were taken at sea by Commodore Barry's

squadron of the infant American navy or were the prizes of the
numerous American privateers that had been preying on British
merchantmen ever since the outbreak of the war. Quantities of cloth,
shoes, hats, and shirts, hundreds of muskets, General Howe's personal service of plate, and the chests of many other British officers
were among the spoil. So, too, were the medical library of a British
army surgeon and the order of the *Lyon d'Or*, which his grateful
sovereign had sent to General Knyphausen. A shipload of British
officers' wives was also captured. There were doubtless grins at Valley Forge over the report of the ladies' fears lest they be given over
to the rebel soldiery, and doubtless the troops felt some envy on hearing of the arrival at Philadelphia of three hundred females, whom
Lafayette described as "*damoiselles*," to solace the British soldiers.

The issue of a gallon of spirits to each officers' mess was the
occasion of "civil jollity" at regimental headquarters dinner tables.
And there were jollifications less civil when, for instance, the maud-
lin antics at an officers' picnic on the banks of the Schuylkill excited
the open contempt of two British bandsmen, deserters, who had
been hired to furnish music for the occasion. Even in the squalor
and misery at Bethlehem the sick and wounded officers evidently
lived so well at the Sun Inn that the services of a dancing master
were in request.

On St. Patrick's Day at Valley Forge the spirit of devilty inspired
the Pennsylvania German battalion to set up a fantastic image
which was immediately recognized as a "Paddy." Every Irishman in
the army—and there were many of them—was infuriated by this
embodied insult to his race. Ignorant of the identity of the perpe-
trators, they naturally suspected the ultra-Protestant New Englanders,
and a serious riot was developing when Washington himself rode in
among them. He knew who the makers of the image were, but he
also knew better than to tell. With ready tact he turned the whole
episode into a joke. He was himself a great admirer of St. Patrick,
he assured the irate Irishmen. He ordered the whole army to celebrate the day and caused an extra ration of whisky to be issued to
every soldier to put him in holiday mood.

4

But even men of the indomitable spirit of those at Valley Forge could not have been held to their duty save by a leader who had earned their unbounded confidence, manifested sympathetic understanding of their miseries, and controlled them with that masterly blending of tact and firmness of which the St. Patrick's Day episode was a conspicuous example. Something of the dry humor which a French officer observed as characteristic of him flavored his orders. In thanking them on March 1 for their perservering fidelity he told the troops: "Occasional distresses for want of provisions is a spectacle that occurs in every army, and perhaps there never was one which in general has been so plentifully supplied in respect to the former as ours."

Every soldier, wrote Waldo, labored through mud and cold with a song on his lips extolling war and Washington. They knew right well that Congress was to blame for the extremity of their sufferings, as they knew that Washington had been unceasing in his efforts for the well-being of officers and men alike. He overlooked few details that might contribute to that end. Each regiment was permitted to send an officer into the neighboring states to purchase wines and liquors. The prices of these were regulated. They ranged from nineteen shillings for a quart of French brandy to two shillings for a quart of Cider Royal; and profiteering sutlers were severely punished and driven out of camp.

To get straw for bedding and transportation to bring it in, parties were sent out to impress both the straw and the horses and wagons to haul it. To meet the need of footgear, other parties went through the country exchanging with the inhabitants the hides of slaughtered cattle at fourpence a pound for shoes at ten shillings a pair. The fat of the animals was mixed with ashes and boiled for soap. Their hoofs were boiled to extract the oil, which was used as a remedy for the itch. When men whose enlistments had expired went home, their blankets were taken from them and given to those who had none.

A policy of gentle dealing with the inhabitants near by proved profitable, although there was a saying in the country that whereas a plague of locusts left something behind it, the American army left nothing. A few farmers were so loyal to King George that they burned their grain rather than sell it to the rebels. Others deferred threshing it for the same reason, until they were warned that it would be taken unthreshed and paid for only as so much straw. But the majority of people, though they lacked the New Englanders' warlike devotion to the cause of Independence and the Jerseymen's thirst for vengeance, were not without feelings of common humanity; and when starvation stared the army in the face, they made collections, almost from door to door, to feed and clothe it. In the course of time markets were established in three places in the camp by the general's orders, and the neighboring country people kept these so well supplied that three market days a week became the rule.

In mid-February, however, it became necessary to resort to drastic methods if the army was to continue to exist. In September, when Congress was about to flee Philadelphia, it had empowered the commander in chief to take, wherever he might be, all such provisions and other articles needed for the comfortable subsistence of his army and to pay for them with certificates drawn upon the Commissary and Quartermaster Departments. This authority had been renewed in November and again on December 12. But Washington was loath to make use of it.

"A reluctance to give distress, and the prevalent jealousy of the military power, may have restrained me too far," he admitted to Congress on December 14. But on the last day of the year he felt so strongly the unwisdom of provoking the people's dislike of military orders that he asked Governor Livingston to use the civil authority to move certain supplies on the Jersey bank of the Delaware out of reach of the enemy. And a week later he was explaining to Congress that the taking of provisions by force not only spread disaffection and dislike of the army among the people but stirred up even among his veteran troops a spirit of plunder and robbery. The small and absolutely necessary seizures he had been compelled to make in the past few days had excited the greatest alarm and uneasiness among some of the warmest friends of the cause.

But both the scruples of humanity and considerations of policy had to give way to dire need. It was learned, moreover, that the

British were about to send out another great foraging expedition between the Schuylkill and the Brandywine, the like of which had already swept through that area; and if the inhabitants were to be stripped of their provender, it might as well be by the patriots as by the enemy. Greene went down along the Brandywine with the intention of foraging the country naked, taking horses, sheep, and cattle, grain and wagons to haul it with. He found the people in a state of poverty and distress. The British had already driven off to Philadelphia most of their cattle and the best of their horses. What remained they hid in dense woods and swamps. But "Harden your hearts," Greene bade his men. "We are in the midst of a damn nest of Tories." He gave a hundred lashes each to two men who were caught taking provisions to Philadelphia, seized without payment of any kind livestock and wagons that had been hidden from his troops, and made prisoners of their owners.

Wayne did the like in New Jersey, where he declared the inhabitants between New Salem and Mount Holly to be even greater Tories, if possible, than those in Pennsylvania, and he burned their hay since he could find no wagons to take it with him. He came close to being caught by the British near Haddonfield but, after a brisk skirmish, got safely over the Delaware once more, and in general so performed his mission that he earned the name of Wayne the Drover. But only by these means was the army at Valley Forge preserved.

By his own way of living, not less than by his efforts for his men's welfare, did Washington support their devotion to the cause. Until the last of them was housed they could look up to the bleak crest of Mount Joy and see his blue headquarters flag, with its thirteen white stars, fluttering and snapping in the icy wind in front of the canvas marquee where he slept, ate, and worked as long as any of his men lacked warmer quarters. When the cabins were finished, he moved down to the village, to what was known as the Isaac Potts house, though it was to Deborah Hewes that he paid his rent. It was one of the few dwellings that had escaped the conflagration kindled by the British.

Lafayette, Knox, and Greene occupied some of the others. Most

of the other general officers lived in cabins near their troops. But
the commander in chief's quarters were not much more comfortable
than theirs. For the next few weeks he lived drearily and crowdedly
in the two small rooms on the ground floor. A seat at his table and
a square on his floor were the best he could offer to General Cadwalader. His Negro body servant Billy looked after him, but the
fare at the headquarters mess was little better than that of the enlisted men. There was no wine, only grog. Plates and knives and
forks were so few that the company had to be divided and the
dishes washed before the second service.

Standards of comfort even among the officers in the American
service were never high. At York Colonel Pickering thought himself fortunate to find near the town quarters in a farmhouse, where
"in a little cabin in a corner of a warm chamber" he slept on a straw
bed, with a bag of straw for a bolster and, for covering, a single
blanket doubled, his greatcoat, and his other clothes over all. But
Washington's situation at this time drew from him one of his few
complaints on that score. "We are in a dreary kind of place and uncomfortably provided," he wrote.

If one accepts the evidence of the John Trumbull portrait believed
to have been painted this winter, Valley Forge told upon Washington
no less than upon his men. It shows no imperturbable Olympian but
a man whom care, anxiety, and worry have harried and aged beyond
his forty-six years. From a portrait that Charles Willson Peale painted
on bedticking in the camp at this time the eyes look out with a
shrewdly watchful if not a quite cynical glance. That his strong sense
of justice and habitual equanimity had ceased in the late autumn to
be what they had been is to be guessed from a letter that Nathanael
Greene wrote to him late in November: "I thought I felt the lower
of your Excellency's countenance, when I am sure I had no reason
to expect it. It is out of my power to command success, but I trust
I have ever endeavored to deserve it."

It was in these early weeks at Valley Forge that Washington is
said to have been discovered alone in the woods, kneeling in the
snow and pouring out his troubles in prayer. The episode may be
apocryphal. But it can hardly be considered out of character in a man

whose private letters abound in references to "the determination of
Providence . . . always wise," though "often inscrutable"; to the
"due sense of dependence we ought to place in that all-wise and
powerful Being, on whom alone our success depends"; and to "the
hand of Providence . . . so conspicuous in all this, that he must
be worse than an infidel that lacks faith."

It might be possible to believe that his orders for morning prayers
in the army and for Sunday morning services, which he urged both
officers and men to attend, were issued with tongue in cheek and
for moral effect only. But if he was not sincere in such utterances
as have been quoted above, they must be regarded as mere cant,
and it would be difficult to imagine a man to whom cant would be
more repugnant than to him.

The passage of time may well have confirmed his belief that
Providence favored the cause of Independence. Eventualities fully
justified his choice of the position at Valley Forge. Weak though
his army became, his dispositions restricted the enemy to little more
than the ground they stood on and made their mere subsistence a
matter of considerable difficulty. Only by expeditions in force could
they collect supplies in Pennsylvania. When their stored hay went sour
from being packed too wet, General Grant had to spend Christmas
Day and the day after, with eight battalions of British infantry,
the Hessian grenadiers, and the 17th Dragoons, collecting a fresh
supply, though his errand took him no farther outside the British
lines than Darby.

To obtain supplies from the neighboring farmers by purchase was
equally difficult, though less so in West Jersey than on the Germantown front, where the people would venture in to town on market
days only if their locality was occupied for the occasion by strong British detachments. Congress had made trading with the enemy an offense
punishable by military law. At Valley Forge the penalty was a hundred
lashes on the bare back. At Lancaster an army lieutenant and a civilian
were hanged for it. A certain amount of this trade did go on, since the
golden guineas with which the British paid for their purchases were
naturally preferred to Continental currency. In Bucks County, it
was said, American officers connived in it. Everywhere horses were

sold to the British when opportunity offered, even by government teamsters if the animals were not branded. But in localities where the patriot sentiment predominated people took the law into their own hands and flogged such offenders, one man so severely that he died.

For the bulk of his provisions Howe had to depend on what was brought him by sea and river from New York. Some of his supply ships were captured at sea. The rest had to pass under the fire of the cannon of Smallwood's division at Wilmington, and parties in small boats fell upon the cattle ships and flour barges by night and set cargoes of hay on fire.

Skirmishes between detachments and patrols were continual throughout the winter and were fought with singular bitterness. On the Germantown front Captain Allen McLane, with a picked force of dragoons and infantry made the country beyond the outpost line unsafe for any British force smaller than a brigade. In General Orders on January 20 Washington thanked Captain Henry Lee and the officers and men of his troop for defeating more than two hundred British dragoons near Darby, though they had surprised his quarters at daybreak and he had not enough men to post one at every window. Attacks on the British outposts were so frequent and daring that when spring came, Captain Montrésor began to build a system of dams by means of which the front lines could be protected by inundations. During the winter, moreover, there was the constant possibility that if ice floes should make the Delaware impassable, the Americans would march down the Jersey shore and bombard the city from the opposite bank.

To Sir William Howe's critics—and these became more and more numerous on both sides of the Atlantic as time went on—the remedy was as simple as it was obvious: namely, a short and vigorous offensive that would destroy Washington's army or at least defeat it and drive it from its position at Valley Forge. Two and a half years later Washington wrote that there had been three times when only British supineness and folly had saved the American cause: at the Delaware in '76, at Morristown in '77, and at Valley Forge when his men were too few to defend the fortifications and so many of his horses had died that he could not retreat.

Howe had now assembled 19,530 troops at Philadelphia. Washington could count only 11,800 on paper; and how many of these were actually present and fit for duty he could only guess, so careless was the keeping of the rolls, so numerous were the unreported sick, the absent without leave, and those on detached service. On December 23 he reported the number of his effectives as not more than 8,200, and for some weeks the fortifications of the camp were little more than shallow tracings in the ground. But although Howe's secret service cannot have left him in entire ignorance of these facts, he saw in them no golden opportunity. The position at Valley Forge was by its nature one of great strength. Only a frontal attack could be made upon it. And that would have to be delivered over a natural glacis which the building of huts had stripped of cover and against troops fighting as they loved best to fight, behind entrenchments which, however incomplete, would give them the opportunity to develop their deadly fire power to its fullest extent. In such circumstances even sick men, who had handled firearms from childhood, could be relied upon to wait until the enemy were within forty yards and then shoot to kill, as the farmers had done at Bunker Hill.

In the late winter, when the fortifications had been completed, the place became a fortress. Entrenchments ran along the entire crest that was occupied by the nine brigades in the front line, with a redoubt where the ground sloped to the Schuylkill, and another behind the right, where Knox's artillery were hutted. A second line turned Mount Joy into a citadel, whose left flank, where the slope was less steep, was strengthened by an abatis more than half a mile in length and as thick and strong as the famous French one at Ticonderoga had been. More entrenchments covered the interval between the abatis and the river, and a star redoubt about halfway between these works and the northern end of the front line frowned from a lesser eminence upon Fatland Ford and the bridge.

In the opinion of Duportail, who laid them out, these fortifications would withstand any attack that might be made upon them. General Charles Grey, who had demonstrated at Paoli and elsewhere that he was not lacking in enterprise, stated after a careful reconnaissance that an attack upon them would be "unjustifiable." Howe, moreover, was still asking why both parties to the conflict could not "sit down like two schoolboys with bloody noses and black eyes" and settle the matter and be friends. But he had already told Germain that the people at large were against him and that he was in the position of a foreign invader, with a long and disagreeable war of conquest ahead of him. It would take ten thousand troops to subjugate New England, he had warned his government, fifteen thousand more to overrun the South, and to these would have to be added strong garrisons to hold New York and Philadelphia. Now, waiting only to be relieved of his command, he had no desire to risk another blot on his already tarnished reputation by marching against such a tough objective as the position at Valley Forge.

Meanwhile the country immediately surrounding Philadelphia became a kind of no man's land. The British and Hessians had not changed their ways since they landed at Elk River. They left a trail of sacked dwellings behind them in their retirement from White-marsh. At Darby they stripped the private houses of furniture, and their cavalry burned the tavern at Jeffersonville after a skirmish with the American light horse. They searched Wayne's house for its owner, to the terror of his wife and children, though they refrained from plundering it. But at General Persifor Frazer's their men were drunk and, although somewhat checked by their officer, sacked the place and carried off all the horses and provisions, two Negro wenches, and other property, for which the general later filed a claim for £287 5 s.

Parties of Tories, based on Billingsport, terrorized West Jersey in the name of the King. Elsewhere American soldiers on furlough and gangs of civilians pretending to be patriot militia committed what Greene called "the most villainous robberies imaginable." Self-styled volunteers went about seizing horses in the name of the patriot cause, and a group of brothers ranged the country in open banditry until they were finally exterminated. Everywhere distrust, fear, hatred, and abominable selfishness were met with, wrote Pastor Collin of Swedesboro: parents and children, brothers and sisters, wife and husband were enemies to one another.

Farther afield, however, closer to the American lines than to the British, there were large districts where peace and harmony reigned through the winter. Quartered in and about Trenton, the American cavalry under Pulaski kept that part of New Jersey free from depredations. The division under Smallwood at Wilmington made British foraging in the Brandywine country difficult and dangerous. In such neighborhoods Whigs and Tories had united in harvesting their crops. In the hills of Gwynedd in the upper Wissahickon country sixteen-year-old Sally Wister had only one visit from the British to record in her diary; and on that occasion, which was in September, their officers were "gentlemanly" and their soldiers "civil" in their behavior. She heard the firing at near-by Whitemarsh on the 7th of December, but the principal events of the winter for her were neighborhood visits on horseback or by carriage or sleigh, times when some of Smallwood's command—"a peaceable sort of men"—made the Widow Foulke's house their headquarters, and the calls of gallant Continental officers of light horse, who contrived somehow to present an "elegant" appearance in white regimentals turned up with blue, and "mighty airish" caps with white crests. Between whiles she had leisure to read *Miss Melmoth, or the New Clarissa* and Henry Fielding's *Joseph Andrews,* though one would hardly have supposed that the latter would have been regarded as fit for a Quaker miss in her middle teens.

The mere presence of the army at Valley Forge, in fact, had accomplished a large measure of what Washington had expected it to do: protecting its friends near-by and behind it, closing large areas to British depredations, and making their capture of Philadelphia a barren conquest. But for all this neither Washington nor his troops got more than grudging credit. What they had failed to do was what was dwelt upon, not only in the country at large but at York, where people ought to have known better, since Congress had taken refuge there.

5

Long gone by were the jubilant days of the previous summer when Washington's success in ridding New Jersey of the enemy had caused him to be likened to Fabius Cunctator, the Roman general who had frustrated the genius of Hannibal by steadily avoiding battle. Before New Year's Day criticism of the army's inactivity had become so vociferous that the temperamental Sullivan, tired of the clamor of the Pennsylvanians, proposed to take the offensive, let the consequences be what they might. Of the stalemate at Whitemarsh one Congressman had written: "It was evident that our army was not inclined to fight," and of Germantown that it was a heaven-sent day of salvation, since it brought discredit on the commander in chief. "Our affairs," he wrote to General Gates, "are Fabiused into a very disagreeable position."

The loss of Philadelphia, the repeated defeats of the autumn, the fall of the forts on the Delaware, followed by the army's enforced inaction, had plunged the country into gloom. "You will know, sir," Richard Henry Lee wrote to Washington, "how weak and divided the people of this state [Pennsylvania] are from various causes. Those of Delaware are still worse"; and in the opinion of the Frenchman Duportail there was a hundred times more enthusiasm for the American revolution in one café in Paris than in all the thirteen American states. The Pennsylvania legislature adopted a "Remonstrance" against the army's going into winter quarters instead of keeping the field to protect their state against the depredations of the enemy.

On that action Washington was moved to comment at length and bitterly in the letter of December 23, in which he announced to Congress the imminent dissolution of his army. The legislature had reprobated his going into winter quarters, he wrote, his frayed nerves showing between the lines, "as if they thought the soldiers were made of stocks or stones, equally insensible to frost and snow; and, moreover, as if they conceived it easily practicable for an inferior army, under the disadvantages I have described . . . to confine a superior one, in all respects well appointed and provided for a winter campaign, within the city of Philadelphia, and cover from depredation and waste the states of Pennsylvania and New Jersey"—and all this in spite of the fact that they had seen with their own eyes the nakedness of the troops and had left unfulfilled their promise to clothe them. "I can assure the gentlemen," he continued, dictating in the frigid air of his marquee on Mount Joy, "that it is a much easier and less distressing thing to draw remonstrances in a comfortable room by a good fireside, than to occupy a cold, bleak hill, and sleep under frost and snow without clothes or blankets. However, although they seem to have little feeling for the naked and distressed soldiers, I feel abundantly for them, and, from my soul, I pity those miseries, which it is neither in my power to relieve or prevent."

As for himself, he went on, he had been chary of giving opinions or lodging complaints. But he thought it high time to speak plainly in exculpation of himself when he found that although the army's inactivity was owing to want of food and clothes, he was being blamed for it, and not only by the people at large but by those in power. The changes in the organization of the Commissary Department had been made contrary to his judgment, he reminded Congress, and he proceeded: "With truth then, I can declare, that no man in my opinion ever had his measures more impeded than I have, by every department in the army."

This was all very well as far as it went. Thus could his critics in Congress at least be answered. But as to the opinion of the country at large, where it was being said that, with sixty thousand men at his disposal, he was doing nothing, he was powerless. To make adequate explanation of his inactivity would be to reveal to the British the completeness of his impotence.

For his enemies both in Congress and elsewhere in the country— and of enemies he had inevitably made not a few in the discharge of his duties during the past two and a half years—it was a situation that might have been made to their order, and they had not been slow to take advantage of it. There were some also who were merely jealous of his great fortune and high position. Others were weary of the unmeasured praise that had been poured upon him by his admirers; and a few—among whom were certain officers in the army at Valley Forge—honestly believed him to have been a failure as commander in chief and wished to see him superseded by the vicariously but spectacularly successful Horatio Gates, the vanquisher of Burgoyne. All of these critics were soon united, though not all of them knowingly, in a campaign of whispering, innuendo, and false rumors directed to that end.

Washington had not long remained unaware of what was going on. It was soon reflected by the actions of Congress. Before he reached Valley Forge that body had more than once flouted his reasonable requests and even gone directly against them. Before the end of

January it had made a promotion that he deplored, limited his
authority as commander in chief, detached troops from his army
without his consent, and initiated an important military project without consulting him. In reply to a friendly warning from President
Laurens he wrote that he knew a malignant faction had for some time
been forming against him. He was chiefly concerned about it, he
said, lest it cause discord among the supporters of the common cause;
as for himself he felt that he had no right to complain: better men
than he had been made to suffer in the same way.

Washington's confidence in himself as an army commander had
never been great. Pickering, who was his adjutant general in the
1777 campaign, wrote of him long after: "The truth is, that General
Washington, not sanguine in his own opinion, and his diffidence
being increased, probably by a feeling of high responsibility as Commander-in-Chief, was ever disposed, when occasions occurred, to con-
sult those officers who were near him, in whose discernment and
fidelity he had confidence, and certainly his decisions were often influenced by their opinions. This is within my knowledge."

Shortly after his appointment to the supreme command—according to Dr. Rush—Washington, with tears in his eyes, had told
Patrick Henry that he was not fit for the position, and had added:
"From the day I enter the command of the American armies, I date
my fall, and the ruin of my reputation." He had begun by abiding
so strictly by the majority votes of his councils of war that Congress
had been moved to pass a resolution to free him from his sense of
obligation to do so. But he was not the man to be maneuvered into
quitting his position by a malevolent clique that lacked the courage
to attack him openly.

"If the people do not want me, I shall go," he told Lafayette,
"but until then I shall resist intrigues." It put a strain upon him to
follow this course, however. For to notice by official word or action
the web of detraction that was being woven about him would be,
he felt, improper in his position. Throughout November and December he bided his time, watching sharply for a turn in events that
would justify him in bringing the situation before the public. It
was late in January before he saw the desired opportunity, and it
was his enemies themselves who gave it to him.

CHAPTER V

☆

The Promise of Spring

1

BACK IN LATE OCTOBER, when General Gates's confidential aide-de-camp, Colonel James Wilkinson, was on his way to Congress with the official report of Burgoyne's surrender, he had no sooner crossed the Delaware than he discovered that Washington was being seriously criticized by a great many people. At Easton Dr. William Shippen, the director general of the army medical service, questioned him about a certain letter that General Thomas Conway, the Irishman from the French army, was said to have written to General Gates, giving thirteen reasons for the defeat at the Brandywine.

At York General Mifflin invited the young aide to tea with two members of Congress, and in the course of the conversation what were discreetly alluded to as Washington's "misfortunes" were dealt with severely. A few days later Wilkinson was writing to Gates of "dissensions, jealousies, calumnies, and detractions" in a quarter which he said he had no need to specify. Gates, availing himself of the fact that Congress, not Washington, had appointed him to the northern command, had neglected to inform the commander in chief, even unofficially, of the capture of Burgoyne, and with a cheap satisfaction Wilkinson added in his letter that the omission had been generally noticed.

His errand at York accomplished, Wilkinson set out by way of Reading to visit the army under Washington. Reading was crowded with such refugees as the Edward Biddles, who lived uncomfortably in lodgings jammed with their family portraits and the most precious of their furniture; and with interned English, Scotch, and German loyalists from North Carolina, and British officer prisoners on parole.

But it was a pleasant place for a young man fresh from the Saratoga wilderness. The British officers talked well of books and told him that Prior was now preferred to Pope by the best English taste. One Hessian officer was a great reader; another played the harp. There were card playing, tea parties, and balls. Officers from Washington's army came and went on business or recreation. And here again Colonel Wilkinson heard of General Conway's criticisms of the commander in chief: how he had spoken at length and publicly of Washington's unfitness for command.

When Wilkinson reached the army, which he finally did at Whitemarsh late in November, he found it rife with jealousies and criticisms of its general, or so he thought. Subsequent events make it seem unlikely that these were more serious than the kind of idle talk and comment that goes on in every camp when monotony, discomfort, and poverty of interests bring out the pettiness of the best of men. But in his youthful partisanship for his own commander the zealous aide-de-camp was all too eager to take them seriously.

Greene and Knox, especially the former, were objects of jealousy and envy to many on account of the confidence which their judgment, military knowledge, and innate military ability had caused Washington to repose in them. In the memoirs which Wilkinson published thirty-nine years later he quoted a letter from Wayne to Gates, dated the 21st of November, 1777, in which the fiery Pennsylvanian expressed the hope that Washington would not "listen too much to some counsel"—Greene's evidently to be inferred.

Washington's conduct of the recent campaign was being freely criticized even among his most loyal adherents, his indecision at the Chew house at the battle of Germantown being cited as the latest instance of what was regarded as his principal failing. De Kalb said it was a pity he was "so weak." When Colonel Pickering said much the same thing to Greene, Greene admitted: "The General does want decision." Hamilton was, for the time being, doubtful of his chief's ability, and among the regimental commanders Aaron Burr added to a personal dislike of Washington the opinion that he was a poor general. But then Burr's regiment was a part of Conway's brigade; and Wilkinson had not been long in the camp before he

heard from Conway's own lips all that the Frenchified Irishman had
been saying about his commander in chief.

All in all, those weeks of late October, November, and December
were a heady experience for "the boy of twenty," as Wilkinson
describes himself in his memoirs. As the bearer of news of America's
greatest victory thus far, and of the greatest disaster to British arms
that anybody could remember, he had been received with celebrations
all the way from Albany southward; and he had not spoiled them
by haste but had taken fifteen days for his passage. An ironic member of Congress, in fact, had proposed that the honorarium cus-
tomarily voted to messengers with such glad tidings should take the
form of a pair of spurs in his case.

Now, with the intelligence he had gathered at York and Reading
confirmed, in his judgment, by what he heard at Whitemarsh, a
dizzying vista of promotion and glory appeared to be opening before
him. For if Washington went down, who must go up if not the
victor of Saratoga? And whom would he take with him in his rise
if not the loyal aide and confidant who had helped him in the
intrigue by which he had superseded the able and devoted Schuyler
in the command of the northern army?

Unfortunately, as things turned out, Wilkinson on his arrival at
York had run across Lord Stirling, who was recovering there from a
fall from his horse, and he had dined that night with Stirling and his
aides, Colonel James Monroe and Colonel McWilliams. Their
mood was convivial, the wine excellent, and the host not one to stint
its consumption. Tongues were loosened, and Wilkinson babbled
out certain damnatory sentences about Washington that Conway
had written to Gates. These the loyal Stirling promptly reported to
his chief.

Wilkinson retained no memory of his indiscretion—or so he
always insisted; and he probably would not have been troubled by it
if he had remembered, so swiftly did his high hopes move toward
fulfillment. The feeling of the thing was in the air. Back at Lancaster and York, where people had illuminated their houses in honor
of the victory at Saratoga, they were dancing a new dance which
they called "Burgoyne's Surrender." The refugees from Philadelphia,

too ignorant of military matters to understand that only the tattered and hungry army at Valley Forge enabled them to dwell in safety where they were, saw only the dark side of the picture: the British rioting and plundering in their beloved homes, ruining furniture, gutting libraries, deflowering virgins, "while our generals and army," as one of them wrote in the late autumn, "are . . . consulting where they shall spend the winter in jollity, gaming and carousing. . . . O America," he lamented, "where is now your virtue? O Washington, where is your courage?"

They knew little and understood less of the army's want and the reasons for it. They heard that thousands of uniforms had been sent to the troops. Strange if these had never reached their destination! When Dr. Benjamin Rush dropped in of an evening, he would tell of a "general murmur in the people, about the city and country, against the weak conduct of General Washington . . . his slackness and remissness in the army," and that "a cry begins to be raised for a Gates, a Conway, a de Kalb. . . ." Too cautious to attack Washington specifically, Dr. Rush assailed his ablest officers and closest friends, calling Greene "sycophant," Sullivan "weak vain braggart," Stirling "lazy ignorant drunkard," Hamilton "paltry satellite," and added that Washington could be judged by the company he kept.

General Mifflin, whom loyal John Laurens described to his father as the head of the party opposing Washington, was ever ready to explain how mistaken the Fabian policy had been. Mifflin had held Washington's stirrup when the newly appointed commander in chief had mounted his horse in Philadelphia in 1775 to ride to Cambridge. But jealousy of Greene had soured him, and he told all who would listen that, owing to Greene's advice, the recent campaign had been a series of blunders.

John Adams had left York that fall to succeed Silas Deane as one of the commissioners in Paris. But his attitude toward Washington had been such that Thomas Paine, who spent that winter at Lancaster, maintained ever afterward that Adams was for Gates as commander in chief. As far back as the February of '77 Adams had deplored the tendency of some members of Congress to idolize, as he put it, an image which their hands had molten. He congratulated himself that Washington could gain no credit by either Burgoyne's surrender or the heroic defense of the Delaware forts, and he stooped so low as to charge him with having worn out the soldiers' clothes and shoes by useless marches during the past summer. As Franklin truly wrote of John Adams: "He was always an honest man, sometimes a wise one, but . . . about some things absolutely out of his senses."

Throughout December and on into January the air grew ever more thick with detractions, canards, and rumors, anonymous letters, accusations, and warnings. Down in Virginia Governor Patrick Henry received an unsigned communication, of which the text was that the northern army had showed what a good general could do, and that a Gates, a Lee, or a Conway could in a few weeks make an irresistible body of men out of the army at Valley Forge, though one of Washington's own major generals had recently described it to the writer as a mob. To President Laurens came an unsigned composition called "Thoughts of a Freeman."

In the letter to Patrick Henry not only were all of the army's troubles—the failure of the Commissary and Quartermaster Departments and the dreadful conditions in the hospitals—artfully deposited at Washington's door, but even the depreciation of the currency. "Thoughts of a Freeman" followed much the same lines, and with all of a singularly benighted civilian's ignorance of military matters, attacked also the conduct of the recent campaign. It demanded an investigation of the enemy's successful turning movement at the Brandywine and of the loss of Philadelphia. It condemned as fruitless and unaccountable the marches of the past summer; the separation of the troops from their baggage during the fall it held to have been largely responsible for filling the hospitals with sick; and it referred to the loss of the Delaware forts as mysterious.

All this, it concluded, argued a great weakness in the head: the head could not possibly be sound, when the whole body was disordered. The liberties of America could be safe only in the hands of the militia. The militia had had a principal share in every victory, and no good could be expected from a standing army "until Baal and his worshipers had been banished from the camp."

Patrick Henry forwarded the anonymous letter to Washington, and Laurens did the like with "Thoughts of a Freeman." Friends at Williamsburg and Port Tobacco wrote to Washington, warning him against the Board of War as the instrument of secret enemies, and against what they called petty larceny attacks by Congress with the intention of forcing him to resign: the eastern and southern members being active in this, and Mifflin and Richard Henry Lee particularly so. It was rumored with increasing insistence that he intended to resign; and if any action short of demanding his resignation could have led him to do so, it must have succeeded, so outrageously did Congress ignore, thwart and snub him.

Congress this winter was far from being what it had once been. Washington lamented the absence of Mason and other able men, who had either gone into the army or taken on duties in their various states, which seemed more important to them than Congressional business. Often there were only sixteen or seventeen members present, sometimes only nine or ten. Power, thoughtful people said, had fallen into low hands. While the people of York made a good thing out of charging the members thirty-seven and one-third dollars a week for indifferent board that did not include the keep of a servant, the more clear sighted of them spoke contemptuously of "King Congress" and called it "a bunch of kings." For as it waned in numbers and capacity, it grew in jealousy of its powers and prerogatives and in a senseless mistrust of military authority. The ruinous changes it had made in the Commissary Department were but the first manifestation of this spirit. They had been followed by what was tantamount to a slap in the face of the commander in chief—the promotion of General Thomas Conway to the rank of major general and his appointment as inspector general.

Conway had arrived at Morristown the previous spring, sporting the Order of St. Louis, loquacious on the subject of his experience in the campaign in Germany in 1761, and insisting that any rank less than that of brigadier would be beneath his dignity. He had commanded a brigade in Washington's army in the recent campaign. But a violent antagonism had developed between him and the commander in chief, and as soon as Washington heard of the possibility of Conway's advancement he had written to Richard Henry Lee to protest against it.

Conway's merit as an officer and his importance in the army, he told Lee, existed more in the man's own imagination than in reality. It was a maxim with him to leave no service of his own untold or to go without anything he could get by importunity. And why, Washington asked, should the youngest brigadier in the army be put over the heads of the eldest and command gentlemen of sound judgment and unquestionable bravery who were at present his seniors.

He did not add—as he might have done, since he was writing a private letter—that according to several trustworthy witnesses Conway had been guilty of cowardice at the battle of Germantown and Washington had quashed the charges lest they be attributed to his well-known dislike of the man. But he warned that Conway's promotion would greatly increase the number of officers' resignations, of which he had received twenty in the past six days; and he concluded: "It will be impossible for me to be of any further service, if such insuperable difficulties are thrown in my way." Lee had replied that he did not think the promotion would be made, since it was likely to have such evil consequences as Washington had mentioned. Conway had resigned, as he had threatened to do if he were not promoted, and Washington wrote to him civilly, wishing him a pleasant voyage back to France. But there is no record of Congress's accepting the resignation, and on December 13 the promotion was made, and with it the appointment as inspector general.

The next move was more subtle in its beginnings. It was proposed to create a Board of War. The idea appealed to Washington as Richard Henry Lee outlined it to him in October. Colonel Joseph Reed, Colonel Pickering, and Colonel Robert H. Harrison, all past or present members of his military family, were suggested to him as members of it. But it turned out far otherwise. Gates was brought down from Albany to be its head; Wilkinson, with the brevet rank of brigadier general, became its secretary; and Mifflin was its most influential member.

Its proceedings were made subject to monthly Congressional inspections and were to be always open to examination by any member of Congress. There was little need of this precaution, however, on the part of Washington's enemies, for the Board was an eager instrument for anything that might insult or injure him. Congress itself soon passed a resolution limiting to 2,500 the number of men the commander in chief might draw from the northern army; it cultivated afresh its old habit of sending orders directly to officers on detached service instead of through army headquarters; and the Board of War was quick to follow suit.

Near the end of January Washington was constrained to write stiffly to Gates: "Agreeably to your request I shall order Hazen's regiment to march from Wilmington . . . towards Albany. As some particular purpose seems to be intended by desiring this regiment, I am induced to part with it, notwithstanding our force will ill bare the smallest diminution." What that particular purpose was he did not find out until some days later, when Lafayette received from the Board of War the appointment to take command of an expedition against Canada and the young Frenchman came to him in great distress as to whether or not he should accept it.

2

When the news of Conway's promotion reached Valley Forge, the indignation was as general and outspoken as Washington had warned that it would be. Arrogant and boastful of his past exploits and superior military knowledge, Conway had made himself almost universally hated. He had a way of looking an officer over and asking: "Did Congress see you before they appointed you?" Greene sent a protest to Congress against the fatal effect on the army of thus violating the rules of promotion by advancing officers who had never distinguished themselves in the field. Nine of the brigadier generals united in a similar protest, and a group of officers at Sullivan's headquarters did likewise. When Wilkinson's promotion was announced, John Laurens wrote his father that everybody was disgusted and many officers were likely to resign. It was cynically observed that those who went to York got the promotions, and so vociferous were the denunciations that Wilkinson resigned his new rank.

Washington did what he could to quiet these angry feelings, and he set an example by his silent endurance of the slights put upon himself. When he was tardily consulted about the proposed expedition to Canada, he contented himself with begging to be excused from giving any advice on that subject, since he knew neither the extent of the object in view nor the means to be employed to effect them. He approved the troubled Lafayette's acceptance of the command of the expedition—telling him that he would rather have him than some other in that position—though the appointment had evidently been intended to undermine the warm friendship between him and the young nobleman whose letters were influential in forming opinion in France.

But of his personal feelings toward Conway, Washington made no secret, and he received him coldly when he visited the camp in his new capacity, though not without all proper respect for his rank and duties. Writing to assure him of his cooperation, Washington had taken the opportunity to tell him that his appointment had caused not the slightest uneasiness to any officer in the army—a point that Conway had had the effrontery to raise. Of the feelings of the brigadiers whom Conway had superseded, Washington continued, Conway might judge from his own feelings when de Kalb was promoted. For Conway had sent a bitter remonstrance to Congress upon de Kalb's appointment as major general.

Conway's letters to Washington on the subject were characterized by a mendacity and insolence hardly to be matched in military correspondence. His only motive in accepting the inspector generalship, he stated, had been his desire to promote the welfare of the cause and Washington's glory by making the troops more fit for their duties. He had not solicited the appointment and was very ready to return to France if Washington was displeased by it. As for his new rank, no inspector general in Europe ranked under a major general, and it was necessary to his possession of sufficient authority to carry out his duties. He made no pretentions, he wrote, to the prodigious height of "the great Frederic in Europe" and "the great Washington on this continent," but he had thirty years of service, which was longer than some of his fellow brigadiers had lived. He did not pretend to be a consummate general, but an old sailor knew more of a ship than admirals who had never been to sea.

Nor was this the only interchange of shameless effrontery and dignified rebuke between the two. On receiving from Stirling an account of Wilkinson's tipsy babbling that October night at York, Washington had sent the following pregnant note:

To Brigadier General Conway 9 November, 1777
Sir,
A letter which I received last night contained the following paragraph. "In a letter from General Conway to General Gates he says, '*Heaven has been determined to save your country, or a weak General and bad counsellors would have ruined it.*'"
I am, Sir, your humble servant,
George Washington

The tone of Conway's reply can be gathered from his principal collaborators' comments upon it. Mifflin wrote Gates with evident gratification that Conway had not apologized and had given no satisfaction. Gates wrote to Conway that he had acted with all the dignity of a virtuous soldier. Two months after the date of Washington's note Conway brought up the matter again in one of his several complaints to the commander in chief at not having been called to Valley Forge to exercise his functions as inspector general.

He understood, he wrote, that Washington's aversion to him was owing to the letter of which Wilkinson had babbled. But there was not a subaltern in Europe that did not state fully his opinions of his generals in writing to his friends and acquaintances, without the least notice being taken of it officially. "Must such an odious and tyrannical inquisition begin in this country?" he asked. "Must it be introduced by the Commander-in-Chief of this army raised for the defense of liberty?" Again he complained of the coldness of his reception at Valley Forge, accused Washington of being responsible for the bitter feeling which his promotion had aroused in the army, and closed with his customary thinly veiled threat to resign.

Conway was riding high at this time, and if his collaborators had possessed more of his skill in intrigue and his boldness in carrying it through, it seems possible that he might have continued to do so. It was said at York that there was one day when Washington's enemies in Congress, if they could have counted on two more votes, would have introduced a resolution calling for his being removed from command and brought to York under arrest to answer certain charges against him.

But ambition must be made of sterner stuff than that which composed the character of General Horatio Gates. From the moment that Gates heard of the first consequences of Wilkinson's tipsy revelations his conduct illustrated the proverb that the guilty fleeth when no man pursueth. Neither his origin nor his past life had given him the steadiness of purpose that his present situation required of him. Gates, wrote Horace Walpole at Strawberry Hill this winter, "was the son of a housekeeper of the second Duke of Leeds, who, marrying a young husband when she was very old, had this son by him. . . . My mother's woman was intimate with that housekeeper, and thence I was godfather to her son, though I believe not ten years old myself." Gates's father was said by some to have been the Duke's butler.

Through many years of sycophancy and intrigue Gates had risen to a lieutenant-colonelcy in the British army, with intervals on half-pay that were passed in drinking and gambling and the adoption of Methodism as an antidote. His importunities had worn out the patience of more than one powerful patron, and in 1772 he had turned Whig and migrated to Virginia, where, as the owner of the plantation named Traveller's Rest, he had been Washington's neighbor and once his guest at Mount Vernon.

Washington had first met him when Gates was a captain of British regulars in Braddock's disastrous expedition and, twenty years later, had found him sufficiently able and efficient as adjutant general of the newly raised Continental army at Cambridge in 1775. In an army in which few native Americans were well grounded in military matters it was easy for a former officer of the British regular service to gain advancement. By the June of 1776 Gates had risen to the rank of major general. But it was by political influence rather than the demonstration of ability that he got on, and the observant soon noted that he had no compunctions about rising by the ruin of other men's careers. When Washington was mounting his desperate

attack on the Hessians at Trenton in the grim December of 1776 and
earnestly begged his aid, if only for a few days, Gates had pleaded
illness and followed the refugee Congress to Baltimore to initiate
the skillful lobbying that culminated in his superseding Schuyler in
the northern command. When Hamilton came to him in the following November with Washington's urgent request for reinforcements,
there had been strange and unaccountable delays in dispatching
them, although the British had evacuated Ticonderoga after Burgoyne's surrender and Gates did not intend to advance beyond that
point. It was evident that Washington would win no conspicuous
success that autumn if Gates could prevent it.

Conqueror of Burgoyne, president of the Board of War, and the
favorite of a powerful clique in Congress, it may well have seemed
to him that only a little more scheming would elevate him to the
supreme command. But late in November a warning from Mifflin
that an extract from a letter to him from Conway had been sent to
headquarters shook his nerve.

He wrote at once to Conway, asking which of his letters had
been copied and begging Conway's help in discovering the person
guilty of such infidelity. To Mifflin he wrote that no punishment
was too severe for the wretch, and that he counted on Mifflin's friendship and zeal for his safety to bring the name of the miscreant to
public light. And within the next week he had appealed to both
Washington and President Laurens for help in detecting a wretch
who might not only betray him but seriously injure Washington's
operations. To Laurens he enclosed a copy of his letter to Washington, in order, he explained, that the whole affair might be communicated to Congress and the criminal the sooner detected. For
he feared that he might be betrayed to the enemy by the same
traitor, if the thief remained undiscovered.

Why he took this extraordinary course is hard to imagine. At most
he needed only to have expressed to Washington his confidence that
Washington was too fair-minded to hold a man in his position
accountable for letters that might be addressed to him by misguided
critics of the commander in chief. Presumably his emphasis on the
necessity of discovering the identity of the "thief" was intended as

a sort of red herring to deflect attention from the contents of the letter and what might be inferred from it.

Washington was mystified. "What could induce General Gates to communicate [to Congress] a copy of his letter to me is beyond my comprehension," he wrote to President Laurens. But Gates's action gave him the long-desired opportunity to bring the intrigue into the open. Hitherto he had felt that his quarrel with Conway must be treated as a purely personal affair. With characteristic magnanimity he had ignored the crucial instances of Gates's failure to support him and had noticed the flagrant slight Gates had inflicted on him in the matter of the news of Saratoga only by adding to his congratulations to Gates on the victory an expression of "regret" that he had heard of the event only by report and letters which lacked "the authenticity . . . which it would have received by a line under your signature, stating the simple fact." But now, freed from his scruples by Gates's blunder, he acted promptly.

He sent to Congress Conway's letters of complaint and accompanied them with the statement: "If General Conway means, by cool reception . . . that I did not receive him in the language of a warm and cordial friend, I readily confess the charge. I did not, nor shall I ever, till I am capable of the arts of dissimulation." To Gates he replied at length, giving him a circumstantial account of how the quotation from Conway's letter to Gates had been brought to his attention and quoting in full his letter to Conway on the subject. He had, he went on, never mentioned the matter to any one outside his military family, excepting the Marquis de Lafayette, to whom Conway himself had showed the letter from which Wilkinson had quoted.

He expressed his surprise that Gates had sent to Congress a copy of Gates's letter to him. But as some end was doubtless to be served by it, he continued blandly, he was compelled to return his answer through the same channel lest some member of Congress should suspect him of having come by the contents of Conway's letter by indirect means. Till Lord Stirling's letter reached him, he explained, he had not known that Conway was one of Gates's correspondents, and he had considered Stirling's information as coming from Gates himself, with a friendly view to forewarn him against a dangerous incendiary, which the country would sooner or later discover Conway to be. "But in this, as in other matters of late," he concluded significantly, "I have found myself mistaken."

The effect upon the plotters, when their machinations were brought out into the harsh light of the Pennsylvania winter day, was devastating. Weak and vain, Gates had been, up to this point, an excellent stalking horse for Washington's enemies, but he lacked the firmness to be a successful villain. Frightened and flustered at finding himself exposed as the head of a movement against the commander in chief, he wrote to Washington that the paragraph in Conway's letter which Washington had quoted to him was spurious, a wicked forgery. He accused Wilkinson of fabricating it; and that unhappy young man, far over his head in matters too deep for his younthful inexperience, challenged Gates to a duel "with pistols tomorrow morning behind the English church." When morning came, however, Gates took him for a walk instead, apologized warmly, and told him that Hamilton had surreptitiously made a copy of the letter when he was at Gates's headquarters in November.

In answer to Gates's statement that the quotation from Conway's letter was spurious, Washington replied that it was strange that Gates should have tacitly acknowledged its genuineness in his earlier letter. Then, through the equivalent of three large and closely printed pages, Washington proceeded to lecture Gates on the error of his ways. Gates's answer was as meek as it was false and as false at it was meek: he had no personal connection with Conway, no interest in him except as an officer in the American army. As for himself, he was of no faction, and he begged, in effect, that the affair might be forgotten. To this Washington agreed readily and could well afford to do so.

Conway's response to the undesired publicity of his scheming was a barefaced denial that there was any such paragraph or anything like it in his letter to Gates, and with his habitual impudence, he advised his commander in chief to be on his guard against flattery and calumny. But President Laurens, who had seen the letter, told Washington's aide, John Fitzgerald, that although it did not contain the paragraph Wilkinson had quoted in his cups, it said as much in substance, and ten times more, including the lament: "What a pity there is but one Gates!"

"The Gentlemen who have been active in this," Fitzgerald wrote to his chief in mid-February, "are by this time heartily sick of it, and plainly perceive that the fabric which they were endeavoring to rear, is likely to fall upon their own heads"; and Washington had already assured an anxious friend that "the design is not only seen through but reprobated." The reaction throughout the country had indeed been unmistakable. As usual in such cases, the noise made by the carpers proved to have been out of all proportion to their number. An overwhelming majority of the people were fairly represented by an inhabitant of York who, when Dr. Rush told him that only some immediate and heroic action could arouse the country from its dangerous torpor, wrote down his own conviction that "G. W. must be the man to put such a scheme in practice." They understood, if certain politicians either could not or would not, that Washington's inaction since the battle at Germantown had been forced upon him by the incapacity and meanness of spirit of the very men who attacked him.

At Valley Forge his officers, though they might discuss his shortcomings among themselves, swore by him almost to a man when it came to an issue between him on the one hand and on the other Conway, whom they hated; Mifflin, who had deserted and neglected them for the past six months; and Gates, the fictitious quality of whose glory they must have heard of as soon as Morgan's riflemen returned from Saratoga. And they were still suffering too keenly from legislative incapacity, parsimony, and jealousy to support a Congressional clique against a chief whom they knew to be their champion against those evils.

Morgan, on being approached by some of Gates's supporters, said roundly that he would serve under nobody but Washington: the Saratoga campaign had given him more than enough of Gates's pusillanimous leadership. When Conway attempted to make capital of de Kalb's criticisms of Washington, the Baron wrote to President Laurens: "I look upon him as the sole defender of his country's

cause." The other French officers, though they quarreled among
themselves with such bitterness that de Kalb shunned their company,
were united in their support of the commander in chief and would
hardly speak to Conway. One of them, Lieutenant Colonel the
Vicomte de Maurois, who disliked both the men and the women in
America, nevertheless wrote, when he was about to sail for home in
the spring:

> J'ai vu Wassington sans armée,
> Devant un ennemi vainqueur,
> Et la cabale envenimée
> Attaquer jusqu'à son honneur.
>
> Du double coup qui le menace
> Ce héros n'est point abattu,
> L'Anglois respecte son audace,
> L'envieux cède à son vertu.

Frightened by the general indignation, the plotters scuttled for
cover so swiftly that Hamilton feared the conspiracy—for so he
called it—had merely been driven underground. But his fears proved
to be needless. Nobody in Congress showed any eagerness to start
an investigation based on the charges contained in "Thoughts of a
Freeman," though Washington asked for one. Dr. Rush, though he
persisted in admiring Conway and regarding Gates highly as an
officer and an army commander, grew busy with efforts to clear his
name of any connection with that despicable paper. Mifflin packed
up and went home in disgust—so he said—at the persistent gossip
to the effect that he was trying to oust Washington from the supreme
command, which he strenuously denied. Wilkinson resigned as secretary of the Board of War. Pickering, a member of the Board,
reported this with evident satisfaction. But although he had been
for months a member of Washington's military family, he added
the wish that America would produce some great patriot like Pitt.
A man under the shade of a lofty tree, is, to be sure, seldom a good
judge of its height. Conway found himself foiled at every point.

He and Gates had made their last fling in the plan to send Lafayette
to command the expedition to Canada and, thanks to that young
man's clearheaded loyalty, had lost. Yet the scheme had looked most

promising. It had the outward appearance of respectability which their other machinations lacked. What could be more fitting than the gallant young Marquis at the head of a force whose purpose was to liberate the French Canadians from the British yoke? But how surely would Washington's reputation abroad be undermined by raising up a French rival against him in the war in America!

Evacuated from Chester after the defeat on the Brandywine, Lafayette had remained at Bethlehem until his wound had recovered sufficiently to enable him to walk about. But before he could wear a boot he had ridden with Greene in the too long-delayed attempt to support Fort Mercer, and in the skirmishing that followed he had handled skillfully his command of riflemen. Washington had already written to Congress that the young Frenchman had never clearly understood that his rank in the army had been intended to be purely complimentary, and that his influential connections in France, his zeal for the cause, his bravery at the Brandywine, and his discretion and increasing ability to speak English made it both wise and proper to give him the command of a division. This had been done, and he had succeeded to the command of the unfortunate Stephen, whose fondness for liquor had cost him his commission.

In the dismal weeks of the late autumn and early winter, homesick for France and his wife and children, Lafayette had found solace in the company of Conway—the Comte Thomas de Conway to him—who had known France from childhood, its army in thirty years of service, and its aristocratic society through the patronage of the Marquis de Castries, one of Lafayette's intimate acquaintances. The adroit Irishman had neglected no opportunity to flatter him, calling himself "my soldier," as Lafayette told Washington afterward, and amusing him—in the eighteenth-century sense of that word—with "shining projects" in which the two were to sail under the American flag to raid the British Indies, both East and West.

The disillusionment that came with the revelation of Conway's machinations was complete and shocking. Inquiry, he wrote to Washington on December 30, had convinced him that Conway was an ambitious and dangerous man. "I am bound by your fate," he went on, "and I shall follow and sustain it, as well by my sword as by all the means in my power." Washington replied appreciatively and reassuringly: a time would come when, if his dear Marquis would give him his company in Virginia, they would laugh over their past difficulties and the folly of others.

In accepting the command of the proposed expedition into Canada Lafayette made his own terms with the Board of War. Received at York with a superfluity of flattery, he nevertheless insisted that de Kalb must be his second-in-command, thus ousting Conway, who had doubtless expected to be the real commander; and he made it plain that, unlike Gates, he would regard himself strictly as subordinate to Washington, and that his dispatches would reach Congress only through the commander in chief's headquarters.

The occasion was celebrated at Gates's own house with a large and lavish dinner, the like of which occurred only in hungry dreams at Valley Forge. Toast after toast was drunk at its conclusion, but none, the watchful young Marquis observed, to Washington. At length he arose and, reminding the company that in their enthusiasm for the new project they had omitted the most important toast of all, proposed the health of the commander in chief. The uncomfortable silence that followed was broken only by the scraping of chairs as the reluctant diners shambled to their feet. Glasses were raised but were set down untasted. The newly made commander of the Canadian expedition drained his, smiled blandly, bowed politely, and left the room.

He departed for the North so filled with enthusiasm for his mission that he was prepared to spend five or six thousand guineas of his own money to ensure its success. According to the representations of the Board of War he was to have a force of two thousand men, lead them across the ice of Lake Champlain, burn the British shipping at St. John's at the foot of the lake, and press on to the capture of Montreal. Gates, indeed, had gone as far as to assure him that Stark would have burned the enemy vessels by the time he arrived at Albany.

Traveling by sleigh and on horseback through rain, snow, and bitter cold, he reached his destination only to be told by Schuyler, Lincoln, and Arnold, who were still recovering from the wounds

they had received in the Saratoga fighting, and even by Conway, that
the expedition could not possibly be ready to start for at least five
weeks and by that time the melting ice on the lake would make it
impossible. There were not twelve hundred men fit for duty, and
the Northern Department was $800,000 in debt.

Lafayette wrote to Congress directly, so anxious was he to inform
them of the situation in which he found himself. Ridiculous, he
called it. He had written enthusiastically to Europe of his mission,
and he would be laughed at there. He proposed henceforth to serve
only as a volunteer in America, unless he should find some opportunity to redeem his reputation. But he need not have entertained
these fears. Both he and de Kalb were promptly recalled to head
their respective divisions at Valley Forge, while Conway was left at
Albany until his habitual impatience moved him once more to tender
his resignation, an action which proved this time to be once too often.

Everywhere now the "mystical darkness" which Greene had observed to be spread over the councils of America was clearing away.
Congress had begun to find out how thoroughly it had been fooled.
Washington was authorized to draw from the Northern Department
as many troops as he thought fit, although Gates was still in titular
command there. To Conway's surprise and chagrin his resignation
was accepted. Charles Carroll told him that any man who did not
support Washington ought to get out of the army, and Conway
complained that there was a cabal against him.

He lingered about the doors of Congress, still loud in criticism of
Washington but trying to get reinstated, until the following July,
when General Cadwalader challenged him to a duel and, as Cadwalader described it, "stopped his lying mouth" with a bullet through
mouth and neck and put an end to his American adventure. Believing that the wound was mortal, Conway wrote to Washington that
he was sincerely sorry for having written or said anything disagreeable
to him. He recovered from his wound, returned to the French army,
served as governor of the French settlements in India, commanded
a Royalist army in the South of France in 1793, and was driven into
exile, where he died seven years later.

The wretched Wilkinson emerged from the predicament in which

his weak head had landed him more happily than he could have
expected, thanks to Washington's habitual thoughtfulness and consideration of all men, especially the unfortunate. He had obtained
from Lord Stirling a statement that his words from Conway's letter
had been spoken in private company and during a convivial hour,
although, Stirling had added, under no injunction of secrecy; and
Washington had had him to dinner and had showed him a letter
in which Gates had accused him of fabricating the quotation from
Conway and had asked to have him punished. With this fresh start
Wilkinson became clothier general to the army the following year.
But he went on, through a life of intrigue that involved him in Aaron
Burr's conspiracy, to be discharged from the army as a major general
thirty-nine years later after unsuccessful campaigning in the War
of 1812.

3

Before February had run its dismal course of rain, snow and ice,
thaw, slush, and mud, the psychological atmosphere at Valley Forge
had been brightened by breezes even more enlivening than the
freshened airs that had begun to blow from York. Mrs. Washington
arrived about the middle of the month and once more, as at Morristown, proceeded to improve the rugged way of life which was the
best her "old man" could be bothered to create when he was left
to himself. She gave a party for him on his forty-sixth birthday, with
music by an army band, to which she paid fifteen shillings for its
services. She turned the Potts house into something like a home—the
staff, one gathers, finding living quarters elsewhere—and she got
a cabin built adjoining it, in which the headquarters mess could
dine in comfort and she could hold social gatherings.

Since the needs of the soldiers were far greater than in the previous
winter, her work for their welfare was the more strenuous. To sew,
mend, and knit for them she assembled in her drawing room every
weekday morning the officers' wives who had begun by this time to
brave the rigors of the camp in order to be with their husbands. Each
afternoon, no matter how foul the weather, she was out on foot
among the hospital cabins, with a single attendant to carry her

basket of comforts, ministering to the neediest cases; and the last hours of many a dying man were eased by her consolations.

The evenings at headquarters became gay. Since card playing was banned in the army and there was neither space nor a floor in the cabin for dancing, coffee and conversation, stories and songs were her only resources. But she had the gift of bringing out the social qualities of her guests. Everybody with any pretensions to a voice was called upon to sing and, such was her persuasiveness, evidently did so.

The handsome and cheerful Lady Stirling and her daughter "Lady Kitty" Alexander, Mrs. Clement Biddle, plump and witty Mrs. Knox, and Mrs. Nathanael Greene ably seconded the efforts of their hostess. Mrs. Greene's own little parlor was a haven for homesick French officers. To them her schoolroom French, which she had acquired only in the previous summer, was a godsend: so much so to one of them that he credited her with an excellent knowledge of both the language and its literature. Hamilton and John Laurens were among the few other Americans with whom they could talk in their own tongue.

All in all, it was a group of people of extraordinary intelligence, ability, and knowledge of the world, as the later careers of many of its members were to demonstrate. Among the foreigners was the brilliant if erratic Marquis de la Rouërie, a member of his king's *Garde du Corps*, who had entered a Trappist monastery for love of a dancer and, serving as the Chevalier Armand, had fought gallantly in the actions of the past autumn. He was to die a leader of the counter-revolutionary Chouans in Brittany in 1793. There was Duportail, the officer of engineers, who was to be Louis XVI's minister of war at the beginning of the French Revolution, and the Chevalier de Ternant, later minister of France of the United States. Presently appeared Pierre Charles L'Enfant, the planner of the city of Washington, and seventeen-year-old Pierre-Etienne Duponceau, who became a citizen of Philadelphia and so distinguished a member of the bar that he was offered the position of chief justice of the United States.

Hamilton was the life of every party. John Laurens had lived much abroad. Among the other young officers were a future President, James Monroe, and a future chief justice, John Marshall. The brilliance of the company was enhanced by the presence of Elias Boudinot, the commissioner for the exchange of prisoners, and by the members of the Congressional committee which spent the first three months of the year at Moore Hall, some three miles from the camp, working with the commander in chief on his fifty-folio report on a proposed reorganization of the army. The forthright "signer" Charles Carroll of Carrollton was of their number. So were Joseph Reed, the former adjutant general, and the courtly and courageous Gouverneur Morris. As minister of the United States to France in the throes of her revolution, Morris was to outface on the steps of his modest legation a Paris mob that clamored for the blood of aristocrats who had fled to the shelter of the flag of his new and feeble republic.

In a gathering of such people the conversation was bound to be lively. Almost all of them were young, or at most not beyond the middle forties. And there was no lack of provocative subjects to talk about: the probability of France's coming into the war; the flood of counterfeit bills with which a Tory printing press in New York was accelerating the depreciation of the Continental currency; the chances that the various states would adopt the Articles of Confederation which Congress had recently formulated; hopes that the Congressional committee would succeed in rectifying the crying weaknesses in the military establishment; and most serious of all, the latest twist in the machinations of Conway, Mifflin, Gates, and their fellow conspirators at York.

On the lighter side was comment on the spurious *Letters of George Washington to his Friends in 1776*, a clever forgery concocted, printed, and circulated in pamphlet form by the British this winter. In its pages Washington appeared as opposed to Independence, referring to King George as "my King," making military preparations only with a view to peace, and resolved to be no longer "the puppet" of Congress. He was represented as contrasting the Southerners unfavorably with the New Englanders and as describing Patrick Henry as "in many respects the unfittest man" to be governor of Virginia.

There were just enough half-truths in all this to make it the blackest of lies. But it fooled nobody. The discriminating observed that one of the letters, which was addressed to Mrs. Washington, bore a date on which actually she had been with her husband at headquarters; and to the general public Washington's actions in the twenty months since the letters were supposed to have been written spoke more clearly than any words could have done. But the letters made amusing reading: one in particular, in which he appeared to be defending himself against his wife's reproaches for neglecting her.

With this animated company around him Washington's mood evidently brightened. Young Duponceau wrote of his impression of him: "I could not keep my eyes from that imposing countenance; grave, yet not severe; affable, without familiarity. Its predominant expression was calm dignity, through which you could trace the strong feelings of the patriot, and discern the father, as well as the commander of his soldiers. I have never seen a picture that represents him to me, as I saw him at Valley Forge, and during the campaigns in which I had the honor to follow him." And Duponceau's presence itself was a token of better days to come. He was secretary to the Baron von Steuben, who arrived at Valley Forge on the 27th of February, and whose genius for discipline and training were to make the army of the United States an efficient and reliable fighting force.

Bearing letters from Benjamin Franklin, in which he was described as a lieutenant general in the service of Frederick the Great, Frederick William Augustus Henry, Baron von Steuben, landed at Portsmouth, New Hampshire, on December 1, 1777, after a voyage of sixty-six days, which had been diversified by a mutiny of the vessel's crew and three occasions when she was on fire. He was two years older than Washington, a veteran of the Seven Years' War, in which he had been wounded at the battles of Prague and Kunersdorf, and he had so distinguished himself as a staff officer that Frederick the Great had made him lieutenant quartermaster general in a class of thirteen selected members who were trained by the King himself.

With the splendid star of the Baden-Durlach Order of Fidelity glittering on the breast of a scarlet uniform turned up with blue, which he supposed to be according to American army regulations, he came ashore accompanied by a staff of three in similar dress and by his Italian greyhound Azor. But he wrote to Washington with becoming modesty that he would serve as a volunteer rather than cause trouble about rank, and that after serving under the King of Prussia he would serve under nobody else but Washington. Washington replied cordially to the Baron's letter, which must have been a welcome change from the arrogance and importunity of the soldiers of fortune who had pestered him in the past, and rode out several miles to meet him on the day of his arrival at Valley Forge.

With Hamilton acting as interpreter, the Baron made an excellent impression from the first. His knowledge of English was extremely limited, but he had managed to read *Robinson Crusoe* during his voyage, and he learned the language rapidly if imperfectly. Careful to avoid giving the slightest cause for offense and evidently aware of the discord in the American service, he had paid his respects to Congress at York and had politely declined an offer of quarters in Gates's house there. If he had been allowed to do so, he would have refused the guard of honor of twenty-five men which was assigned to him at Valley Forge. "I am only a volunteer," he protested. Prussian though he was, and with the Prussian training, he was shocked by the number of men kept on such duty at the various division and brigade headquarters, by the many detailed as officers' servants— mere quartermasters having as many as three—by the number of officers who lived not in the cabins built for them but in more comfortable quarters miles away, and by the practice of making the men work before breakfast.

His spontaneous geniality and kindliness were not long in winning the liking and confidence of both officers and men. Often he and his staff fed the sentinel at his door. He gave frequent dinners for the officers of the lower grades, who were frequently as hungry as their men, and in the spirit of ironical humor that prevailed in the camp he made a feast to which only guests in ragged breeches were invited. *"Sansculottes"* he called them, coining thereby—according to Duponceau—the word to which the French Revolution was to give currency. No wine was served at these affairs, only "salamanders," a concoction that was set on fire and drunk, it was said, flame and all.

Washington was quick to recognize in him exactly the temperament and professional qualifications required to give the army the uniform drill and training he had so long desired for it; and soon von Steuben was "in a manner domesticated in the family," wrote his secretary, dining at headquarters three times a week to discuss the details of the task.

It was a herculean one, as even the optimistic von Steuben saw it: to impose upon a collection of regiments that had been trained, some by French, some by English, and others by Prussian drill books, a uniform system of drill and maneuver. And only two months could be counted on in which to accomplish it, for active hostilities must be expected to begin by the 1st of May. But the material had been tempered by hard fighting and unparalleled hardships, and he appreciated its excellence. He had begun his service in Germany with a *Frei Corps* of volunteers, which dealt in swift raids and other perilous special missions. So he was not unprepared for some of the idiosyncrasies of his new pupils and soon understood the rest of them, learning quickly that the best results were to be obtained by explaining the reasons for what he taught.

He set to work at once at preparing a set of drill regulations which, though it was based on the Prussian system, was simplified to teach only the essentials. The number of commands in the manual of arms was reduced to ten. The prescribed step, as Ensign Ewing of the New Jersey brigade noted approvingly, was halfway between quick and slow time, an easy and natural step. The mere manual labor of turning out enough copies of these instructions for every company in fourteen brigades was, of course, enormous. But written in French by their author and translated into English military terminology by Laurens and Hamilton, the sheets were divided among numerous copyists whose assiduous quills had the first of the weekly installments in which they were issued ready for distribution in a fortnight.

Training was begun gradually with a hundred of the most intelligent and soldierly men of American birth, these being selected from the entire army and attached temporarily to the Commander-in-Chief's Guard. This unit, composed of sixty foot soldiers under the command of Captain Caleb Gibbs, Washington had created at Morristown in the previous spring as absolutely necessary, he explained rather apologetically, for the security of his baggage and papers. Wear, tear, and weather had doubtless ruined long since their smart buff and blue uniforms, red vests, and white bayonet and body belts. But they remained an excellent nucleus for training, all native-born Virginians as they were, carefully selected and of a uniform height of five feet and nine or ten inches. When the first hundred pupils had received some days of training, they were replaced by a second hundred, and so on until the whole army had been leavened by men who knew something of the new drill.

The officers were required to attend these exercises as observers. They remained as admiring, and often amused, spectators. Somehow the Baron's modest rank of lieutenant quartermaster general had been transmogrified into lieutenant general—a misconception that both Washington and President Laurens, though they did not share it, fostered. Nor was it made known that von Steuben had not come directly from the Prussian service. Consequently the American officers were amazed to see one of such exalted rank doing the work which, following the custom of the British army, they had relegated to their sergeants, and doing it with such a will that they could not always restrain their laughter at the mingling of French, German, and English vituperation with which he emphasized his instructions.

"*Viens*, Valker, *mon ami, mon bon ami!*" he would exclaim in utter frustration to Captain Benjamin Walker, who acted as his interpreter. "*Sacre!* Goddam die *gaucheries* of dese *badauts. Je ne puis plus*. I can curse dem no more."

But there was no mistaking the man's ardor, skill, and judgment as an instructor. He paid little attention to the niceties of the school of the soldier but dwelt upon practical details: loading and firing, the use of the bayonet, in which the American troops had always been weak, and the precise execution of the essential foot movements. To obviate difficulties arising from the lack of uniformity in the size of the various units—one regiment had only thirty privates, one company only one man—he formed instruction battalions. Within less than a month he had the whole army drilling by the new regulations: by regiments in the morning under the direction of subinspectors, and in the afternoon by brigades, to each of which he gave an hour of his personal attention; and only indispensable formations were permitted to be conducted in the old ways. As early as the 1st of April John Laurens wrote of "the enlivened scene of our campus martius." The old straggling march by files, which had caused the fatally slow deployment at the Brandywine, was gone forever. Detachments of as few as six men were made to march in double rank and closed up. By the end of the month the troops could cross the roughest ground with ranks and step unbroken, without the aid of music.

Nor were the Baron's activities confined to the drill ground. There was no defect that escaped his trained eye and inexhaustible energy. Every morning at daybreak he was out and all over the camp on horseback, observing the persistent ignorance of guard duty, the slovenliness of the roll calls, and the queer mixture of arms in many organizations—muskets, rifles, and sometimes even fowling pieces in a single battalion. He gave instruction in guard mounting and conducted a school for adjutants every evening at six o'clock. Assisted by Greene, who became his fast friend, and by Hamilton and Laurens, he put into effect a system of accountability. Punctuality, that fundamental military requisite, which cold and bad weather impair in the best-disciplined armies, he insisted upon. Brigade majors were required to set their watches by that of the adjutant general, who took the time from the clock at headquarters, and the regimental adjutants set theirs by the brigade adjutants'.

Stragglers were rounded up. Neatness and soldierly appearance were required of the men. Adjutants whose guard details were dirty and unsoldierly were put under arrest. If noncommissioned officers failed to set an example of cleanliness and discipline they were reduced to the ranks. The rank and file were told that even in rags they could at least shave, wash their hands and faces and keep a clean camp. And in mid-April Washington, with his customary courtesy to his major subordinates, "requested . . . for the last time" a general cleaning up of the cabins, daily airing of bedding, the ridding of streets and alleys of filth, and the daily burning of garbage. In a ride through the camp, the General Order stated, the commander in chief had noted with pleasure the respect that some of the brigadiers had paid to his similar orders in the past. He wished that it had been general, "but the case was otherwise."

But although von Steuben's work was justified by its results, it was not accomplished without opposition and some heartburning. True to his self-chosen role of volunteer, he had made his beginning in a sense unofficially. On the strength of his earliest accomplishments Washington had the approval of all the brigade commanders in recommending to Congress, as he did early in March, that the Baron be appointed inspector general with the permanent rank of major general; and pending the action of Congress, a General Order announced that von Steuben was to be respected and obeyed as such. In April, however, several of the brigadiers grew resentful of his activities as infringements of their rights and prerogatives.

They were called upon to render exact accounts of arms, accouterments, and clothing, lists of men absent sick or on furlough, and the names of officers who were keeping soldiers as servants. Inspections by regimental commanders were ordered to be held weekly, and brigade inspections fortnightly. The granting of furloughs was restricted to the commander in chief and his deputies. And when the regimental adjutants were required to furnish headquarters with returns of men fit for duty, the brigade commanders complained of what they described as a "progressive encroachment." The French officers, many of whom had fought in the Seven Years' War, were hostile to von Steuben as a former enemy. When the Alsatian de Kalb, with his French army background, returned from Albany, he spoke slightingly of the Prussian's "methodic mediocrity." But there was no gainsaying the results of his work. The improvement of the troops was so great and rapid that even its creator was surprised by it; and there was little complaint when, on May 5, Congress formally ratified his appointment and rank.

4

Even von Steuben's energy and genius might have failed, however, if an improvement in the living conditions at Valley Forge had not taken place. Men who are hungry and half-clad make dull pupils. About the time the Baron's work got well started, Greene became quartermaster general, and it was not long before food began to come in with greater regularity and in larger quantities; and supplies of clothing followed. Greene took on the work with the greatest reluctance and only at Washington's earnest persuasion, seconded by that of Gouverneur Morris and Joseph Reed. Nobody, he objected, had ever heard of a quartermaster general in history. He feared, moreover, that if he were not successful, Washington's enemies, who were only too ready to attack the commander in chief through him and Knox, would make capital of his failure. He hated the place, he told Knox, and accepted it only out of compassion for Washington, who had often been compelled to act as his own quartermaster.

Even so, he insisted that, although he would receive no additional pay, he must retain his rank as major general, have the right to choose his subordinates, and have nothing to do with the accounts. These terms Congress not unnaturally rejected. They offered him, however, the power to select all forage masters, wagon masters, and the rest of the department personnel, including two principal assistants, with whom, as the three might determine, he was to divide compensation which should consist of 1 per cent of all monies spent by the department; and on March 2 the appointment was made. Congress instructed Mifflin to assist him by furnishing him with a report on the preparations that had already been made for the next campaign. But if Mifflin made any other response than to sneer that Greene had taken the post to be out of the way of the bullets, it is not on record.

Greene put one of his assistant quartermaster generals in charge of purchases, the other in charge of accounts, and himself attacked the fundamental difficulty of transportation. He sent orders as far as Virginia and New England for wagons, got a law through the Pennsylvania legislature to relieve from militia duty teamsters who were working for the army, and set the engineers to work on the repair of the bridges and roads between Valley Forge and Lancaster, on which he saw wagons sunk in the mud, their horses strained and almost ruined in the effort to move them. To meet all imaginable exigencies of the approaching campaign he established magazines of oats, corn, and rye at convenient points all the way from Head of Elk to the Hudson, installed screws for the packing of hay, and ordered boats and forage carts to be built for the distribution of supplies.

Upon taking up his new duties he warned Congress that, with the opening of hostilities so close at hand, he would have no time to haggle over contracts, that the heavy expenditures were bound to increase the depreciation of the currency, and that he must have money, a great deal of money, and at once. But frugal Rhode Island ironmaster that early training and environment had made of him, he was, as he said, "startled" by the enormous sums for which he was compelled to draw upon "The Honorable, the Board of Treasury of the United States." He hoped that that form of address was the correct one, he wrote on April 3, and that, anyhow, he would get the money. Fifty thousand pounds was what he needed on this occasion, not having thus far received a single shilling. Somewhat later, when he asked for $150,000, only $50,000 was sent him, although there was a large sum of money in the hands of the loan officer at Bordentown.

But he managed somehow to pay for all he bought, and his efforts yielded prompt and remarkable results. Wagons abandoned by the roadsides, quantities of tent cloth left in a farmer's barn, spades, shovels, and tomahawks by the thousand, and many other items of supply and equipment, which the Congressional committee with the army had reported as dispersed over the whole country, were rounded up and carted to the camp, where there had long been a scarcity of every essential.

Early in April Congress, by that time fully aware of its past mistakes, appointed Colonel Jeremiah Wadsworth of Connecticut commissary general and restored to that office all of the authority of which it had so foolishly deprived Joseph Trumbull. Wadsworth, who had been Trumbull's deputy for purchasing, brought to the position experience, ability, and devotion; and thanks to the transportation with which Greene supplied him, the troops at Valley Forge could thenceforth count on having enough to eat.

With full stomachs, spring weather, the consciousness that they were getting sound training, and the stimulation of morale that always results from strict discipline intelligently administered, the spirit of the troops rose from dogged and sardonic endurance to optimism and gaiety. There were pranks such as setting fire to a twist of hay that had been tied to the tail of an unpopular quartermaster's horse. There was a stage play at the bakehouse, at which there was standing room only. An order of Congress setting aside April 22 as a day of Fasting, Humiliation, and Prayer must have caused amusement among men who had lived through three months with seldom a square meal or a shirt to their backs. But, anyhow, there was no work that day.

Things had turned so fine that four days later Waldo was moved to celebrate the aspect of the camp in verse:

> Camp, hills and dales with mirth resound;
> All with clean clothes and powdered hair
> For sport and duty now appear,
> Here squads in martial exercise,
> There whole brigades in order rise.
>
> . . . .
>
> Where all the varying glitters show
> Of guns and bayonets polished bright.
>
> . . . .
>
> One choix at Fives are earnest here,
> Another furious at Cricket there.

The 1st of May was dedicated to "mirth and jollity." Every regiment had its Maypole. Reveille was answered throughout the camp with three cheers for King Tammany. With hats wreathed with the white blossoms of the dogwood, the troops paraded through the streets of the camp, escorting the Indian king, a tall sergeant who was decked out as an Indian chief and had a guard of honor of thirteen other sergeants in Indian costume. They marched down the road to headquarters to pay their respects to the commander in chief. But on being told by one of his aides that he was indisposed, they turned back up the hill—"with the greatest decency and regularity," according to Ensign Ewing—to General Stirling's headquarters, with halts to hurrah at every Maypole on the way.

Washington himself could now relax enough to join his officers in a game of cricket. When a miniature painter came to the camp, he took time on several occasions to sit for his portrait. But Boudinot wrote of him in mid-April: "worthy man, he has both heart and hands full." For as one cause for anxiety was disposed of, another rose to demand his attention. All winter the wretched plight of the prisoners of war whom British neglect was slowly starving to death in Philadelphia had lain heavy on his heart, and he was still striving vainly to accomplish the exchange of as many of them as possible. More pressing was the need of more troops with which to fight the campaign whose opening could be hardly more than a month away. And now appeared a danger unforeseen, whose consequences might prove to be more disastrous than anything that had gone before it.

In a letter dated April 17 Mr. Boudinot told his wife of the arrival at the camp of what he called "a grand piece of news." If it proved to be true, it might mean the early and happy ending of the war. But in the judgment of Washington and President Laurens it strongly resembled a Trojan horse, a mere peace offensive, as it would be called today, "meant to poison the minds of the people, and detach the wavering at least from our cause." It emanated from New York, that prolific source of forgeries, and was sponsored by Tryon, the progenitor of so many despicable stratagems. It first appeared at Valley Forge in the form of a handbill purporting to present certain Conciliatory Bills, which the British Parliament had passed at Lord North's insistence, offering peace to the rebellious colonies on the most generous terms. And it soon became known that large shipments of these handbills had been sent out from Philadelphia for distribution thoughout the country.

It proved to be entirely genuine, however. Tryon himself certified this in a letter to Washington in which he enclosed two copies of the bills themselves and had the impudence to suggest that Washington make their contents known to his troops. Washington replied crisply that, with the approval of Congress, the bills had already circulated freely among his officers and men, since he had the most perfect confidence in their fidelity to the United States. Congress had indeed been too wise to give the offer importance by making a mystery of it and had themselves caused it to be printed and distributed. But Washington considered it more dangerous to the cause of Independence than any armed efforts of the enemy. It was intended, he felt sure, only to divide the country, and he greatly feared that it would succeed. In his opinion there was no trick so low that the British Government would not resort to it to accomplish their ends.

But even supposing the proposals to be sincere, Washington wrote to various correspondents, nothing short of Independence would be a sound basis for peace. The injuries done to America were too great to be forgotten; and no other country would ever help the colonies in the future if they accepted peace with dependence now. In any event the army must be maintained and strengthened, if only as a support to Congress in the peace negotiations. By this means also the peace propaganda could best be combated. Moreover, it was the best means of encouraging France to come into the war.

The response to the peace proposals proved Washington's fears to be groundless. People everywhere recognized the Conciliation Bills for what they were, a product of the fears and weakness of Lord North's Government. At Providence a crowd of ardent patriots burned copies of them under the public gallows. Congress replied to them with a resolution declaring that only after the independence of the United States had been acknowledged and the fleets and armies of Great Britain withdrawn from the country would the said states hold conference with peace commissioners. The reasons that the proposals had been made was too easily to be guessed. The commissioners at Paris had not been idle. Saratoga and Germantown had made their impression abroad. And April was hardly over before these surmises were confirmed by the news that France had signed a treaty of alliance with the United States.

Crossing to Falmouth in a French frigate that bore the appropriately Yankee-sounding name *Sensible*, Simeon Deane, Silas Deane's brother, had brought over copies of the treaty for Congress to ratify, and from Bethlehem on his way to York he had sent Washington the gist of the glad tidings. "I believe no event was ever received with more heartfelt joy," Washington wrote to President Laurens on the 1st of May. His own emotion, one who was with him at the time observed, came close to breaking down even his iron self-control. Now, at last, after four terrible months, had come justification for the faith expressed in his General Order at the Gulph that "the period is not far distant when France will take a more active part, by declaring war against the British Crown." For nobody could doubt that the treaty meant war between France and Britain.

CHAPTER VI

"Philadelphia Has Taken General Howe"

1

HORACE WALPOLE HAD NOT been exaggerating when he wrote of the frustration of the British campaign in New Jersey in the summer of 1777: "France sits by and laughs . . . and winks on Franklin." From their beginning, Great Britain's troubles with the American colonies had been a delight to the French. For years the French, both Government and people, had been yearning for an opportunity to revenge themselves for the loss of Canada and the other humiliations of the Seven Years' War. Under the powerful patronage of the Marquise de Pompadour the Duc de Choiseul had worked steadily to that end, improving the army and building up the navy until, in 1770, it numbered sixty-four ships of the line and fifty frigates.

But to intervene openly in the struggle involved a risk that Louis's XVI's foreign minister, the Comte de Vergennes, hesitated to take. There was a century-old hatred of France in the English colonies in America, and in the war that was bound to follow French intervention they might suddenly become reconciled with their mother country and France might lose her own colonies in the West Indies. Encouraged, however, by the news of the British evacuation of Boston, Vergennes sent Caron de Beaumarchais to Spain in the June of 1776 with a million francs of French Government money and instructions to give the rebels all possible help surreptitiously. In Spain that many sided genius proceeded to organize Roderigo Hortalez and Company, through which he began shipping to the Americans large quantities of arms, artillery, ammunition, clothing, and shoes, which he purchased from the surplus stocks in French arsenals and storehouses.

The British ambassador at Paris, Viscount Stormont, was kept well informed of what was going on by his secret agents and protested vigorously against these palpably unfriendly actions. The lethargic young Louis XVI, impressed by the arguments of Turgot, his minister of finance, consented only with reluctance to a policy which might involve his country in a war that it could not afford. But Frederick the Great, in fear of a Franco-Austrian combination that would give Bavaria to Austria on the death of its ailing king, was anxious to have France fully occupied otherwise and kept striving to impress Louis with the idea that here was a heaven-sent opportunity to cripple Great Britain at little cost.

Louis's queen, the frivolous Marie Antoinette, succeeded in ousting Turgot from his ministry and made the American cause fashionable. The Comte d'Artois, heir presumptive to the throne, declared himself a "Bostonian." The younger nobles, disciples of Montesquieu and Voltaire, were filled with enthusiasm to fight for liberty in America; the older ones thirsted for revenge on Britain by any means. So not only did the clandestine aid go on, but by stationing French naval squadrons so that they could maintain the right of American ships to enter French harbors France had, in effect, recognized the American colonies as belligerents in the summer of 1776.

Such was the atmosphere in which Benjamin Franklin arrived in France on the 3rd of December of that year, and the manner of his coming did nothing to decrease the warmth of his welcome. He was probably unique among envoys in bringing with him a cargo of indigo to pay the expenses of his mission and sailing into Quiberon Bay with two prizes, British merchant ships, which, forgetful of his own safety, he had permitted his vessel, well-named *Reprisal*, to capture in the course of the voyage. "And we French allow ourselves to be afraid!" Beaumarchais exclaimed in admiration of the old man of seventy, who was ill and suffering from boils at the time.

He was received enthusiastically. The "Poor Richard" of his almanac, the stoves of his invention, and his investigation of electricity had long ago given him a reputation throughout Europe. During his several years in London as colonial agent for Pennsylvania he had made the acquaintance of many of the prominent European statesmen and diplomats. He had visited France twice in the past, had been presented to King Louis XV, had been made much of by the *Franklinistes* among the scientists, and had been cultivated by the economists. His French, though inaccurate, was fluent enough to be serviceable.

Now there were crowds to welcome him at Nantes. The friends of America gave a grand dinner and ball for him. In Paris the expectation of his arrival was tremendous, and his appearance did not disappoint his admirers. In his brown coat and spectacles, with a walking stick instead of a sword, and his straight gray hair hanging below his fur cap in contrast to the powdered heads of the Parisians, he seemed to them the embodiment of those primitive virtues which Rousseau had made popular. Soon his picture was on everybody's mantelpiece, on the lids of snuffboxes, and in miniature set in rings.

His mission, specifically, was to ask for thirty thousand muskets and the loan of eight French ships of the line, the latter request being put forward as justifiable since the German princes had leased their soldiers to Britain. But his real object was the negotiation of a treaty of alliance between his infant country and France. Vergennes received him and his colleagues, Silas Deane and Arthur Lee, with cordiality, though with nothing more tangible at the moment. The news of the American defeat on Long Island and the loss of New York had made King Louis's ministers hesitant about proceeding further with the American affair until the situation became clearer.

But it was not long before two million francs passed into the hands of the American commissioners on the easiest terms. In January of the new year the port authorities at Le Havre and Nantes were instructed to stop asking embarrassing questions about the cargoes of ships bound ostensibly for the West Indies. The *Reprisal* was permitted to go to sea, where she joined the American cruisers *Lexington* and *Dolphin* in ranging the Channel for British shipping. The *Dolphin* was armed with French cannon and manned by a French crew, and all three vessels were allowed to use French ports as bases and sell their prizes in France in spite of Lord Stormont's vehement protests. Moreover, the waters of the Caribbean soon became infested by privateers that flew the American flag, to be sure, and bore letters of marque granted by the Continental Congress, but sailed out of

French West Indian ports and preyed so fiercely on British commerce that the value of captured cargoes in one month amounted to £140,000 and in London the insurance rate for the West India trade rose to 28 per cent, higher even than in the Seven Years' War.

By making but few appearances in public Franklin kept up the popular interest in himself and the cause which he represented. He lived quietly, at first at the Hôtel d'Hombourg on the Rue de l'Université in Paris, later in the suburb of Passy in a pleasant house where, despite his years, he kept up his habit of walking a league every day, in the large garden if the weather was fine, indoors if it was foul. He kept a carriage and pair, but he seldom used it except to attend meetings of the Academy of Sciences.

Diderot, Turgot, and d'Alembert became his friends. Walpole's old friend, Madame du Deffand, received him. He met the Duc de Broglie and Choiseul, Lafayette's relatives-in-law the Noailles, and the young Duc de La Rochefoucauld d'Enville. He liked gay company and the French liked him for liking it. John Adams wrote home of him in the spring of 1778: "Being seventy years of age, the ladies not only allow him to embrace them as often as he pleases, but they are perpetually embracing him." Not for nothing had George III called him "that insidious man" and Lord Stormont warned the French ministers that Franklin had got the better of three British foreign ministers.

Stormont kept him surrounded by spies, some of whom he knew for what they were, some he suspected, and a few he failed ever to detect. But he refused to be disturbed by their machinations. To a friend who warned him of them he wrote: "I have long observed a rule which prevents any inconvenience from such practices . . . to be concerned in no affair that I should blush to have made public, and to do nothing but what spies may see and welcome. . . ." His refusal, however, to play the game of cloak-and-dagger diplomacy according to the rules gave the enemy a decided advantage over him. By means of writing in white ink between the lines of letters apparently concerned with "gallantry," which were deposited in a hollow tree on the south terrace of the Tuileries, Lord Stormont was furnished with the names of the masters and the sailing dates of the ships employed by the American commissioners. Information about American privateers and their prizes, on which he based his protests to the French Government, reached him in the same way. About half of the American diplomatic correspondence was captured by British cruisers at sea; Stormont often knew of the proceedings of Congress before the commissioners did; and on one occasion a packet of blank paper was substituted for the dispatches of the commissioners and went on its way to America while the dispatches themselves were spirited across the Channel to the ministers of King George.

The jealous and suspicious Arthur Lee got himself expelled from Spain, had his papers stolen by British agents in Berlin, confused Deane's negotiations with the French military contractors, and undermined his colleagues so seriously at home that Congress recalled Deane to report on the progress of American affairs in Europe. But Franklin kept steadily at work with his deceptively easygoing air that was to annoy John Adams's bustling New England temperament more than a year later. He thoroughly understood the situation of Vergennes during the summer of 1777. King Louis would not consent to a war with Great Britain unless Spain would join him in it; Spain, with an anxious eye to her own colonies, was opposed to the idea of independence for any colonies in the Americas; and the news from across the Atlantic was the reverse of stimulating to the idea of intervention.

Its effect was somewhat lessened by the extravagant claims of successes that emanated from the British embassy. On one occasion Lord Stormont announced a British victory in which four thousand rebels had been killed together with their leader. *Stormonter* became a synonym for *mentir* (to lie) in Parisian slang. But when Ticonderoga fell, it seemed that nothing could prevent Burgoyne's continued advance and the isolation of New England. Franklin, however, continued to pronounce his habitual *"Ça ira"* with apparently unshaken confidence. Late in November, when a gentleman remarked to him that General Howe had taken Philadelphia, he answered with smiling calm: "I beg your pardon, sir. Philadelphia has taken General Howe." And on December 4 came word of the surrender of Burgoyne and his whole army, and shortly afterward accounts of the excellent behavior of Washington's troops at the battle of Germantown.

Vergennes promptly sent the commissioners his congratulations and invited them to renew their proposal for a treaty of alliance, which he had rejected in September. They met with him in the utmost secrecy in a lonely house a half-mile outside Versailles. Five days later the Royal Council approved the alliance, and a courier went galloping to Madrid to get Spain's concurrence, without which the treaty could not be concluded. But Spain persisted in her obduracy, and again the weeks went by without anything being accomplished. It was the evening of Friday, the 6th of February, 1777, when the treaty of alliance was finally signed.

Its terms provided that France would help the United States of America to win their independence; that if a war between France and Great Britain should result from this action, the United States would make common cause with France; and that neither party to the treaty would make either a truce or peace without the consent of the other, or lay down their arms until a treaty with Great Britain had assured the United States of their independence.

His Most Christian Majesty, Louis XVI, informed King George of the treaty in a message of which Washington wrote gloatingly that it was "conceived in terms of irony and derision more degrading to the pride and dignity of Britain than anything she has ever experienced since she became a nation"; and on March 20 King Louis received Franklin and his fellow commissioners publicly at Versailles.

The wily old negotiator was careful to maintain his character of homespun philosopher and statesman on this occasion. He wore a coat of brown velvet and white stockings and carried a white hat under his arm, but he went without a sword, kept his spectacles on his nose, and his lank gray locks were without wig or powder. He appears to have fascinated Marie Antoinette. She kept him at her side throughout the evening and talked with him in the intervals of placing her bets on the gaming table.

2

Although the negotiations had been surrounded by all possible secrecy, Lord Stormont had managed to keep pretty well informed of their progress. According to the British agent who sent it, a copy of the treaty of alliance was in London forty-two hours after it was signed. Meanwhile the American commissioners had been repeatedly assailed in letters from English friends and in personal interviews with secret agents with proposals for reconciliation. It had all been carefully unofficial, but "the grand basis of the Navigation Acts," or indeed almost any other basis for reconciliation short of Independence, had been suggested, and it had been strongly hinted that there would be titles of honor, wealth, and high positions in the Government for those who brought it to pass. Before the end of February that authority on the fall of empires, Edward Gibbon, observed peevishly from his seat on the Government benches in the House of Commons that Great Britain and France were "fairly running a race for the favor of America."

Britain had need to run. For the treaty meant war with France— a war for which Britain was altogether unprepared. The danger had long been foreseen by naval and military men. It was more than a year since Sir John Jervis, the future famous Earl of St. Vincent, had written from England to Sir Henry Clinton at Providence that France and Spain were evidently arming for war, and the military situation both at home and abroad had become increasingly alarming since then. For years it had been the policy of Lord North and the Earl of Sandwich, the corrupt First Lord of the Admiralty, to starve the naval dockyards. The war in America had absorbed so large a part of the British army that only ten thousand soldiers remained at home to defend England against an invasion for which France had made great preparations. At Dieppe she had gathered a fine new fleet of thirty ships of the line and twenty-five frigates, and an army of twenty-five thousand picked troops stood ready to board their transports and cross the Channel, while at Toulon a powerful expedition was preparing to sail for America.

No general was available in whom England had confidence. Lord Amherst, the conqueror of Ticonderoga in the French and Indian War, refused to take command against the Americans, who had been his comrades. He told the King, moreover, that it would require a reinforcement of forty thousand men to subdue the Americans, and the situation over there went far to bear him out. The rebels were

once more in possession of Ticonderoga and were guarding the
Hudson Highlands more strongly than ever. Britain had lost a whole
army, and her remaining troops were cooped up in Newport, New
York, and Philadelphia. Horace Walpole, whose hatred of Lord
North's Government probably fathered his pessimism, thought that
both Quebec and New York might be lost, or Washington might
decide "to overwhelm Howe."

By the time Parliament adjourned for Christmas the probability
of war with France had grown so great that Lord North announced
that henceforth his American policy would be one of reconciliation.
The country was shocked and amazed. Consols dropped twenty
points. On February 17 Lord North proposed to the reassembled
House of Commons that Parliament retract all measures displeasing
to the Americans, from the Stamp Act to the opening of hostilities,
and that a Royal Commission be sent to the colonies with full powers
to arrange for immediate pacification, instructions to proclaim a truce
during the negotiations, to address all members of the American
Government and military forces by any titles they had seen fit to
assume, and to offer full pardon to all who had taken part in the
rebellion.

How changed would have been the feelings of the men at Valley
Forge if they had known of these proceedings! There on that same
17th of February an officer was sentenced to dishonorable discharge
for stealing an enlisted man's ration of whisky; two days earlier it
had been necessary to send out parties to impress straw for bedding;
and a week later the brigade commanders were called together to
make "a just distribution" of the available clothing.

Parliament passed the Conciliation Bills in an atmosphere of
gloom. The King signed them. Great Britain declared war on France.
The French ambassador's carriage was pelted by the mob as he
passed through Canterbury on his way to take ship for home. The
nation, long divided on the American issue, became united against
its hereditary enemy, and after some delay the Peace Commissioners
set sail, hoping to reach Philadelphia in time to forestall the effect
of the arrival in America of the treaty of alliance with France.

They were not ill-chosen for their mission. Their chief, the thirty-year-old Earl of Carlisle, had lately entered public life after a career of roistering in the company of Charles James Fox, and was intelligent, well educated, traveled, and by temperament sympathetic with people less fortunate and exalted in rank than himself. Among the other members were George Johnstone, who had been governor of West Florida, and William Eden, later the first Lord Auckland, who was a brother of Sir Robert Eden, a former governor of Maryland. Their secretary was Dr. Adam Ferguson, professor of what would seem to be singularly mismated subjects, Pneumatics and Moral Philosophy, at the University of Edinburgh. That nothing conciliatory might be lacking, the seal of the Commission bore the persuasive device of a mother blessing her children. But, unknown to them, the situation in which they were to negotiate had been undermined by the government that sent them out; and above all, they were too late.

At Philadelphia the guns that saluted their arrival on June 6 had hardly ceased to boom before they learned that the treaty with France had beaten them across the Atlantic, that the Continental Congress had already ratified it, and that the Conciliation Bills had been received throughout the country with scorn and derision. Washington refused with frigid courtesy their request for a passport to enable Dr. Ferguson to go through the American lines for the purpose of laying their proposals before Congress. Johnstone's efforts to make contact by means of personal letters to acquaintances among the Congressmen were rebuffed. The commissioners were reduced to forwarding their papers to York under a flag of truce.

This they proceeded reluctantly to do, in a packet which contained also a number of private letters to members of Congress from friends in England, and which was secured, as John Laurens noted, by that propitiatory seal of theirs. The answer was slow in coming but it was unmistakably positive: no peace negotiations while British armies and fleets remained in American territories and waters and the independence of the United States remained unacknowledged by Great Britain.

More disappointing still, if that was possible, was the revelation of a fact of which they had been kept in ignorance until they reached their destination. Their expectations of the military situation they were to arrive in cannot have been brilliant. But they had grounds for believing that, supported by a victorious army, they would be offering peace from a conquered capital to rebels who, in spite of one brilliant success, had been repeatedly and soundly beaten. They were shocked by the actuality. As they sailed up the Delaware in the fine weather of early June through a beautiful country of evident richness, they observed with amazement the chain of warships anchored at frequent intervals to protect the army's supply ships from the raids of the rebels, who infested both banks of the river, made communication by land impossible, and actually fired on their vessel with rifles.

At Philadelphia Lord Carlisle discovered that a ride of eight miles carried him "beyond our possessions," he wrote to his friend George Selwyn: "Our lines extend only two." The American army, he learned, was posted very strongly twenty-six miles away, but so active were its flying parties that it was safe for him to ride out as far as Germantown only because it was a market day and two thousand British troops had been sent out to protect the countrypeople, who would otherwise have been afraid to bring their provisions in for sale. And to crown all else, the Earl and his colleagues were informed that the army had received orders from home to evacuate Philadelphia and return to New York by sea. Indeed, preparations for this movement had already been begun.

So instead of being supported by an aggressive military policy the Commissioners found themselves handicapped from the start by a spectacular withdrawal which gave their offers of peace what Carlisle described as "the appearance of supplications for mercy from a vanquished and exhausted State." And there was "nothing," Johnstone wrote in his anger and chagrin, "more contemptible than a retreating army, or a supplicating prince."

The morale of Sir William Howe's troops moreover, must have been disheartening to any member of the Commission who was able to observe it with the eye of a professional soldier. Not only were they discouraged by the order for evacuation; the tone of both officers and men, with few exceptions, had suffered severely from the frustration, idleness, and easy living of the past winter. Philadelphia had not ruined Howe's army as Capua ruined Hannibal's. But its effects were evident.

3

In the whole British Empire, outside of London, the officers and soldiers of Howe's army could hardly have found a pleasanter place than Philadelphia in which to spend the winter. It afforded a delightful contrast to last winter's crowded quarters in the dull little towns of New Jersey and bleak, half-burned New York. The city had long been known as a center of wealth and culture. While Congress was sitting there Richard Henry Lee had discribed it as "an attractive scene of debauch and amusement." But John Adams found its society "happy, elegant, tranquil, and polite." Its Medical School was justly celebrated. The observation of the transit of Venus by the members of its Philosophical Society in 1769 had won the praise of the Astronomer Royal.

The city was pleasantly interspersed with groves, hills, ponds, and gardens which formed a setting for handsome country houses. The principal streets were well lighted at night, paved, and frequently brightened by the passage of smart coaches whose panels sported heraldic devices. The stately, three-story red brick houses had an air of London about them. Their mistresses, members of the Society of Friends though they might be, dressed in bright colors and as nearly in the prevailing mode as the distance from Europe permitted. They danced at assemblies that had been an institution for eighteen years. Visitors from abroad wondered at the skill of hostesses who were able to maintain conversation in their drawing rooms without the aid of cards, a thing that was no longer possible in London; and Philadelphia dinners were famous for their turtle soup and Madeira.

The doors of most of the best houses opened wide in welcome to the British officers. For Philadelphia, though strong for constitutional rights, had listened apathetically to the clang of the Liberty Bell on the Fourth of July, 1776. The round of "drums," "routs," and dances lasted through the winter. There was skating on the Delaware, and heavy snows gave the opportunity for sleighing parties. To discharge their social obligations the officers organized a series of weekly balls at Smith's City Tavern and in fine weather gave dinners at Springettsbury, the Penn manor house, near the junction of the present 20th and Springgarden Streets.

They organized handicap races on the Commons, in which dashing, twenty-three-year-old Banastre Tarleton, brigade major of the cavalry, made a pleasanter name for himself than that of "a butcher and a barbarian," which the young Comte de Rochambeau gave him for his exploits in the South a few years later. Captain John André and Captain Oliver Delancy of the 17th Dragoons, who had been the animating spirits of the Theatre Royal in New York the previous winter, took over the shabby little playhouse on South Street, whither it had been relegated by the stricter sect of the local moralists of an earlier day.

With the help of other staff officers, they opened it on January 14 with *No One's Enemy But His Own* and *The Deuce Is in Him* and followed them with a varied repertory that included *Henry IV*, Part I, Dr. John Home's *Douglas*, *The Minor*, and *The Wonder, or A Woman Who Kept A Secret*. Delancy painted the scenery, as he had done in New York, and for the opening André wrote a prologue in which a grim allusion proved to be curiously prophetic:

> In lofty terms old vaunting Sadler's Wells
> Of her tight rope and ladder dancing tells,
> But Cunningham in both by far excells.

Cunningham was the provost marshal and as jailor and executioner had become notorious for his brutality. In England years later he perished on the gallows, as André did at West Point in 1780.

Prices of admission ranged from a dollar for a seat in a box or the pit to half as much for one in the gallery. The proceeds, as in New York, were devoted to the relief of the widows and orphans of the army. The theater became so popular that people had to send servants at four o'clock in the afternoon to hold places for them, although the curtain did not rise till seven; and it was May 19 when *The Citizen* brought the season to a close. After each performance the members of the cast and their friends supped gaily in the players' clubrooms at the City Tavern, where, one spring evening, they had the doubtful honor of entertaining General Charles Lee as he passed through the city to be exchanged for the British General Prescott.

In their relations with the townspeople the British officers—excepting one whom the others detested—generally behaved with courtesy and consideration. Cornwallis moved to another house when Mrs. Isaac Norris, on whom he had been billeted, complained that his suite did not leave her enough room to live comfortably. But in the circumstances it was inevitable that there was another side to the picture. Young Charles Stedman, back in his home town as an officer in the British service, deplored the lack of discipline and subordination that pervaded the whole army, and the prevailing atmosphere of indolence and luxury.

For those for whom more innocent amusements had little attraction there were club dinners at the Indian Queen and wild supper parties at the Bunch of Grapes after boisterous evenings at the Cockpit in Moore's Alley. At a faro bank that made the fortune of the foreign officer who operated it many a young officer was so "plucked" that he had to sell out of the service and go home penniless. Several officers kept mistresses openly, even establishing them—to Stedman's indignation—in their billets in the houses of decent people.

Good-looking bondwomen found in this a convenient way of escaping servitude. Two officers advertised in the newspapers for a housekeeper, a young woman "who can occasionally put her hand to anything." They promised "extravagant wages" and required "no character." A Major Williams of the artillery had a lovely English girl, whom he paraded down the line at a review, dressed in the regimental colors with plumes to match, in an open carriage with fine English horses and an English coachman and footman. The winter was not far advanced before a Hessian lieutenant called the city "a confluens cannaillorium" that did "not yield to Sodom and Gomorrah in respect to all the vices."

The dissipation among the officers was reflected, as it is invariably, by slackness and insubordination among the rank and file. But for an occasional foraging expedition in force, there was little to relieve the monotony of the soldiers' life, which might have been much the same as garrison life in England had it not been for the extra fatigues that were owing to their situation and the climate. The frequent and heavy snows had to be shoveled from the banquettes and platforms of the redoubts, with care that it was not merely thrown upon the parapets; and firewood had to be cut, by torchlight sometimes in the short winter afternoons or out across the Delaware at the risk of being sniped at by guerrillas.

In the city expensive fences, fruit trees, and even some vacant houses vanished by night to rise in smoke from the stoves of barrack-rooms and company kitchens, though flogging was the penalty when British soldiers were caught at such destruction. As at Valley Forge, courts-martial ground steadily through the winter. A few men were hanged for stealing and more serious crimes. A number were tried for desertion and sentenced to a thousand lashes of the cat-o'-nine-tails on the bare back: a punishment tantamount to death by torture, which their comrades, in locked ranks and with frozen faces, were forced to witness. But even the performance of guard duty, that fundamental of military efficiency, so deteriorated that General Orders complained of sentinels who were not only careless but ignorant of the etiquette required of them.

For looting, the British soldiers were severely punished. But General Knyphausen—who, by the way, had the intriguing habit of buttering his bread with his thumb—took little trouble to control his Hessians so long as they performed their military duties smartly. Without the slightest discrimination between loyalists and those of rebel sympathies, these troops humiliated and infuriated the people by their rudeness and arrogance and their wanton destruction of what they did not plunder. They stabled their horses in fine houses and disposed of the manure by dumping it into the basements through holes in the floors and leaving it there to fester.

So slack was the enforcement of sanitary regulations that the city stank to heaven in the following June. The fine public libraries were pilfered, though not ruined like those in New York the previous winter, and private libraries did not go scot free. Even so decent a person as John André took two books of Benjamin Franklin's with him when the army departed. The damage to private property during the occupation was estimated at £180,000, without counting the losses of the loyalists.

The primary cause of this state of affairs was not far to seek. It was simply a case of like master, like man, from the top down. Of Sir William Howe, Charles Lee wrote not altogether unjustly: "Howe shut his eyes, fought his battles, drank his bottle, had his little whore, advis'd his Counsellors, receiv'd his orders from North and Germaine [sic], one more absurd than the other, shut his eyes and fought again." Sir William's way of life in New York had become notorious, and he made no change in it at Philadelphia. Far from prohibiting cards and other forms of gambling in the army as Washington had done, he was himself a habitué of the faro bank that ruined so many of his young officers; and it was not long before he was joined by his light-o'-love of Boston and New York days, Mrs. Loring. "The Battle of the Kegs," a lampooning ballad in which Francis Hopkinson celebrated the Americans' attempt to blow up the British warships at Philadelphia this winter with floating kegs of gunpowder, jeered at Howe's infatuation:

> Sir William he, snug as a flea,
> Lay all the time a snoring,
> Nor dreamed of harm as he lay warm
> In bed with Mrs. L——ng.

Before her arrival at Philadelphia Howe appears to have found a local substitute for her, but she was soon re-established as a sort of maitresse en titre. Observers described her as a "flashing blonde." In the army they called her "the Sultana," and the strictest hostesses soon discovered that she must be among their guests if they wished Sir William to attend their parties. Her husband, the former high sheriff of Dorchester, Massachusetts, was Howe's commissary of prisoners, a position that brought him in some $30,000 a year by way of compensation for his complaisance.

Howe was living comfortably, at first in General Cadwalader's house on Second Street, later in Richard Penn's, and he drove about in Mrs. Mary Pemberton's carriage. His portliness and lethargy had grown upon him. He was smarting under "the many mortifications" which his brother the Admiral said that the Government had put upon both of them; and only waiting to be relieved of his command after a year of failures for which he felt that he was not responsible, the enterprising officer who had led the assaults at Quebec under Wolfe and at Bunker Hill was by way of becoming an arrogant and morose proconsul.

He did nothing to make out of Philadelphia the citadel of loyalism to the Crown that it might have become under tactful management. There was no attempt to reconstitute the civil authority, or even to recognize the loyal spirit among the inhabitants who had remained in the city. The leading Tory citizen, Joseph Galloway, who had been Howe's faithful and busy agent for the past twelvemonth, received no higher position in the administration than superintendent general of police and of imports and exports, and he was placed under the authority of the provost marshal.

The city was treated like a mere fortress. The artillery and the 42nd Highlanders were quartered close to the State House. The State House yard was filled with cannon, limbers, and tumbrels. The government was wholly military. Arbitrary, frequently insolent, wrote the disgusted Stedman, it was given to plunder, with no compensation, and blighted legitimate business, while a hundred and twenty-one new shops which were opened by Scotchmen and Tories from Virginia, flourished under the patronage of army headquarters.

Like all indolent and self-indulgent men in high places, Howe was swarmed about by the inefficient, the corrupt, and the cruel: surrounded, it was said, by "a pack of self-interested puppies," who went home rich enough to set up estates after a few months of juggling with army contracts. His enemies believed him to be in secret partnership with one Coffin, a military shopkeeper in a large way of business, and upon Howe's return to England Horace Walpole wrote that he had come home "richer in money than in laurels."

Whether that was true or false, the peculation that went on under his indulgent eye was described as "enormous . . . indecent . . . both the troops and the treasury robbed," the hospitals "pesthouses," the provisions "poison." For want of proper hospital supplies the condition of the wounded became so shocking that the Quakers came to their relief. In the great prison at 6th and Walnut Streets the prisoners of war would have literally frozen and starved to death but for the Quakers' donations of blankets, clothing, and food.

It was, of course, true, as Burgoyne had written airily to General Gage in the first summer of the war, that "by the law of the land" the captured rebels were "destined to the cord," and that the British had "overlooked the criminal in the captive." But this seeming magnanimity was spurious. While hundreds of British officers and men were prisoners in American hands, ready subjects for reprisals, it would have been unwise to proceed against captive Americans as had been done with the Jacobites in England and Scotland after the risings of 1715 and 1745. They were treated, however, with a barbarity that John Laurens regarded as incredible.

To Washington's repeated protests and threats of reprisals, Howe replied with bland indifference to the facts, denying that the prisoners were mistreated. He stated that they were under the supervision of a field officer, who was instructed to receive their complaints and report them to him, and that their rations were the same as those issued to British troops when on board of men-of-war or transports.

Actually they were under the unchecked authority of the abominable Cunningham, the provost marshal, who, with his "Kennel, ye sons of bitches, kennel," had made floating hells of the prison hulks in New York Harbor. They were crowded by hundreds into rooms without ventilation, and while they slept the sleep of exhaustion their guards picked their pockets. Their daily allowance of food consisted of from four to six ounces of pork and a half-pound of biscuit, which some of them in their desperation strove to eke out with mortar scraped from between the stones of the walls; and each day some of them were carried out to fill graves in the near-by potter's field, now Washington Square.

Since December, amid the destitution of Valley Forge, officers and men had from time to time been scraping together what they could to send under flag of truce to their captive comrades. Washington had been untiring in his efforts to bring about the exchange of as many of them as possible. But Congress had demanded that the maintenance of prisoners held by the United States should be paid for in gold, but that the British must accept Continental paper money for the maintenance of prisoners in their hands, and had declined to authorize exchanges on any other basis, although many Americans had been in captivity for more than two years.

To complicate the business still further, a party of British officers and men bringing clothing to British prisoners under a flag of truce was arrested at Lancaster with such violence and indignities, in Hamilton's opinion, as would have been a disgrace to Hottentots. Commissioners from both armies met at King of Prussia Tavern on March 10 and several times after that. They agreed that all accounts should be settled in kind. Mr. Boudinot wrote to his wife in the middle of April: "I have been so long with the gay accomplished proud Englishmen, that I ought to be a foot higher than I used to be." But Howe refused to bind his Government to any agreement; so no cartel of exchange could be arrived at.

To the atmosphere of slackness and corruption that prevailed in Philadelphia those sound patriots who had remained in the city did all they could to add discomfort and frustration; and they were active and subtle in their efforts. Knowledge of the whereabouts of hidden stores of lumber, which was badly needed for the building of more comfortable quarters for the troops, had to be paid for *sub rosa*. "Secrecy is the word or Death," wrote the badgered Montrésor about such transactions; and twenty years later he was still in the toils of His Majesty's treasury department to account for monies thus expended. It proved to be impossible to prevent the forwarding of military information, though examining posts were established at all of the entrances to the lines and women were employed to search the skin of those of their own sex who passed out. Few foraging parties or other expeditions left the city before ample warning of their purpose, destination, and time of departure reached headquarters at Valley Forge.

There was bitter disappointment among the Tories everywhere at Howe's lethargy, and it was not soothed by his cool disregard of the sacrifices which their loyalty to the Crown was costing them. Galloway believed that if Washington's army were defeated or driven across the Susquehanna, three hundred gentlemen in Pennsylvania, Maryland, Delaware, and New Jersey would come out for the British cause, and that he himself could raise ten thousand loyalist troops among the inhabitants. As things were, Howe refused even to receive a deputation of fifty gentlemen from New Jersey's Monmouth County, a Tory stronghold, and less than a thousand men enlisted in the Provincial battalion that was organized in Philadelphia.

Galloway, who stood to lose a fortune of £70,000 if Britain lost the war, bombarded the authorities all winter with pleas and arguments for aggressive action. The Americans had lost between forty and fifty thousand men since the beginning of hostilities, he asserted; the rebellion in the middle colonies was in its last, languishing state and would be ended in another year, with vigorous and proper management. Only the defeat of the Hessians at Trenton had prevented the submission of Pennsylvania the previous winter, he wrote; and now only Washington and his "miscreant troops" kept the rebellion alive.

And even Washington's army, small and wretched though it was, was kept in being, Galloway maintained, only by impressing the lowest, or next to the lowest, class of men, under penalties of imprisonment and heavy fines. This was proved, in his opinion, by its deserters. Of the 1,134 of them who had slipped into the British lines by March 25, not more than one in ten was a native-born American: the rest were Irish, English, Scots, Germans, Canadians, and Frenchmen. As for the people in general, they were weary of their new tyrants. Did they not hide their provender from the rebels and risk their lives to bring it to market in Philadelphia?

It does not seem to have occurred to the wishful-thinking Tory gentleman that a preference for British gold rather than Continental paper had something to do with the countryfolk's marketing of their provender, and that the proportion of native-born Americans among the deserters was so small because most of them were sticking to their colors. At all events the loyalists' estimate of the situation was fully shared by the officers of the British army. They were deeply discontented at Howe's inaction. They read with chagrin a query in the London *Morning Post* as to why they had not swept away Mr. Washington's army, which had been so often described as sickly, ill-clothed, dispirited, and by no means so well armed as their own troops. Late arrivals from England doubtless told them how in London drawing rooms it had been humorously suggested that Sir William Howe be elevated to the peerage with the title of Lord Delay-ware.

Lord North's new policy, which was to restrict the war in America to the conquest of the South, while New England and the middle colonies were merely to be harried by coastal raids, they called "a buccaneering war" and liked less than before the idea of fighting people of their own blood. Officers and men alike shared the disgust and mortification of the Peace Commissioners at the order for the evacuation of the city. Sir William Erskine considered it "devoid of all Honor, Spirit, and Policy." The army at Philadelphia numbered about 19,000 British, German, and Provincial troops all told. In Erskine's opinion, which was shared by General Grant, the spirit of the rebels had never been so low as it was this June, and their army was as nothing in comparison with the British. But had they been better informed of what had been going on at Valley Forge in the past three months they might have thought differently. Philadelphia had indeed taken General Howe, and to a degree that these gentlemen had yet to realize. In fact by June Sir William was no longer at Philadelphia.

4

The order relieving Howe of his command, which he had asked for in November, had reached him in April. Shortly before the arrival of the Peace Commissioners Sir Henry Clinton had succeeded him, and he had sailed for home. There had been no joy among his troops at the change. Clinton's record in the war had not been brilliant. They thought him a cold-hearted man of limited vision, whereas Howe's manner toward his troops was genial and outgiving, and though his officers and men might grouse at his inactivity and lack of enterprise, he never lost their liking. His very vices aroused the envious admiration of the rank and file. In the past three years he had led them to victory in six pitched battles. Under him they had taken the rebel capital. He had been considerate of their comfort, appreciative of their loyal and devoted service. Had he been listened to there would have been no need for the hateful order for evacuation that branded their past two years of strenuous campaigning as a failure. With more enthusiasm than good judgment they set about giving his departure the air of a triumph; and they shed tears of genuine sorrow when he boarded H.M.S. *Andromeda* on May 24 and set sail for England to become the scapegoat of Lord North's blundering.

A committee of wealthy field officers arranged and paid for the festivities that signalized the army's approval of his conduct of the war and its regret at his departure. A *Meschianza* (Italian for medley) they called the affair. It consisted of a tournament and a ball conceived in a spirit of rococo medievalism that would have done credit to Horace Walpole in his *Castle of Otranto* period. Taking over Walnut Grove, Mr. Thomas Wharton's fine place on the river, they drew upon Montrésor's sappers and miners for the construction of lists and barriers on the four-acre lawn. At either end stood pavilions for British and American Queens of Beauty, each of whom was attended by six damsels of honor in Turkish costumes. Twelve champions, equally divided between Knights of the Blended Rose in crimson and white silk, mounted on gray horses, and Knights of the Burning Mountain in orange and black, on black horses, contended for their favors.

Captain André designed the ladies' costumes: towering headdresses decked with pearls and jewels, polonaises of white silk, spangled pink sashes, spangled shoes and stockings and veils—these last edged with silver lace for the ladies of the Blended Rose; and similar dresses for the ladies of the Burning Mountain, except that their polonaises were bound with black and that they wore black sashes.

Evidence of Howe's failure was obvious in the presence of the guardian men-of-war and the transports anchored in the river in preparation for the evacuation. But it was blithely ignored. The vessels' yards were manned, their rigging gay with flags, when, between three and four o'clock in the afternoon of the 18th of May, a procession of decorated barges laden with the participants in the pageant, the notables, and the other guests passed down their line from Knight's Wharf to the landing place at Old Fort to the strains of military music.

From the shore to the lists a grand avenue a hundred yards long and lined with troops in the various uniforms of the British army led the company in procession under two triumphal arches, also of André's design, each of which bore a figure of Fame, star-spangled like the ladies of honor and blowing from her trumpet the motto: *"Tes Lauriers Sont Immortels."* A herald presented Howe with a laurel wreath and declaimed his praise in lines of André's writing, which did not forget to make tactful allusion to the new commander in chief:

> Chained to our arms, while Howe the battle led,
> Still round these files her wings shall Conquest spread.
> Loved though he goes, the spirit still remains
> That with him bore us o'er these trembling plains
> .   .   .   .
> Nor fear but equal honors shall repay
> Each hardy deed where Clinton leads the way.

For an hour or more the champions contended in mimic combat with lance, sword, and pistol; subalterns in heralds' tabards proclaimed the victors; and knights received their ladies' favors between solid hedges of British infantry. Then the procession was formed once more and proceeded to the near-by mansion, where dancing began at six o'clock in a ballroom which the brushes of André and Delancy had made gorgeous with garlands of roses against a background of blue and gold. Some eighty or ninety large mirrors had been assembled to reflect the brilliance of the scene, and a thousand wax candles shed their flattering illumination upon it when darkness fell.

At ten there were splendid fireworks on the lawn, and at midnight four-and-twenty black servitors in Oriental costume, with silver bracelets on their arms and silver collars around their necks, served a supper of four hundred covers, twelve hundred dishes. The heralds proclaimed the toasts—the King and Queen, the Navy and Army, the Commanders, the Knights and Ladies. Then the dancing was resumed, and it was kept up until four o'clock in the morning, though the sound of distant cannon fire and of drums beating the long roll caused some of the ladies to ask awkward questions. They were told that the shots were salutes from the redoubts in honor of

the occasion. Actually it was Major McLane and his picked force
of Continental infantry and dragoons, who had been keeping the
outposts on tenterhooks ever since January. This night he celebrated
by setting fire to the abatis.

There were few young ladies of beauty and position in the city
who declined an invitation to take part in the affair, let the family
politics be what they might. Captain Montrésor's wife, the former
Miss Achmutty, was one of the ladies of honor. Another was the
handsome and witty Miss Franks. She married Colonel Johnson of
the 17th Foot but told Winfield Scott in England many years later
that she was sorry she had not been a patriot. Notable among the
girls of Whig families should have been beautiful seventeen-year-old
Peggy Shippen, who was soon to become the unhappy Mrs. Benedict
Arnold, and whom, twenty years after, Tarleton called "the hand-
somest woman in London." She attended all the rehearsals, but at
the last minute her father put his foot down and forbade her par-
ticipation in the performance. Those who did take part earned
Anthony Wayne's withering disapproval and were pointedly omitted
from the invitation list of the ball that was given to celebrate the
recovery of the city by the Americans a few weeks later.

People less interested in having a good time than in getting on
with the war girded at the whole affair. Many of the older, sober,
and seasoned officers were mortified by its fantastic extravagance.
"Why, child," a veteran artillery officer replied to a little boy who
asked what was the difference between the two contending parties
in the tournament, "the Knights of the Burning Mountain are Tom
Fools, and the Knights of the Blended Rose are damned fools. I
know no other difference between 'em. What will Washington think
of all this?"

What was thought of it by the rank and file, turned out in their
stiff parade uniforms, with cued and powdered hair, to sweat for
hours under a strong May sun in a living frame for the cavortings
of their betters, is not recorded. They were not used to being treated
with much consideration, and doubtless there was an extra ration
of beer for them at the end of the day. But that General Sir William

Howe should have countenanced such a garish performance in his honor added nothing to his reputation among his colleagues in rank. Five years afterward, at the end of the heroic defense of Gibraltar, when its commander, Sir George Augustus Eliott, was approached by his officers with regard to giving him a suitable farewell, he replied: "Anything but a Meschianza." The disappointed, disillusioned, and nearly ruined Galloway called it "a farce of Knight errantry" and "a triumph of leaving America unconquered."And the other Tories who had joined him in supporting the cause of the Crown shared fully in his feelings.

For them and their kind in Philadelphia the order for evacuation meant the end of the world. They had staked their all on Howe's promises and the strength and valor of the British army. They had made the best of the occupation, in which they had suffered little less in humiliation and material losses than if they had been the stubborn victims of conquest. A good many of them had taken up arms and fought for the Crown. And for their pains they had learned, first, that the Crown was offering the rebels free pardon as the price of peace, and then that they and their city were to be given up and left a prey to their enemies.

For a time they might strive to comfort themselves, as young Stedman did, with the belief that the traditional fear and hatred of France, especially in New England, would make the prospect of a French alliance so unpopular that reconciliation on the liberal terms that were offered would be preferred to it. When the French alliance, disliked though it was, received grateful acceptance, they turned to Howe and asked his advice as to what they should do. He replied negligently that they had best make such terms as they could with the rebels.

As soon as Washington became convinced of the genuineness of the peace proposals, he had, with his customary wisdom and tolerance, proposed that Congress advise the several states to offer pardon to all Tories who would swear allegiance to the United States by a certain date. They were frightened, he wrote, and such an offer would detach them from the enemy and hasten the conclusion of the war. But the Tories knew only too well how frail a shield such a pardon would be against neighbors eager to pay off old scores of insult and injury. At best they could hope to be no more than tolerated, under constant suspicion until the war came to an end, and forever scorned as the castoff supporters of a lost cause.

Flight and exile were preferable. But, for a time, even flight appeared to be impossible. The evacuation order directed that the army should go to New York by sea, and there would be no room for refugees on the transports. To go by sea, however, would expose Britain's only field army in America not only to the vagaries of wind and weather but possibly to attack by the French expedition from Toulon, which was known to be approaching the American coast. It was composed of twelve ships of the line and a squadron of frigates under the command of the Comte d'Estaing and carried four thousand French infantry. If Clinton's transports should be scattered by a storm, Admiral Lord Howe's escorting squadron of warships could not possibly defend them all. The movement of the army by sea, moreover, would leave Washington free to attack New York, which he could threaten by so few days of marching that any delay of the transports by calm or bad weather might cost the British the loss of the city. It was decided therefore that the army should march across New Jersey, preferably by way of New Brunswick, while the ships carried the heavy baggage, the great guns and mortars, and the refugees and their possessions.

Again, as twice before in the past nineteen months, the sidewalks of Philadelphia were heaped with furniture, family portraits, china, and bedding, awaiting cartage to the wharfs or for sale at public auction. But now it was the Tories who must avert their eyes from this indecent exposure of their household goods. Out at Valley Forge they heard that every available vehicle, from wagons to wheelbarrows, was rolling to the waterside day after day with the goods of the refugees. Nothing but misery and sorrow were to be seen in the city, wrote Mr. Serle on May 23. Sympathy for these innocent victims of their government was general among their British friends.

On the night after the *Meschianza* hearts were somewhat lightened by the brief prospect of at least a minor success. The drums beat to arms, and under cover of darkness strong columns commanded by

Grant, Grey, and Clinton himself moved out by the Germantown and Whitemarsh roads and up the Schuylkill. It was reported that Lafayette and his tattered retinue had abandoned their mudholes and taken up a position at Barren Hill, about halfway between Valley Forge and Philadelphia, in which it seemed likely that they could be surprised and captured.

Sir William Howe, whose sailing was now but a few days off, was in high spirits at the probability of having the famous young French noble to take home with him as a trophy. He told the ladies that he expected to have a real French marquis to present to them at the dinner he planned to give on the morrow. But plans miscarried. The Americans made good their escape with an orderliness and skill that they had never shown before in like circumstances. Sir William had to sail without a distinguished captive. He left his blond enchantress to the care of one who should have been a grateful husband, all things considered. And the melancholy business of the evacuation went on.

It was a slow and tiresome operation and as mortifying a spectacle as any Englishman ever saw, one of the members of the Peace Commission thought. The refugees—men, women, and children—numbered not less than three thousand. A generous amount of cargo space was allotted to their goods and chattels, and the loading of these required much time and care. As the transports were filled they dropped down the river and anchored to await the completion of the convoy. There they lay for a fortnight in the steaming heat of a tidewater Pennsylvania June, their unhappy passengers devoured by mosquitoes and sweltering in their crowded quarters between decks. It was little wonder that Mr. Serle saw none but doleful faces among them. Lord Carlisle wrote home that the sight of them from his cabin window was enough to tear a kindly heart to pieces.

5

Meanwhile preparations for the army's departure from the city had gone steadily forward. At Cooper's Creek on the Jersey bank of the Delaware redoubts were built to form a beachhead for the crossing, and some five or six hundred sailors from the fleet were busy for a week at ferrying thither the army's wagons, the five thousand horses that had been collected during the winter, and finally the field guns that were left in the fortifications until the latest possible hour of the night before the evacuation. Two nights earlier the shipyards had been destroyed in a conflagration that included some of the neighboring dwellings.

Orders were issued for every soldier to carry four days' rations in his haversack and for the wagons to be loaded with supplies for twenty days. For the route which the army was to follow crossed some difficult and highly defensible country; most of the Jersey people were bitterly hostile; and in all probability Washington's troops would soon be hovering on the British flank and rear. There was a report, moreover, that the American troops at Peekskill were already on the march to join the Valley Forge army, in which case things might come to a pitched battle, and Clinton was determined to be prepared to fight his way through, let the opposition be what it might.

On the night of June 17 the army was marched out beyond the streets of the city and bivouacked. There should be no foundation for such stories of plundering and outrage by his men as were told of the American troops after the evacuation of New York in 1776, if Clinton could help it. But owing to the numbers that had been quartered in the city, the neglect of sanitation, and the absence of natural drainage, Philadelphia was left in a condition which Captain Montrésor described as "very offensive"; and Mrs. Knox, who came in for a visit a few days later, found it impossible to remain there.

The men were still discontented over Howe's departure and the order to retire to New York. Two of the German battalions, Anspach troops, had become too unreliable to be trusted in the field and had been placed on board the transports. A good many other Germans, and some British soldiers, who had married Philadelphia girls in the past six months, took the opportunity to desert. But of the fifteen thousand men with whom Clinton took the field that June there were relatively few who were not spoiling for the fight which Howe's do-nothing policy had denied them throughout the winter.

At three in the morning of the 18th the troops marched to Gloucester Point, where the boats from the fleet awaited them. "It was," wrote one who was present, "the finest and the saddest night I ever knew." But no time could be lost in vain regrets or in brooding over its beauty. Clinton spent those early morning hours seated upon a rock in momentary expectation of an attack. But no attack came. Admiral Lord Howe, with his peculiar talent for such operations, supervised the ferrying, as he had done their landing, with such high hopes, at Head of Elk nearly ten months before. By ten o'clock every man and gun were over the river, and the army marched unmolested the five miles to Haddonfield, where it remained until next day.

But the last of the British troops had no more than got ashore when some of Henry Lee's cavalry galloped through Philadelphia and down to the landing on the Pennsylvania bank. On the 16th the son of the laundress who washed the Peace Commissioners' shirts had brought word to Valley Forge that the British were about to leave the city. This had been confirmed by McLane's observations in front of the enemy outpost line, and early in the morning of the 18th one George Roberts galloped up to Washington's headquarters with the news that they had actually gone.

That evening Mrs. Eliza Drinker heard the bellman going about the Philadelphia streets announcing that by order of Colonel Morgan of the Continental service all persons found abroad after nightfall would be arrested. Next day, behind an escort composed of a whole regiment of infantry, Major General Benedict Arnold rolled in in a coach (because of the leg that had been wounded at Saratoga) and assumed the military command of the place, with headquarters at Richard Penn's house, which had so lately been vacated by Sir William Howe. And on the 20th, up in the Gwynedd country, Sally Wister's cousin, Owen Foulke, saw General Washington ride eastward with a life guard of fifty troopers with drawn sabers.

His army was already on the march for the hills of New Jersey on a route parallel to that of the British some thirty miles to the south of them, and there must have been exultation behind the thoughtful imperturbability of his countenance that day. For behind him lay the full justification of the boldness and foresight that had led him to take and keep his post at Valley Forge throughout the past terrible winter, "as if," his critics had sneered, "he had bought a freehold of it." By that course, desperate though it had been, he had nullified the effect of the capture of his country's capital, its largest and richest city; he had prevented the British from dominating the central states, as otherwise they might easily have done; he had, for all practical purposes, reduced their superior army to the condition of a beleaguered garrison; and he had finally compelled them to abandon even the meagre gains that a whole year's campaigning had won them. For the fourth time in eighteen months they were in full retreat across New Jersey.

How this success was to be capitalized was his next problem.

BOOK THREE
The Proof of the Forge

CHAPTER VII

★

☆

Glorious Summer

1

OUT AT VALLEY FORGE that May and early June spirits were as gay and hearts as high as they were discouraged and depressed in Philadelphia. To the celebration of the alliance with France Washington gave all the pomp and circumstance in his power to command.

It having pleased the Almighty Ruler of the Universe propitiously to defend the cause of the United States of America and finally by raising us up a powerful friend, among the Princes of the Earth, to Establish our Liberty and Independence upon lasting foundations; It becomes us to Set apart a day, for fully acknowledging the Divine Goodness, and celebrating the important event, which we owe to his Benign interposition. . .

So began "General After Orders. 6 o'clock—P.M.—" on the 5th of May. Muskets and bayonets now kept clean and shining thanks to von Steuben's inspectors, were given an extra polish for the occasion. A call had already gone out for combmakers to supply that article so necessary to soldierly appearance. Clothes, though some of them might still be patched and threadbare, were washed and brushed. Each officer and enlisted man was instructed to deck his hat with a nosegay. Blank cartridges were issued for the firing of *feux de joie*.

At nine the following morning the glorious news was read to the several brigades by their chaplains, who then, pursuant to orders, proceeded to offer up thanksgiving and deliver discourses suitable to the occasion. A cannon shot terminated the eloquence of any one who had not finished in half an hour. Battalions were formed and inspected, muskets loaded with blank charges; and at half-past eleven the brigades, wheeling to the right by platoons, marched in five columns to the parade ground, where they formed in line, with Stirling in command of the right wing, Lafayette of the left, and de Kalb of the second line.

The artillery fired a salute of thirteen guns, to which the infantry responded with a running fire that rattled from right to left down the front line and from left to right along the second. On signal the whole army united in a "Huzza: Long live the King of France!" A second thirteen-gun salute was echoed by a second running fire and "Long live the Friendly European Powers!" A third salute by the artillery, a third running fire by the infantry, and "Huzza for the American States!" brought the ceremony to a close.

There were no drills or other exercises that day, and each man drew an extra gill of rum. Two soldiers under sentence of death were pardoned as having been "misled by designing Traitors." All other prisoners were released for the general joy, and a spy who was caught in the act was sent back to his employers in the belief that an account of what he had seen would pain the enemy far more than his detection and execution.

Washington, accompanied by his staff, other officers, ladies, and distinguished guests, watched the ceremony with an expression Nathanael Greene remembered as never so radiant as on this day. Then at the head of a column formed by all the officers of the army, marching thirteen abreast, with arms linked as a symbol of union, he led the way to a sumptuous banquet of fifteen hundred covers, which was served in a great enclosure under tent cloth on poles, with marquees to shelter the higher ranks, the ladies, and the other guests. Mrs. Washington, Lady Stirling and "Lady Kitty," and Mrs. Greene were among "the intruding fair," as Mrs. Greene called them, who graced the feast. The soldiers lingered about until it was over and then followed their commander in chief to his headquarters with cheer after cheer, while he halted repeatedly to bow his acknowledgments.

That Arnold and Lincoln, who had not yet recovered from their wounds, might not feel altogether neglected in their convalescence, Washington sent them handsome epaulettes and sword knots which

a French lover of the American cause had requested him to give
to generals whom he wished to honor. There was a set for himself
also; and ten days later he received from another French admirer "a
very elegant plumage," as John Laurens described it, set in gold and
inscribed with Henri IV's celebrated words to his troops at the battle
of Ivry: *"Ne perdez pas de vue mon Panache blanc: vous le trouverez
toujours au chemin de l'honneur et de la victoire."* It would be interesting to know whether the modest Virginia planter ever wore it.

In General Orders next day Washington commended the troops
for their fine appearance and performance and thanked von Steuben
and his assistants for what they had accomplished. The march and
deployment from column into line were executed with a speed and
precision of which the brigades had been incapable two months
before. The running fires along lines ten thousand strong gave proof
of the excellent fire discipline that had been instilled into the
individual soldier. In marked contrast with the parade through
Philadelphia the previous August, the men were well set up, and
their step and cadence had the uniformity and swing that long hours
on the drill ground had made a thing of second nature to them.

Arms and equipment, thanks to Greene's reorganization of the
Quartermaster Department, were complete and uniform. Every infantryman now had a bayonet—except the riflemen, whose weapons
were not adapted to it—and had been so well trained in its use that
he felt a confidence in it which he had never had before. All were
equipped with knapsacks, cutting swords or tomahawks, cartridge
pouches, and two fine American flints, each worth half a dozen of
the European variety.

As to clothing, however, much was still to be desired. There was
enough for forty thousand men at Boston, Mr. Boudinot heard, but
shipments en route to the army had been stalled for want of money
to pay the teamsters. Nearer at hand the Board of War's meddling
with the clothier general's business had resulted in the delivery of a
supply of hats too small, blankets too narrow, and shirt material short
in quantity and poor in quality. A week after the alliance celebration
Wayne wrote: "For God's sake send us linen to save the men from
vermin." And when good clothing was issued, the men had become

so used to patched and tattered garments that they seemed to have forgotten how to take care of it. They had to be warned in General Orders against spoiling their hats by carrying water and provisions on their heads.

A few special corps from New York, Virginia, and Philadelphia sported the regulation buff and blue, but green or brown was the prevailing tone of the uniforms. Washington, indeed, favored the so-called "rifle dress": a hunting shirt with ruffles at neck, shoulders, elbows, and wrists; long breeches and leggings, which were warmer and wore better than stockings; a round dark hat, turned up in three places and decked with a cockade or a green twig; a black stock; hair in a cue; and a white belt over the left shoulder for the cartridge pouch. Thus the army had little of the splendor of the European armies of the time, but at least the men had no longer the look of unlucky tramps.

The indefatigable Knox had repaired those losses which the artillery had suffered through its invariable gallantry and *esprit de corps*. But the cavalry continued to cause the commander in chief great dissatisfaction. To be sure, the troop under Henry Lee had done so well that Washington had expanded it into two troops. The performance of McLane's dragoons against the British outpost line had been excellent also, and Pulaski's light horse had cooperated with spirit in Wayne's great raid to Haddonfield in February. But although Governor Livingston had praised the gallant Pole for his management in the difficult and crowded conditions at Trenton, where his command passed the winter, his insufficient knowledge of English had made harmonious relations with his subordinate commanders impossible.

He had resigned and had turned his attention to the raising of a special corps: a legion composed of sixty-eight lancers and two hundred light infantry that went by his name. But his former command failed to benefit by his departure. Early in April Washington wrote sternly to the colonels of two of these regiments that he was determined to make examples of those who were responsible for the "shameful neglect of the cavalry"; that he had gone without their services in order to rest the horses and build them up, but that both officers and men had been galloping about the country for their own amusement until the animals were in a worse condition than those that had been kept at work.

But the most serious want was the fundamental one, perennial in the American Revolutionary armies, the want of adequate numbers. The Congressional committee on the reorganization of the army, Washington wrote to President Laurens, had led him to expect forty thousand troops. "Instead of these, what are my prospects?" he asked. Some of the states had not yet decided even on the means by which they would fill their regiments. The total number of troops in the Continental service at the opening of the summer's campaign was only twenty thousand, and but little more than half of these could be assembled at Valley Forge.

Until May, moreover, it had seemed probable that experienced officers would be lacking for even this inadequate force. Since the previous August between two and three hundred had resigned, and it had been difficult to dissuade as many more from doing so. In April there were ninety from Virginia alone who planned to go home. Having seen their troops through the winter, Greene's able and devoted brigade commanders, Weeden and Muhlenberg, whose steadfast resistance at the Brandywine had kept the American retreat from becoming a rout, were about to leave the service.

The reason was not far to seek. In the frequent letters in which, throughout the latter half of March and the whole of April, Washington urged upon Congress the adoption of its committee's report on the reorganization of the army, he had dealt with it with unsparing realism. Patriotism, he pointed out, was not enough in a prolonged struggle. Self-interest had to be considered. Commissions must be given some of the material value they had in other armies. In England, for example, the commission of a captain of dragoons was worth four thousand guineas. And if this were not done, he would have few officers left to him by the opening of the campaign. The committee had recommended a provision for half-pay for officers at the end of the war. But the weeks had gone by; Congress, held back by the New Englanders' jealous fears of a standing army—fears which, as Washington observed, were entertained in other countries

only in peacetime—hesitated to adopt the committee's report; and
no officer in the Continental service knew where he stood.

In the first week in May, however, after long hours of niggling and
criticism, the report was adopted. Half-pay, to run for seven years
after the end of the war, was granted to all officers, though with the
stipulation that generals should receive no more than colonels; and
enlisted men were promised a bonus of eighty dollars. The New
Establishment the reorganization scheme was called, and it looked
quite beautiful on paper. The strength of the infantry battalions was
fixed at 477 men, artillery battalions at 336, cavalry regiments at 342,
and the engineer company of 60 which Duportail had organized during the winter, was regularized. But the units from the several states
continued to vary so greatly in strength that it was necessary to
organize the army for combat purposes into brigades made up of
battalions of from 80 to 111 files each. So tardy were the new levies
that the total of 11,800 men at Valley Forge this month was largely
due to the return of several hundred from the hospitals. And of that
total, three thousand were on the sick list one day.

By the middle of May training had reached a point where it was
felt that drills could be called off on Friday afternoons, and the
sergeants were instructed to take their men by squads to wash their
linen and bathe in the Schuylkill—with the caution that no man
was to be allowed to remain in the water more than ten minutes.
Early June saw the troops move out of their dismal cabins and go
under canvas a mile in front of their old lines to escape the stench
that arose from the ground, which was filled with the buried carcasses
and accumulated filth of the winter. They left behind them also,
Wayne wrote grimly, "some hundreds we thought prudent to deposit
six feet underground." But new tentage at the rate of a tent for every
six men now furnished commodious and airy shelter for all, and the
general health improved rapidly.

The whole army was under arms at five o'clock each morning.
Furloughs had been prohibited since April. A flea had been put in the
mustermaster's ear as to his slipshod methods of performing his
duties. Soldiers who thought it easier to clean a loaded musket by
firing it instead of drawing the charge were given the biblical thirty-

nine lashes. A captain was discharged from the service for threatening the life of another "in an ungentlemanly manner"—the dueling code furnished the proper way of doing such a thing in those days. Regimental commanders were required to have the latrines of their units screened by boughs or, more durably, by hurdles.

Games that the men could not play without taking off their accouterments were forbidden to those on guard duty. An elaborate code of paying honors to officers of various ranks was promulgated, the Commander-in-Chief's Guard paying none except to him. A General Order required the attendance of all enlisted men at the eleven o'clock religious services on Sunday mornings. Since a good many chaplains had gone home during the winter on the plea that it was too great a hardship for the men to be kept standing in the cold to listen to sermons, those organizations which lacked chaplains were ordered to attend the one nearest to their tents. Officers of all ranks were expected to set their men an example by their presence. "To the distinguished Character of the Patriot," ran the order, "it should be our highest glory to add the more distinguished Character of Christians."

As the opening of the campaign drew nearer, Mrs. Washington and the other officers' wives took their departure, although Mrs. Knox who traveled under General Arnold's escort from New Haven, did not arrive in camp until May 20. She was fatter than ever, Greene wrote to his wife, who had already gone home, and Knox, being equally fat, they could laugh at each other. "She professes her regard for you," Green wrote in another letter. "You will judge the regard from former circumstances: but she really seems sincere." Evidently the warm friendship that existed between the quartermaster general and the chief of artillery was not reflected in the social relations of their wives.

May and early June were punctuated with orders preparatory to taking the field. With a reminder of the losses of baggage which officers had suffered after the Brandywine campaign, headquarters had been urging them for several weeks to rid themselves of everything they would not need on campaign and to substitute for trunks and boxes valises, which could be obtained through the quartermasters, since it was intended to substitute packhorses for wagons so far as possible in the baggage train.

Regimental and corps commanders were instructed to draw all arms and accouterments that might be lacking in organizations, and the battle allowance of ammunition was issued to each man. By the end of the month brigadiers had received orders to apply to the quartermaster general for wagons, the commissaries to have field rations of hard bread and salt meat ready for issue, and the whole army was ordered to be ready to march at a moment's notice.

Eager to be done with the boring round of fatigues and drills, the troops hailed these preparations for action with delight. The news that the enemy were about to evacuate Philadelphia had not been long in reaching Valley Forge, and the men saw in it a confession of weakness. People better informed than they were wrote home: "Our glorious struggle is almost over." Success was in the air. Hardly a week had passed since a strong force of von Steuben's pupils had justified in the most trying circumstances the confidence with which his training had inspired them. It was the affair that had given Sir William Howe the false hope of taking Lafayette home with him as a prisoner.

On May 19 Washington had sent twenty-one hundred men and five guns to occupy a position at Barren Hill, some eleven miles east of Valley Forge and only two or three from the British advance post at Germantown. Their mission was to cover the country between the Schuylkill and the Delaware, intercept communication with Philadelphia, and gather intelligence of the enemy's dispositions and intentions. Perhaps with the idea of emphasizing the alliance with France, Lafayette was given the command. He must have welcomed it as a distraction from his personal troubles at this time. For on the heels of the joyful tidings of the alliance had come the sorrowful news of the death of his infant child, and he had felt constrained to hide his private grief lest it mar the rejoicing of his comrades.

His position at Barren Hill was highly vulnerable, if he should be surprised. Behind him was the Schuylkill; his nearest avenue of retreat was a road that followed the course of the river to Matson's Ford, three miles to his left and rear; and in that generally loyalist territory he had every reason to expect that his movement and location would be promptly reported to the enemy, as indeed it was. A Quaker at whose house he fixed his headquarters, and an officer lately dismissed from Proctor's artillery, were believed to have carried the information. But he had taken proper precautions against such an eventuality. He could hardly have foreseen that an outpost of militia, which should have given him ample warning of an enemy advance, would leave its position without orders and even without informing him that it had done so.

Daybreak on the 20th brought the sound of firing from his right flank and front, and word came in that a heavy column was pushing swiftly toward his left to cut his line of retreat. In fact, ten thousand British troops were about to surround and crush his twenty-one hundred. With the clumsy maneuvering and march by files of Brandywine and Germantown days his entire force must have been destroyed. But now the troops fell in without confusion, formed column and marched to the ford with such steadiness and swiftness that they were deployed on the commanding opposite bank, with their guns laid to cover the crossing, when the enemy came in sight, although that column of the British had been nearer the ford than they were when they began their retreat.

When the sound of distant firing broke the stillness of the dawn at Valley Forge, it took the troops there only fifteen minutes to get under arms, and they were soon marching to Lafayette's assistance. As the sun came up, young John Marshall, who was a lieutenant in his father's regiment, saw Washington on a hilltop watching through his telescope the distant clouds of powder smoke and the dust of the marching columns with evident anxiety. But it had been only the prospect of an easy victory that had tempted Sir Henry Clinton to come out, and when that disappeared, he marched quietly back to Philadelphia.

The American troops returned to their camp in high spirits. They had a hearty laugh at a comic episode in the affair. A small band of Indians in the American service had collided unexpectedly with a troop of British dragoons. Neither party had ever before seen anything like the other, and both fled the field in terror. The whole incident had amounted to no more than a skirmish, a small rear guard action, and an orderly retirement. But the men of Valley Forge were old enough soldiers to understand that no military maneuver is a severer test of discipline and training than a forced and sudden withdrawal in the face of an active and enterprising enemy. They were correspondingly elated. Just give them the chance for one good stand-up fight and they would end the war then and there.

A month later, when they took the road for the Delaware at Coryell's Ferry, and the Jersey hills beyond it, the day was hot, and there were violent storms of rain. But nothing could damp their spirits. To the shrilling of the fifes they sang as they tramped along, first, "Yankee Doodle," then, to the tune of a new march:

> Come, join hand in hand,
>   Brave Americans all.
> And rouse your whole band
>   At Liberty's call;

and finally, and less decorously, a salty lyric called "Nothing Like Grog."

2

At army headquarters the situation appeared less simple than it did to the latrine and campfire strategists. On April 20 Washington had sent a circular letter to all the general officers in the camp, asking their opinion of three possible courses of action for the forthcoming campaign: (1) to attempt to take Philadelphia and destroy the British army there; (2) to attempt to shift the field of operations to the North by moving against New York; (3) to remain in a fortified camp, perfecting the training and organization of the army until the enemy began operations, and then to act accordingly.

The opinions he received differed greatly. Wayne headed a group that favored attacking Philadelphia, whether by storm, siege, or blockade. Knox had equal support in favoring New York as an objective. Greene thought that the main body should be kept at Valley Forge while Washington in person led four thousand Continental troops and the militia of New York and New England against New York. Stirling was for an attack on both cities. Lafayette, von Steuben, and Duportail, the last of whom doubted the ability of the troops to stand against the British in the open field, considered that any offensive would be unwise until the army was stronger and in better condition.

Three days later the word came in that Sir William Howe had been relieved of his command and that Sir Henry Clinton would succeed him, and Washington called a council of war, which met on the 8th of May. It was a particularly interesting assemblage, for it included two faces which had not been seen in such a gathering for many months, and which should have been rather red if their owners possessed a decent sense of shame. One was that of Horatio Gates, the other Mifflin's.

Their presence at the council gave rise to much hard feeling and some uneasy speculation. Officers who had stuck by the army through the past terrible winter were furious at Mifflin's reinstatement. The two men had come at Washington's invitation. But Congress had ordered them to attend, and Washington's most ardent admirers saw in that action the same desire of "certain great men" to humiliate him that John Laurens had suspected a few days before, when Congress had failed to inform the commander in chief fully on the state of affairs in Europe.

Greene called Mifflin's reinstatement "a phenomenon in politics." Washington commented on it dryly: "that gentleman's stepping in and out, as the sun happens to beam forth or become obscure, is not *quite* the thing, nor *quite* just, with respect to those officers, who take the bitter with the sweet." But he could afford to be philosophical about the matter. Congress had stipulated that both Mifflin and Gates should be directly under his authority and, upon his orders, should resign from the Board of War. With confidence in Gates's military ability, he sent him promptly to take command in the Peekskill area.

Another general who had long been absent from the army made his reappearance this month. He was Major General Charles Lee, upon whose exchange Sir Joseph Yorke, the British ambassador at the Hague, had observed that he was "the worst present the Americans could receive." Charles Lee, wrote Mrs. Mercy Warren, who had known him at Cambridge in the early months of the war, was "without religion or country, principle or attachment; gold was his deity and liberty the idol of his fancy: he hoarded the former without taste for its enjoyment, and worshiped the latter as the patroness of licentiousness rather than the protectress of virtue."

Cherishing a grievance against the Tory government in England when he resigned his commission in the British army, Lee had migrated to America and bought an estate in Virginia. With a brilliant reputation, which he had won in the Seven Years' War, and a somewhat vague record of service against the Turks and under the King of Poland—all of which lost nothing by his own account of them—he had sold his sword to the Continental Congress for $30,000 and a major general's commission that placed him next in rank to Washington.

But he had expected to be made commander in chief, and he had been unceasing in his efforts to undermine and supersede the Virginia planter whose military ability he held up to open scorn before anybody who would listen to him. But for his capture Washington might have been crushed at the Delaware in December, 1776, before Lee's troops came to his support. That scheme of his—"Mr. Lee's plan"—which had motivated Howe's move against Philadelphia the following summer, was a fair measure of his loyalty to the cause of the United States. His exchange and return to the Continental service proved to be one of the worst things that happened to the American army that year.

Washington, though he was, of course, ignorant of Lee's treachery during the past winter, was well aware of his conduct toward himself. But he had continued to treat Lee not only with all the consideration due his rank and his anomalous position as a prisoner of war who had been an officer in the army of his captors, but with thoughtful kindness. He took pains that his captivity should be made as comfortable as possible, wrote him friendly letters, and even saw to it that the small pack of dogs of various breeds that always accompanied him were properly looked after.

Released on parole until the formalities of his exchange were com-

pleted, Lee made straight for York and Congress, with but a brief halt
at Valley Forge. Washington rode out to meet him, welcomed him
warmly when he returned, and gave him the room behind his own
in the little Potts house, although Lee's superabundant luggage and
his numerous canines, which were now reunited with their master,
can have added nothing to the peace and comfort of the establishment.

Lee had been reading Marshal Saxe and "Machiavel's *Institutions,*"
as he called it, during his captivity and was boiling over—the northern Indians had once given him the name of Boiling Water—with
a plan for winning the war by a more extensive use of the militia
than had been made in the past. "A hobby horse of my own training,"
he wrote to Washington from York. Washington, though he had
suffered severely from the wastefulness and unreliability of the militia in the past and was deferring calling them out until the latest
possible moment, replied with tolerant humor that he hoped Lee's
hobby would not prove to be "so limping a jade, as the one on
which you set out for York."

The sight of Lee's countenance—it had been rated second only
to Lord Rawdon's for ugliness in the whole British army—cheered
Greene with the thought of the difference between the state of the
troops this spring and their condition—ragged, barefoot, and cower-
ing behind the Delaware—at the time of Lee's capture fifteen months
before. But Lee, true to form, declined to be impressed by what
von Steuben and Greene had accomplished. In his opinion, which
he expressed freely, the army had gone to the dogs in his absence.
Washington, he told Mr. Boudinot, was "not fit to command a
sergeant's guard." As for the alliance with France, he overlooked no
opportunity to throw cold water upon the exultation it had created.

Perhaps it was his criticisms that made it necessary to issue an
order requiring strict adherence to von Steuben's regulations at this
time and led John Laurens to write to his father as late as mid-June
that certain jealousies had retarded von Steuben's work. But it was
one thing to run down the beaten commander of the disastrous
summer and fall campaign of 1776 and quite another to assail the
reputation of the general who had cleared New Jersey of the enemy .

without a battle, kept the army in being throughout the past winter, and by its mere presence at Valley Forge made the possession of Philadelphia useless to the enemy. Soon after Lee's arrival in camp, moreover, he behaved in a manner that should have brought suspicion upon him, if any one had known of the double game he had been playing, but which seemed only ridiculous at the time.

In order to assure the French Government of American constancy Congress now required of all officers under its authority, civil and military alike, an oath by which they not only abjured allegiance to the King of Great Britain, his heirs, and successors, but also swore to maintain and defend the United States against the British Crown *in the offices they held at the time they took the oath*. The phrasing was unfortunate. Many officers, especially in one of the Virginia brigades, though all were ardent patriots, hesitated to sign lest they should thereby incur an obligation to remain in the army till the end of the war. And to this objection a no less devoted champion of Independence than Lafayette added three others: the officers' past conduct made the oath unnecessary; it might prevent them from working for desirable changes in the service; and there were many who had been passed over for promotion who could not afford to remain in the army on the pay of their present ranks.

Discussion and persuasion, however, mollified the most scrupulous, and the oath was finally taken by all concerned. But when the generals assembled at headquarters for that purpose, Lee advanced a new reason for his hesitation in signing. He was quite willing, he explained, to renounce his allegiance to King George, but he could hardly do the like conscientiously with regard to the Prince of Wales. His words raised a general laugh. It occurred to nobody that they were those of an undetected collaborator who had become for the moment slightly confused in his game of playing both ends against the middle.

Lee had missed the council of war on the 8th of May but had returned from York in time to sign its decision, which was unanimously against any offensive movement at that time. Against Sir Henry Clinton's upwards of nineteen thousand men in Philadelphia Washington could bring less than twelve thousand from Valley Forge, and the Commissary and Quartermaster Departments were still functioning so imperfectly as to make a greater concentration of troops impracticable. The works defending Philadelphia, moreover, were too strong to be taken by storm, heavy artillery was still lacking for a siege, and it would require thirty thousand men to blockade the city effectually.

Washington's secret service had been prompt in reporting the British intention to evacuate the city. But whether their destination was to be New York or the West Indies remained unknown at Valley Forge for several days. When that point was settled, there was still uncertainty as to whether they would move by land or sea, and up to the end of May reports indicated that in any event they would strike at Valley Forge before they left. In early June the probability of such an attack disappeared, and the signs that Clinton intended to march across New Jersey became unmistakable. Only his route remained uncertain.

It was assumed, however, that one of the British columns would go by way of Trenton and Princeton, another farther to the eastward, with New Brunswick or Amboy as their immediate destination. New Brunswick, with the natural barrier of the Raritan, would be an excellent place to head Clinton off and fight a battle to prevent his reaching New York, if the Americans could get there before he did. It would be a close race. The British had the advantage in distance: New Brunswick was fifty-eight miles from Philadelphia, sixty-six from Valley Forge. The Americans would have somewhat the better roads, and they had repeatedly proved themselves the better marchers. But, supposing they won it, would it be wise to risk a battle at this juncture?

The troops Sir Henry Clinton had taken with him numbered about fifteen thousand. With the militia, Washington could lead about as many into battle. But the problem was not merely one of numbers. Whereas Clinton's was Britain's only field army in America, there were nineteen thousand other British and Hessian troops in the country, and Washington's army was the only effective military force possessed by the United States. Might not the wiser course be to resume the war of maneuver which had been so successful last summer?

The question was still unanswered on the morning of June 18

when the news reached headquarters at Valley Forge that the British were actually out of Philadelphia and across the Delaware. But whether for battle or maneuver, the army must now take the road for New Jersey. By early afternoon Charles Lee at the head of Poor's, Varnum's, and Huntington's brigades, and Wayne, with his Pennsylvanians and the brigade that had been Conway's, were marching toward Coryell's Ferry. The rest of the troops—Lafayette's division, Knox's artillery, and the divisions of de Kalb and Stirling—followed them next morning. Lee's orders were to halt for further instructions when he had crossed the Delaware, unless he received authentic information that the enemy had headed for Amboy instead of New Brunswick. In that event he was to continue his march to the Hudson.

3

The 24th of June found the American army assembled in the neighborhood of Hopewell, ten miles east of the Delaware and six miles northwest of Princeton. The troops had been much delayed by terrific heat and rainstorms that turned the hilly roads into torrents and made quagmires of the botton lands. But Greene, who had added many of the duties of a present-day chief of staff to those of quartermaster general, had chosen the route and the halting places with skill. The army had marched forty-seven miles since leaving Valley Forge, while the British, who were reported to have reached Crosswicks, about eighteen miles to the southward, on the previous day, had covered but little more than thirty.

By two or three days of rapid marching Washington could now throw his army across Clinton's path and compel him to fight. Now, if ever, was the time to decide between giving battle and merely countering Clinton's move by continuing the march to the Hudson. The latter course was obviously the safe one. It was even possible that Clinton was moving so slowly in the hope of luring Washington to attack him. On the other hand, a decisive American victory might win the war.

Following his invariable custom in such circumstances, Washington called a council of his generals. "Councils of war," said Napoleon, "never fight": and this one was no exception to that rule. Its proceedings, Hamilton said contemptuously, would have done credit to "the Most Honorable Society of Midwives." Greene, Wayne, and Lafayette spoke for taking the offensive. But Lee spoke against it vehemently. He had continually bragged and vapored about the prowess of the army to which he had once belonged. Long after the intention of the British to evacuate Philadelphia had become a certainty he had insisted that they were not going to retreat. When they were actually out of the city, he maintained that their crossing of the Delaware was a ruse to lure Washington into New Jersey while they marched down the river and boarded their transports with Maryland as their objective. "Mr. Lee's plan" died hard in the mind of its author, or else he was purposely darkening counsel. Now he dwelt upon the maxim of building a bridge of gold for a retreating enemy, pointed out that the French alliance was now a certainty and no longer needed victories to bring it to pass, and asserted that to bring the highly trained British regulars to bay would be criminal folly.

Still greatly esteemed for his reputation of wide experience in war, he carried the majority of the generals with him. Washington seemed to assent their decision. "The fate of posterity, and not the illusive brilliancy of military glory," Knox wrote to his brother William next day, "governs our Fabian commander, the man [to whom], under God, America owes her present prospects of peace and happiness." But when the council had broken up Washington changed his mind. According to tradition, Greene, who had gone off to his tent to put his dissenting opinion in writing, came back with it; and upon seeing him, Washington exclaimed: "I know what you have come for: you wish me to fight," and proceeded to issue the appropriate orders.

A force of 2,500 men, which included Maxwell's brigade, Morgan's riflemen, and a considerable detachment under Brigadier General Scott, was sent off to cooperate with the New Jersey militia and Cadwalader's Pennsylvania volunteers, who were already annoying and delaying Clinton's columns. Next day, the 25th, the main body of the army marched to Kingston, three miles to the northeast of Princeton, while Lafayette, with an advance guard of nearly 4,000, pushed on to Cranbury, eight miles farther to the eastward. Heat and heavy thunderstorms continued to make progress slow, and that evening Lafayette wrote to Washington that he greatly needed either rum or whisky to get the necessary speed out of his men in such conditions.

In these positions the American army stood directly across Clinton's route to both New Brunswick and Amboy. But now, from out in front of the British column, Hamilton reported that Clinton had changed the direction of his march and was moving up the road to Monmouth Court House, the present day Freehold, which lay only a day's march east of Lafayette's bivouac. Von Steuben, who, since he lacked a tactical command, was scouting with Moylan's light horsemen like a junior lieutenant, sent the same intelligence to Washington from Hightstown, a few miles to the south. The forty-eight-year-old veteran was fresh from a brief holiday in Philadelphia, where he had taken great pleasure in speaking his native tongue with the inhabitants of German extraction and was now enjoying himself thoroughly at the risk of his liberty and life. He pushed so close to the British column that both Clinton and Knyphausen caught glimpses of him and identified him by his brilliant star of the Order of Fidelity. With the professional courtesy of the time, Knyphausen checked his Hessians when they were about to fire on him, and Clinton sent out some dragoons in a vain attempt to capture him.

Together with his intelligence, von Steuben sent Washington a recommendation that he push forward to Hightstown immediately and fall upon Clinton's flank. But a cloudburst combined with a breakdown in the supply column forced Washington to remain at Cranbury through the whole of the 26th, and that afternoon the weary British army arrived at Monmouth Court House. There they halted, closed up their long column, and rested for an entire day.

The direction of his last two marches had made it clear that Clinton had given up all idea of reaching New Brunswick or Amboy. Evidently he was now headed for Sandy Hook, whence Howe's fleet could ferry his army to New York; and it was now too late to head him off in that direction, for he lay nearer that point than Washington did. His position, its flanks guarded by impassable morasses, was too strong to be attacked. But if he could be caught as he was moving out of it, his long baggage train intervening between the troops in front of it and those in rear, it might be possible to inflict a serious defeat upon him.

Throughout the 27th von Steuben on a hilltop two miles away kept his spyglass fixed on the British camp for signs of departure but saw none. Horses were grazing, and even a few tents had been pitched. Washington that day was able to push forward the nine miles to Englishtown, which brought him within striking distance of the enemy. Lafayette lay three or four miles to the south of him with what was called "the flying army" and was acting in concert with the militia that had been hanging on the British flanks and rear.

Lafayette's force, which now numbered about five thousand, included not only strong detachments under Wayne, Poor, and Scott but also Maxwell's brigade and Morgan's riflemen. The command had been offered to Lee. But Lee, in his mood of bitter opposition to any offensive movement at all, had refused it. Now, however, it appeared to promise an opportunity for distinction, and his effrontery was quite equal to asking for it. He thus placed Washington in a situation of extreme delicacy. As ranking major general after the commander in chief, Lee had a certain right to the post. But to supersede Lafayette at the moment when his labors and responsibilities as advance guard commander were about to bear the fruits of glory was to risk affronting not only him but France, which he in a sense represented.

As soon, however, as Lafayette heard of Washington's dilemma, he declared, with a magnanimity remarkable in a young man whose enemies blamed him for an insatiable thirst for glory, that he would be perfectly willing to serve under Lee. Lee took over the command with instructions from Washington to allow Lafayette to carry out any plans the Marquis might have made for attacking or annoying the enemy. On the afternoon of the 27th Washington rode over from Englishtown and, after a consultation that included Lee, Lafayette, Wayne, and Maxwell, issued orders that were to be executed at dawn the following morning if Clinton should resume his retreat. According to these, Lee was to attack the British rear guard, no matter how strong it might prove to be, as soon after daylight as possible, and fight a holding action until Washington came up with the main army. These orders were sent to Lee in writing later that night, but Lee outlined no definite plan of action to his subordinates. When they came to him for instructions, he was surly and vague, and they lay down for the night with only the most general idea of what was expected of them on the morrow.

Years later George Washington Parke Custis heard a strange story from a Colonel Nicholas of Virginia, a former officer of the Commander-in-Chief's Guard, who was on duty at headquarters that night. According to Colonel Nicholas, the Reverend Doctor David Griffith, who was both a chaplain and a surgeon in the Virginia Line, came to Washington's tent near midnight and warned him against trusting Lee with command in the next day's battle. But if this warning made any impression on Washington at the time, he did not show it.

4

That whole day of rest at Monmouth Court House was a godsend to the weary British soldiery. The village, with its thirty dwellings, old English church and court house, wheelwright's and blacksmith's shops, three stores and two schoolhouses, must have looked very pleasant after the many miles of sandy roads through scrub oak and pine since they left Philadelphia behind them. The marches had not been long in distance—seldom as much as ten miles in a day. But for nine mornings in succession they had been under arms at three o'clock, and each day they had spent endless hours plodding through mud or sand, or, worse still, halted under a blistering sun or in rains of tropical violence, while bridges were repaired under the fire of lurking enemies or the interminable baggage train closed up the gaps in its column.

The load of the British infantryman, armed and equipped and provisioned for a long march, weighed more than a hundred pounds. His uniform was of thick wool. The clothing and equipment of the Hessians were even heavier. The temperature ranged in the upper nineties; and one out of every three of the Hessians dropped exhausted or sunstruck by the roadside. The drenching rains only added humidity to the heat. When the march was over, there was no place to rest but the scorching or sodden ground. The nights were hot and breathless, the only shelter the huts of the men's own building, which gave no protection from the clouds of mosquitoes that had tormented the troops throughout the day.

With the complacency of the typical staff officer, Captain John André wrote a few days later that the Americans were "perplexed" during the whole retreat, their militia and light troops unable "to find an opportunity to give the least annoyance to a column eight or ten miles in length," in spite of "their boasted knowledge of the country and dexterity in hovering around us." But another story is to be gleaned from Clinton's orders, and one that would doubtless have been corroborated by the advance and rear guards and the flanking parties.

Straying beyond the sentry lines was absolutely forbidden: so sure was it to incur capture, wounds, or death. Morgan's riflemen hung upon the right of the column, sniping at every opportunity and shooting up the bivouacs, while Maxwell's brigade pestered the left, and Cadwalader's Pennsylvanians made life miserable for the rear guard. Dickinson and the New Jersey militia delayed the advance by frequent ambuscades and such stubborn skirmishing that more than once they had to be driven off by artillery fire, and on one occasion it took the dragoons, the light infantry, and the grenadiers to clear them away. When near-by trees were big enough to make troublesome obstacles, they were felled across the road; and so thorough was the destruction of the numerous bridges that it was necessary to attach a force of eighty pioneers, with their tool wagons, to the advance guard.

At Haddonfield and elsewhere along his route Clinton had issued orders threatening with death any man caught in the act of plundering. He offered a reward of twenty-five guineas for the conviction of anyone accused of that crime. But if he hoped thus to placate the local inhabitants, it was in vain. At the farmhouses well ropes had been cut, or the ropes and buckets had been carried away, and some of the wells had been filled. The farmers had fled, taking their families and stock with them, and along the way were scattered papers warning the troops that they were going to be "burgoyned."

The army advanced through an atmosphere of desolation of which Sir Henry was to be reminded fourteen years later, when he marched with the Duke of Brunswick to the battle of Valmy through the desolation of revolutionary France.

Although two men were hanged for the burning of a house, several other houses were burned, two at Crosswicks. Many more were wantonly damaged; and at every opportunity the soldiers took vengeance for their hardships by plundering. A good many men, especially among the Hessians, availed themselves of the favorable circumstances of the march to slip away—though one man was hanged for attempting to do so—and turned up happily in Philadelphia a couple of weeks later.

Far from wishing to lure Washington into battle, Clinton's one earnest desire was to get his army back to New York with as little loss as possible. As far as Crosswicks the Delaware had covered the left flank of his column. But there he learned that Washington was across the Delaware and at Hopewell, where he was nearer to New Brunswick than Clinton was. Clinton's intelligence, moreover, informed him that Gates, at the head of the troops in the Peekskill area, was about to join Washington in barring the crossings of the Raritan. This was not true; Gates was marching to White Plains. But Clinton had no reason to doubt it, and at Allentown on the next day but one he changed his route and took the road to Monmouth Court House, with the intention of putting his army on shipboard at Sandy Hook, as Washington was quick to guess.

As far as Allentown parallel roads had enabled him to move in two columns. But from that point onward there was only a single road. On this his enormous train—baggage and provision wagons, bakeries and blacksmith's shops on wheels, pontoon train, and numerous private carriages and wagons—stretched out for a distance of eight or ten miles, and the breakdown or stalling of a single vehicle in the deep sand of the narrow road brought the whole to a halt. A great many of the camp women, who had been placed on board the transports at Philadelphia, had slipped off again and rejoined the troops, and whether they were marched at the head of their regiments or on the skirts of the baggage train, they were a continual nuisance, inciting the men to plunder and distracting them with their troubles.

At Allentown also Clinton reversed his order of march. Up to that point he had kept his most reliable troops—the 16th and 17th Dragoons, the light infantry, Brigade of Guards, Royal Highlanders, Queen's Rangers, and four brigades of the British Line—in the van. But on leaving Allentown, on the 25th, he moved out "by the left," sending Knyphausen and the Hessians, whom he stiffened with a couple of British brigades, to the head of the column and placing the rest of the British troops at the rear, which he now regarded as the post of danger.

This reversal of the order of march took precious time. But Clinton believed that the capture of his train rather than a battle was what Washington aimed at, and he had a report that the American army that day was at Princeton and Cranbury, whence, by a rapid march, they could fall upon the highly vulnerable flank of his column. The British, however, were spared the cloudburst that kept Washington in his bivouacs on the 26th. By that evening Clinton had the satisfaction of seeing his entire command concentrated at Monmouth Court House and felt safe in giving his men and horses a much-needed rest. He knew that the American forces were now close by, at Englishtown and near it: their leading elements were in touch with his outposts. But when he resumed his march, Washington would be behind him instead of on his flank; his route ran by way of the Middletown hills; and it was only eight miles to that difficult country, in which it was unlikely that the Americans would pursue him. It does not seem to have occurred to him that Washington would attempt to bring on a general action.

At four in the morning of Sunday, June 28, refreshed by their day in bivouac, Knyphausen, the Hessians, and the two British brigades under his command took the road, and the wagons of the train began to follow them. At five the rest of the British troops were under arms, ready to bring up the rear. But the formation of a convoy of several hundred vehicles, many of them the property of civilians, takes time, and the British troops were still waiting for the road ahead of them to be cleared, when the sound of brisk firing came from the outposts. Firing at the outposts had become a matter of course these days. But now, to the astonishment of the watching staff officers, a dense mass of American troops, marching swiftly and in admirable order, appeared over the hills to the westward, with strong columns moving out to the right and left of it, as if to overtake and attack the train.

5

It was Lee's troops that made so formidable an appearance. But it was more by good luck than by his good judgment that they had arrived in time to accomplish their mission. Lee appears to have done everything that an experienced officer could have thought of to cause them to fail to do so. The previous night he had shuffled his subordinate commanders about until none of them knew the men whom they were to lead or were known by them. With an entire day at his disposal, he had neglected to examine the ground over which he was to advance, and this morning he had repelled an offer to show him a short cut with a curt "I know my business." He had been inexcusably tardy in sending out an observation force for which Washington had sent him an order during the night. Yet afterward he complained that he had been "betrayed" into crossing some narrow defiles in the belief that there would be only two or three enemy battalions to oppose him.

When Dickinson, who was watching the British wagon train, reported at 5 A.M. that the enemy were on the move, and Steuben, who had their rear guard under observation, reported simultaneously that they were still in their bivouacs, Lee lost his temper and apparently his head as well. His orders, wrote the disgusted John Laurens, succeeded one another "with a rapidity and indecision calculated to ruin us." Morgan in his position three miles away on the enemy's left received no orders and missed the ensuing action altogether. It was seven o'clock when Lee finally set his troops in motion. But he was still apparently unable to make up his mind and he wasted a priceless hour in marching back and forth. It was half-past nine by the time he had swung his command northward off the road leading to the village and, about a mile short of the Court House, had

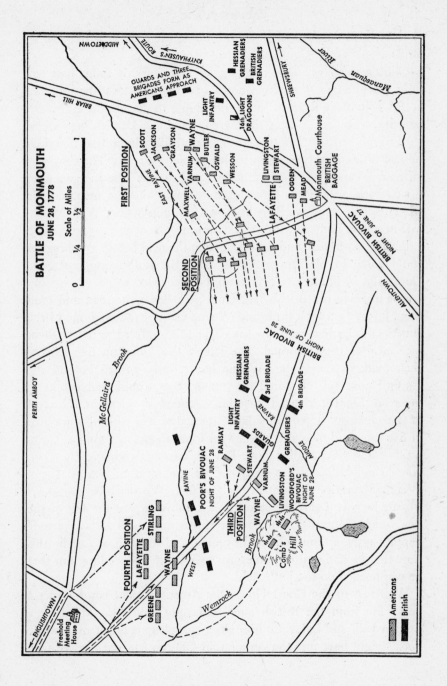

BATTLE OF MONMOUTH
JUNE 28, 1778

Scale of Miles
0   ¼   ½   1

Americans
British

deployed them against the rear and the northern flank of the retiring British.

Clinton, who was still obsessed by fears for his train, had left only the Queen's Rangers, a corps of American loyalists, and the 16th Dragoons in front of the Court House to dispute the American advance. The rest of the British troops and the Hessian grenadiers, with whom he had strengthened the rear of his column that morning, he had hurried up the road after his precious wagons. The dragoons charged valiantly but were ambushed and routed. The Rangers were driven back. Soon Lee's forces were in a position that menaced the whole British column. His guns were already in action. With Washington's main body close at hand, Clinton's one chance of preventing a disaster was to turn and drive Lee from the field before Washington could come to his support. This, with the skillful and energetic Cornwallis in immediate command, he proceeded to do.

But to bring the British regiments back down the road and send them into action took time, and Wayne was not the only one of the American brigadiers who saw the chance thus offered to defeat them piecemeal as they returned. The left of the American line flanked their road. In the center, Wayne had already pushed beyond the Court House and clamored for support that would enable him to press on. On the right, Lafayette, seconded by Captain L'Enfant of the engineers, urged immediate attack. Lee had with him upwards of five thousand men and ten guns, a force almost as strong as Cornwallis could lead against him. But he answered impatiently: "Sir, you do not know British soldiers. We cannot stand against them. We shall certainly be driven back at first. We must be cautious." Finally he gave Lafayette permission to move against the left of the line which Cornwallis had now begun to form, and Lafayette rode happily away, although he had become so distrustful of Lee by this time that he had sent off a message to Washington, telling him that he was needed on the battlefield.

Well east of the Court House the American right came under a heavy fire from the British guns. Lafayette's aide was killed by a cannon ball, and Lafayette himself, a conspicuous target on a white horse, might have met the same fate if Clinton had not guessed who he was and forbidden the British gunners to fire at him. He was about to lead his men forward when, to his amazement, he saw the American troops on his left going to the rear. A few minutes later he received an order from Lee to retreat.

Farther up the line, which stretched for a mile to the northeastward, Lee's brigadiers got no orders whatever. But they could see the troops on their right retiring and the enemy—light infantry, Guards, grenadiers, brigades of the Line, and a fresh regiment of dragoons—deploying against them. Some of them sent their adjutants for instructions; some rode off in person on the same quest. Not all of them succeeded in finding Lee; and one who did so was astonished by being told: "Take your men any place where they will be safe." Others, seeing their commands in danger of being cut off and captured, acted on their own responsibility and fell back to the highway by the route by which they had come.

The troops under Lafayette covered the retirement. There was a brief halt a little to the west of the village while Lee was deciding against making a stand at that point. But soon the road back toward Englishtown was filled by the long column of troops and guns that had so lately left it, while behind them the British swept forward in pursuit on a wide front, with heavy columns of infantry on both flanks and their cavalry and light artillery between them.

Thanks to the hours on the drill ground at Valley Forge, there was no panic among the retreating troops, only a sullen resentment at what Laurens, who had been scouting with von Steuben for the past three days, described as "a senseless retreat without firing a musket over ground which might have been disputed inch by inch." But as the soldiers plodded rearward in the dust of that narrow road and the heat grew more terrific as the sun reached the meridian, there was disorder and some confusion; and the angry Hamilton wrote of it: "Even rout would not be too strong a word." As the various units fell helter-skelter into the column, the elements of some brigades became separated from each other. Officers lost touch with their men. Duportail viewed the congested highway with a shudder at the thought of the slaughter that must ensue if the British guns got close enough to open fire with grapeshot.

All but a very few regiments, however, preserved their formation, and the men needed only the word of command to turn and give battle. But that word Lee refused all entreaties to give. "The enemy have too much cavalry for us," he replied, when he was urged to make a stand some two miles west of the Court House. At this point the road was intersected by what was known as the Middle Ravine, in which a brook and adjacent swamps reduced the crossing, at least for artillery, to the width of the causeway that traversed it. About a mile beyond it lay a similar obstacle, the West Ravine. But between the two the ground was high and sufficiently commanding to cause Duportail to recommend it as an excellent place to turn and fight. "An execrable position!" Lee snapped, after giving it no more than a quick glance. He covered the crossing with artillery fire and got his men safely over. But from this point the retreat continued with increasing disorder.

Lee appeared to be possessed by anxiety for the safety of his flanks and to be searching for a position in woods thick and extensive enough not only to protect them from the charges of the British cavalry but to shelter his men from the burning sun: the thermometer now stood at 97 degrees in the shade. Careless or forgetful of the confusion that must follow if his disordered column collided without warning with the main army, which must now be advancing from Englishtown, he had sent no word of his movements to Washington except a single optimistic message at the beginning of the action. He explained afterward that he thought it would be "presumptuous" to do so. Yet to all but the indignant Laurens and the furious Hamilton he appeared calm and self-possessed. His self-possession, however, lasted only until he had ridden about three-quarters of a mile farther. There it vanished in an encounter with his commander in chief, who was an embodiment of blazing wrath.

By the standards of armies in the field it had been late when Washington breakfasted that morning at the house of Dr. English. He did not like fighting on Sunday, he said, but must do so for the good of the country. He took time to dictate a short letter to the President of Congress, telling him of Lee's mission. But he had overtaken and passed the main body of his troops, which was already beyond the village, when he received the news, first from a fifer, whom he put under arrest, and then from a more reliable source, that Lee's troops were in full retreat.

He had heard no firing except a few cannon shots, had evidently not received Lafayette's two messages—the worried Marquis had sent him a second one at the beginning of the retreat—and he was astounded. He sent Fitzgerald and Harrison off at the gallop to learn if the news could be true. But what he saw for himself as he rode forward made a report from them unnecessary. Down toward the bridge over the West Ravine streamed regiments of Virginians and North Carolinians and Maxwell's whole brigade. One of the colonels told him that the retreat was by order, though he knew no reason for it. Maxwell, who was riding at the rear of his brigade, confessed that he had received no orders and was just moving with the column, since he did not know what was expected of him. The appearance of the soldiers told the same story. They were caked with dust and sweat, many of them staggering from heat and weariness. But their eyes gleamed with anger rather than fear. The more disorganized units Washington ordered into a near-by grove for rest and an issue of rum. The others he faced about and led back up the slope.

At what he saw when he reached the crest—all that had been accomplished by the winter's privations, by the army's reorganization, by von Steuben's training and Greene's labors, thrown away by one man's incapacity, cowardice, or treachery—a suspicion flashed through Washington's mind that Lee had intentionally ruined the operation which he had outspokenly opposed. Hamilton dashed up to him on a horse dripping with sweat, exclaiming: "General Lee has betrayed you and the army!" A couple of hundred yards farther on, Washington met Lee himself.

The desire of the nineteenth century to turn its heroes into graven images has drawn thick veils over that encounter. It has been related as the single instance of Washington's giving way to his naturally violent temper and exploding in an oath. The formal testimony at Lee's subsequent court-martial fails to support even this mild version of the episode. "I desire to know, sir, what is the reason, whence arises this disorder and confusion?" was Lee's statement of Washington's first words to him. Officers who were present at the time testified that after a stammered "Sir—Sir!" Lee replied that the confusion was due to disobedience of his orders but that he did not think a general action was in the interests of the army or of America and that the attack itself had been against his expressed opinion. Apparently this was followed by a brief discussion of the probable strength of the pursuing enemy, which Washington terminated by telling Lee that he ought not to have asked for the command if he did not mean to fight.

But a humble eyewitness's account of Washington's opening words has the ring of authenticity: "My God, General Lee, what are you about?" According to this man, who was a soldier in the ranks: "The whole thing occurred as quickly as I can tell it to you"; Washington cut short Lee's explanation, waved his hand angrily over his head, exclaiming: "Go to the rear, sir!" and rode swiftly away in the direction of the enemy. Many years afterward General Scott, on being asked whether Washington ever swore, replied that he did once, at Monmouth. "Sir, on that memorable day he swore like an angel from heaven." And others believed that as Washington rode off they heard him mutter: "Damned poltroon!"

Of Lee's physical courage, however, there seems never to have been any question. He was riding with the rearmost elements of his command, and Washington had not far to go before he could see the British light infantry and dragoons pressing upon the right, left, and center of the retreating Americans—only four hundred yards, and in some places but two hundred, behind them. They must be checked if the main body of the army was to have time to take position and deploy to face them.

Fortunately both the nature of the ground and the disposition of Lee's troops were well suited to fighting a delaying action. Since crossing the Middle Ravine the American column had spread fanwise and its various units were retiring through the fields, some of them as much as four hundred yards to the north and south of the road; and six of the field guns, whose crews had fought and maneuvered them throughout the retreat with the swiftness and daring of skirmishers, were within reach of Washington's orders. To right and left galloped his aides, and he followed them in person. "Never," wrote Lafayette, "was General Washington greater than in this action. His presence stopped the retreat; his dispositions fixed the victory; his fine appearance on horseback, his calm courage roused to animation by the vexations of the morning, gave him the air best calculated to excite enthusiasm. . . . I thought then as now that never had I beheld so superb a man." The soldiers hailed his appearance with cheers. Some of them perhaps could remember the bitter recklessness with which he had striven to stay their flight at Kipp's Bay and the calm daring that had turned defeat into victory at Princeton.

Two regiments, under the command of Lieutenant Colonel Ramsay, he stationed with four guns on a wooded rise to the north of the road, with orders to hold on there until Greene's and Stirling's divisions could take position on the hills behind the West Ravine. South of the road Varnum's brigade, a New York regiment, and the light troops under Wayne, with two guns, lined a hedge fence that formed an excellent obstacle to cavalry. The remainder of Lee's troops were directed to retire to Englishtown to rest. The American guns opened fire; the British artillery unlimbered and replied; and as Washington rode back to organize the position at the West Ravine, the whole front was shrouded in the smoke of the cannonade.

Ramsay's men disputed the British advance foot by foot. Driven from the wood, they retired in such close combat that to those who watched them they seemed to be intermingled with their assailants. Von Steuben's training with the bayonet yielded bloody returns that day. All ten of the guns that had marched with Lee that morning were now in action, and not one of them was lost, although they unlimbered and fired at every halt. It was here that twenty-two-year-old Molly Pitcher, her husband dead at her feet, dropped the bucket in which she had been carrying water to his piece, caught up his rammer, and served the gun in his place. General Joseph Reed, who had rejoined the army at Hopewell, had his horse killed under him here. A shot brought Hamilton's horse to the ground. Ramsay went down under the sabers of the dragoons and was taken prisoner.

South of the road, behind the hedge fence, where Wayne was in command, his men held their fire until the last minute and then so blasted the dragoons that in their flight they rode over the grenadiers, who were advancing to support them. Varnum's brigade and the New Yorkers covered the retirement of Ramsay's troops and followed them when, according to orders, they withdrew beyond the West Ravine.

There the main body of the American army, which numbered about seventy-five hundred men, was now taking position: Greene to the west of the road to Englishtown, Stirling about a half a mile to the east of him, and Washington himself in the center, facing the bridge with Wayne's division and supported by a second line formed by Lafayette's. In front of them the swampy margins of Wemrock Brook presented a somewhat serious obstacle to attack west of the bridge. But on Stirling's front it was easily passable, at least by foot soldiers, and against this sector of the line Clinton sent his light infantry and the 42nd Foot, the Royal Highlanders.

Stirling's men, steadied by their general's habitual vociferation on the battlefield, by young James Monroe, who acted as his adjutant general that day, and by von Steuben, their old drillmaster, wheeled into line with admirable precision, checked the advancing enemy with the cool and well-distinguished volleys they had learned to deliver at Valley Forge, and presently drove them back down the slope to the brook. There three of Stirling's regiments struck them in the flank with a bayonet charge.

Abandoning the attack in that sector of the field, Clinton tried the right of the American line, sending Cornwallis against Greene's position with two regiments of the Line, a battalion of grenadiers, and both battalions of the Guards. Greene had anticipated this movement and had occupied a hill to his right front with infantry and a battery of six guns under the command of Duplessis-Mauduit, Knox's brigade adjutant, who had distinguished himself so brilliantly at the Chew house in October. Knox himself had been all over the field, reconnoitering the enemy and directing the movement of the guns, and he now rode with this detachment. With marshy ground covering its front, it opened so deadly an enfilading fire on Cornwallis's columns that a single cannon ball is said to have knocked the muskets from the hands of all the men in one platoon.

On the right front of this attack Wayne, with the picked force he had led thus far in the fighting, had retired to a barn and an orchard enclosure belonging to the Tennant Church parsonage and situated on a little rise. There he had been joined by some remnants of Scott's and Maxwell's brigades. Barricading doors and windows and knocking loopholes in the walls, his men turned the place into a strong point, against which the British attacks broke repeatedly and in vain. "Steady. Steady. Wait for the word. Then pick out the king birds," Wayne cautioned as, sword in hand, Lieutenant Colonel the Honorable Henry Monckton led the grenadiers in what proved to be the final charge at that point. The volley crashed. Monckton fell dead only forty yards from the buildings. His men wavered. The coatless Continentals, with rolled-up shirtsleeves, counterattacked with the bayonet and in a furious hand-to-hand struggle captured the grenadiers' battalion colors and the body of their leader.

With this hornet's nest on their right and Duplessis-Mauduit's battery raking their lines with flanking fire, Cornwallis's troops pressed forward to the margin of the brook, but only to be halted there by the same steady, well-aimed volleys that had repulsed Stirling's assailants. For more than an hour the fire fight raged, the artillery of both sides winning the high praise of their respective commanding generals. But the ordeal of Valley Forge had so welded the American ranks that they were not to be shaken, although it was only when most of the British infantrymen had shot away the whole of the eighty rounds with which they had entered the battle that Clinton ordered his troops to retire.

This might have been a difficult operation. The Queen's Rangers and some of the light infantry were deep in the American position. The whole force had been under arms since sunrise, marching swiftly or fighting most of the time, and it was now past five o'clock. The men were worn out, exhausted by their efforts and the appalling heat. Of the British dead whom Clinton reported, almost half had been killed by sunstroke. Many of the horses had dropped dead in their tracks.

But the Americans were in no state to take advantage of the situation. They had shed their coats and blankets before going into action, but for almost half of them the emotional stress of the inexplicable retreat had been added to the strain of combat, and all had been under fire for many hours. "It was found impracticable with our men fainting with fatigue, heat, and want of water to do anything more that night," Washington wrote to his brother Augustine. The Americans' horses had suffered like those of the British. Washington's splendid white charger, which Governor Livingston had presented to him at Cranbury, fell dead under him as he rode about organizing the position at the West Ravine.

The American artillery moved up and opened a galling fire on the new front which the British formed on the far side of the Middle Ravine. The other troops followed the guns across the ground which had been the scene of the fighting in the early afternoon. Those units of Lee's command which had been sent back to Englishtown to rest were ordered to return, and brigades were sent forward to threaten the enemy's flanks. But darkness was about to fall by the time these movements were completed. "We remained looking at each other, with the defile between us," wrote Laurens of the close of the day.

Stretched on their cloaks beneath a tree, Washington and Lafayette discussed by the light of the setting moon various possible explanations of Lee's mismanagement of his mission until they fell asleep. The infantrymen lay down upon their arms, the gunners beside their guns, in line of battle. All was ready to recommence the conflict at the crack of dawn. But at dawn it was discovered that under the noses of the drowsy American sentinels the enemy had slipped away, and scouting parties returned with the report that the British were so far on the road to Middletown that pursuit would be useless.

CHAPTER VIII

☆

Hope Deferred

1

> He forms his camp with vain parade,
> Till ev'ning spreads the world with shade,
> Then still, like some endangered spark,
> Steals off on tiptoe in the dark. . . .

So JEERED JOHN TRUMBULL, the Westbury, Connecticut, lawyer and poet, at Clinton's retreat on the night after the battle at Monmouth Court House.

Repulsed at right, left, and center by the regular volleys of the American infantry and the well-aimed fire of Knox's cannon, Clinton had withdrawn to a strong position just east of the Middle Ravine and there gone into bivouac. But he had no intention of renewing the battle. More anxious than ever for the safety of his baggage train, he allowed his exhausted troops to rest only until the setting moon brought darkness. By midnight he was well on his way toward Middletown, and he stood not upon the order of his going. Four of his officers and forty of his enlisted men too seriously wounded to survive transportation he left with surgeons in improvised hospitals in the Court House and the English Church at Monmouth. Most of his dead remained unburied; and the discarded equipment that strewed the road of his retreat bore witness to the demoralization of his men. "Lost in action" would seem to have been as sound an excuse for missing articles in that day as it has been since.

Soon after sunrise the troops with Clinton overtook the baggage train and Knyphausen's force, which had bivouacked three miles to the south of Middletown, and by the evening of the next day, June 30, the whole army was camped on the Navesink Highlands, with

223

Sandy Hook and the vessels of Admiral Earl Howe's fleet at anchor below them.

Since dropping down the Delaware, the ships had lain steaming in the heat inside the Delaware Capes, waiting for a favorable wind to carry them to their destination. In the nick of time, on the morning of the 29th, it had begun to blow, and so freshly that in another twenty-four hours they had anchored off Sandy Hook, a sight to gladden the weary troops as they topped the Navesink hills that afternoon.

The embarkation presented certain difficulties. The winter storms had converted the Hook into an island, and the bridging of the turbulent tidal inlet was a troublesome task. Time pressed. For word came that the fleet under d'Estaing was now in American waters, and although the naval reinforcements which Admiral Howe had asked for months ago were known to have left England, they had not yet put in an appearance. But by July 5 troops, guns, and vehicles were all on board and headed across the Lower Bay for New York. On the 7th the small American force that had been keeping the British under observation reported to Washington's headquarters that nothing remained of them on the shore except abandoned wagons and the bodies of a great many horses, whose throats had been cut lest the poor beasts should be made use of by the Americans.

When news of the campaign reached England, the Earl of Shelburne described it as "the shameful retreat from Philadelphia, when the General escaped with his whole army, rather by chance and the misconduct of the enemy, than by the natural ability of the force under his command." Walpole sneered to his friend Sir Horace Mann that "upon the whole the Royal army has gained an escape." But there was no denying that Sir Henry Clinton had accomplished his mission, which was to get his army to New York, whatever happened by the way being merely incidental to that purpose. A speaker in the House of Commons said it was "universally allowed to be the finest thing performed during the present war." The English public, which had long been starving for a bit of good news from America, hailed it as a brilliant success. From the days of the Ana-

basis to those of Dunkirk successful retreats have always had a certain
glamour about them.

King George professed to be delighted. In acknowledging Clinton's
report of the movement Lord George Germain assured the general
of His Majesty's "highest approbation of your whole conduct . . .
Choice of Route . . . and the highly Military and spirited Resolution
you took of attacking the enemy in their main body. . . ." Clinton
had reported Washington's total strength at an estimated 20,000,
Lee's detachment at "near 12,000."

That report was, indeed, a masterpiece of face-saving. The march,
it stated, had in general proceeded "without interruption" from the
enemy, "except by what was occasioned by their having destroyed
every bridge on our road" in a country "much intersected by marshy
rivulets," where "the excessive heat rendered the labor of repairing
the bridges severely felt." He had been wrong, Clinton admitted, in
encumbering the army with so long a baggage train; but, he noted
with pride, he had lost not even a single cart.

He implied that the fighting at Monmouth was a mere rear guard
action, asserting that his later movements that day were made only
to extricate the light infantry and the Queen's Rangers. As for his
not remaining to resume the action next morning: he had, "for
various reasons," ventured to disobey the order to take his army to
New York by sea, and "the principle of the British army was to
retreat at this period." The promptness and celerity of his retirement
—the troops that had been engaged in the battle marched twenty-four
miles in the next two days, whereas they had averaged only seven
miles a day between Philadelphia and Monmouth—he explained by
his anxiety lest Washington, by a rapid night march on a parallel
road, should strike him on the flank at Middletown.

The report made no mention of plundering and desertion by his
men, although he deplored them in an order issued at Navesink in
which he thanked the troops for their exertions. They had, in fact,
left a blackened trail of depredation behind them, and the number
of desertions was disgraceful. By July 8 more than six hundred of
them, of whom three-fourths were Hessians or other German auxiliaries, were back in Philadelphia. The total British losses during the

retreat, Washington, who was never prone to exaggeration, estimated at not less than two thousand all told—close to 15 per cent of Clinton's entire strength.

Sir Henry might report what he liked. But the American army, from commander in chief to drummer boy, knew that his retirement from Philadelphia had cost him dear, and that they had fought and won no mere rear guard action but a pitched battle. Victors do not leave the vanquished in possession of the field. The rear guard phase had ended with Lee's disorderly retirement. Clinton might then have resumed his retreat. But it was then, and not to extricate the light infantry and the Queen's Rangers near the end of the fight, as his report asserted, that he had sent to Knyphausen for reinforcements. His fighting blood was up. He rode everywhere with the advance troops under the heaviest fire, pressing the action, quite evidently in the belief that, having put so large a part of Washington's army to flight, he might defeat and perhaps destroy the whole of it.

Next morning Washington dashed off a brief and happy dispatch to President Laurens:

> FIELDS, NEAR MONMOUTH CT HOUSE
> 29 June, 1778—
>
> SIR:
> I have the honor to inform you, that, about seven o'clock yesterday morning, both armies advanced on each other. About 12 o'clock they met on the grounds near Monmouth Court House, when an action commenced. We forced the enemy from the field and encamped on their ground. They took a strong post in our front, secured on both flanks by morasses and thick woods where they remained until about 12 at night, and then retreated. I cannot at this time go into a detail of matters; when opportunity will permit, I shall take the liberty of transmitting to Congress a more particular account of the proceedings of the Day. I have the honor to be, with gt respect
>
> Sir, your most obt. servt.
> GO WASHINGTON

To his brother Augustine he wrote of the battle: "from an unfortunate and bad beginning [it] turned out a glorious and happy day."

Knox wrote to his wife: "Indeed upon the whole it is very splendid. The capital army of Britain defeated and obliged to retreat before

the Americans." Wayne wished the Philadelphia ladies to be told
that "the heavenly sweet pretty Red Coats—the accomplished gentlemen of the Guards and Grenadiers—have humbled themselves on
the plains of Monmouth. The Knights of the Blended Rose and the
Burning Mountain have resigned their laurels to the Rebel officers,
who lay them at the feet of the Virtuous Daughters of Liberty, who
gave up ease and affluence for Liberty and peace of mind in a cottage."

More encouraging than even the material success, however, was the
moral achievement of the troops. They had turned from disorder and
retreat to disciplined resistance and final victory. For the first time
in the war they had driven the best troops of Britain before them
with the bayonet and had inflicted on them losses far greater than
their own. In his later report to Congress Washington wrote: "The
behavior of the troops in general, after they recovered from the first
surprise occasioned by the retreat of the advanced corps, was such
as could not be surpassed." The usually captious and jealous Charles
Lee rushed off a letter to the Trenton *Gazette*, in which he said:
"The behavior of the whole army, both men and officers, was so
equally good, that it would be unjust to make distinctions; tho' I
confess it is difficult to refrain from paying compliments to the
artillery, from General Knox and Colonel Oswold, down to the very
driver." High praise, especially since the veteran artillery opposed to
the American gunners received in orders their general's "best thanks"
for their conduct on that field.

The day after the battle was spent in burying the dead, including
four British officers, who were interred with military honors—Colonel
Monckton in the near-by Tennant Churchyard. Clinton, with the
lack of candor that had characterized his predecessor in command,
reported his losses as 147 killed, 170 wounded, and 64 missing. But
the American burial parties counted the corpses of 247 British enlisted men, though the British had buried some of their dead before
their departure. British bodies were still being found in the woods
and thickets a week later. The number of their wounded whom the
British had carried off with them could only be guessed. Including
the wounded they had left behind, they had lost a hundred men
taken prisoner. The American losses Washington reported as 58

killed, 161 wounded, and 131 missing. But of these last, many reported for duty in the next three or four days, some of them doubtless having been overcome by the heat, which had caused a few deaths among their comrades. The casualties among the American officers were notably high: seven killed and seventeen wounded.

In spite of his victory, however, Washington decided against pursuing the enemy. Clinton had gained almost a whole day's march during the night after the battle. The best information indicated that the Middletown–Sandy Hook area was a country of deep sand, almost destitute of water; the soldiers were tired out; and rapid marching in the great heat, which still prevailed, was bound to add greatly to the number already dead or disabled from that cause. To follow the British more deliberately would be both useless and imprudent. For Clinton, once more possessed of the advantage of sea power, would now be able to move against the forts on the Hudson with an ease and a swiftness that the marching columns of the Americans could not hope to match. "Being fully convinced by the gentlemen of this country, that the enemy cannot be injured in their embarkation at Sandy Hook . . . and unwilling," Washington wrote to Congress on July 1, "to get too far from the North River, I put the troops in motion early this morning and shall proceed that way." He had, however, sent Morgan's riflemen, Moylan's cavalry, McLane's corps of light troops, and Maxwell's brigade of Jersey men to the northeastward with orders to keep the enemy under observation, to assist deserters, and to prevent depredations as far as possible.

After the policing of the battlefield the army was given a day of rest. The men bathed in the brook, washed their clothes, and cleaned their arms and accouterments. The local inhabitants complained that some of the American soldiers had taken to plundering, robbing them of articles that they had succeeded in hiding from the British. There was a search of knapsacks, and it was Washington's turn to threaten death to any man convicted of the crime. Molly Pitcher's gallantry was rewarded with a sergeant's warrant. The New Jersey militia, whose term of service expired that day, went home, and early the following morning the army took the road for the Hudson.

Two days later the troops reached New Brunswick after a march of twenty miles through deep sand, which Washington described as "inconceivably distressing" to both men and animals. There was not a drop of water to be had, except at South River, which was halfway. The intense heat kept up; a few men died of it; many were disabled; and it killed more of the horses than could be spared. With headquarters on the pleasant banks of the Raritan, opposite New Brunswick, Washington halted for several days to rest his men and give Greene an opportunity to replace the dead animals. There in the late afternoon of July 4 the army celebrated the second anniversary of their country's independence with a thirteen-gun salute, a parade, with a sprig of green in every hat, and a *feu de joie* which young Dr. James McHenry, Washington's secretary of war eighteen years later, described as "a beautiful and brilliant exhibition."

By the end of another week the whole "family"—by which McHenry meant Washington and his staff—were picnicking pleasantly under a spreading oak at Passaic Falls, on cold ham and biscuits and water from a bubbling spring with which to mix their grog. For by this time there was no longer any need for haste. Instead of moving up the Hudson, where he could have at least delayed Washington's crossing of the river, Clinton had encamped his troops in three divisions on Manhattan Island, Long Island, and Staten Island, and had set them to building entrenchments and redoubts: a course of action which was presently explained when a flag-of-truce boat arrived from New York. The French fleet had been sighted off Chesapeake Bay, and on July 11 it came to anchor off Sandy Hook.

By way of Paramus (now Ridgewood) and Haverstraw the army marched slowly to King's Ferry at Stony Point, crossed the Hudson, and on July 24 joined Gates's command at White Plains. Thus, as Washington wrote to General Nelson, "after two years maneuvering and undergoing the strangest vicissitudes, that perhaps ever attended any one contest since the creation, both armies are brought back to the very point they set out from, and that which was the offending party in the beginning is now reduced to the spade and pick-axe for defense." He had good reason for this quiet exultation. The last time he had seen White Plains Howe had worsted him there, Fort Washington and Fort Lee had been about to fall, and he was soon to be leading the dwindling remnants of a thrice-defeated army in a desperate retreat to refuge beyond the Delaware. Now it was he who had lately been the pursuer, and the enemy were digging in to defend their only important base of operations on the continent.

2

There was, however, another side to this happy picture. With success and the return of rest and leisure, came, as they always do, irritability, personal ambition, jealousy, and petty spite among the very men who had been self-forgetful heroes in adversity, hardship, and danger. The old bickering over rank and seniority broke out afresh. The French alliance had brought a new influx of foreigners seeking positions out of all proportion to their worth. There was murmuring among the American officers when, owing to a temporary shortage of major generals, von Steuben was put at the head of a division for a short time; and when he went on leave to Philadelphia, whither Congress had now returned, and began to lobby for a permanent divisional command, Washington wrote to Gouverneur Morris that he wished there were not a single foreigner in the army except the Marquis de Lafayette.

The commander in chief's nerves showed once more the strain they had been under, and Greene, in a letter of quietly reasoned protest against what appears to have been an outburst of unjustifiable criticism of his management as quartermaster general, was not above bringing up an old grievance—Washington's omitting to praise Greene's brigades in General Orders for saving the army from rout at the Brandywine. But most regrettable of all—or it would have been so, if the end result had not been to rid the American cause of a worse than doubtful supporter—was the case of Major General Charles Lee. On the second day after the battle Lee was put under arrest, charged with misbehavior in action and afterwards. He was court-martialed, and his trial dragged on through the various halts in the army's march all the way from New Brunswick to White Plains.

In that hectic noontide on the battlefield, as Washington was riding back to form his main body, he had again met Lee and had made what was in effect an *amende honorable* for his recent outburst of temper by asking him if he would assume command of the retirement of the troops then in action. This Lee had consented to do. Later in the day Washington had sent him back to Englishtown with the more disorganized and exhausted elements of his command. At Englishtown Lee had continued to air his defeatist opinions, had openly doubted the report that the British were retiring in disorder, and would have prevented von Steuben from going forward with reinforcements if he had not been shown Washington's order for that movement. But Washington had evidently been willing to allow the whole affair to pass without further notice on his part. As late as the morning of the 30th he had named Lee as major general for the next day.

But the whole army was boiling with resentment against the man but for whose blundering, or worse, they felt sure they would have won a victory that might have destroyed the enemy's army. The troops whom he had led to disgrace would have liked to see him shot. Wayne and Scott put in a part of the day after the battle on a joint letter to their commander in chief, in which they stated the facts of Lee's retreat. It was a duty which they owed to the country, themselves, and the officers and soldiers under their command, they wrote. The retreat had not been owing to want of numbers, position, or the wishes of both officers and men, they went on; no plan of attack had ever been communicated to them, or any notice of a retreat, until it had taken place in their rear, they supposed by General Lee's order. Knox wrote home mildly that Lee was "obliged to retreat" and "after some circumstances not yet explained, thought it proper to retire." But very few were inclined to be so lenient. Grossly exaggerated versions of Washington's rebuke on the battlefield were bandied gleefully from mouth to mouth; and Lee, like most detractors, was highly sensitive to criticism of himself.

Before nightfall, so angry that he misdated his letter July 1 for June 29, he sent Washington an insolent demand for reparation for the expressions he had used to him on the battlefield. They implied, he wrote, that he was guilty of disobedience of orders, misconduct, or want of courage; and unless this act of cruel injustice were rectified, he would retire from a service that had at its head a man capable of inflicting such injuries.

The next day brought a crackling interchange of notes between the commander in chief and his disgruntled second-in-command. Replying to Lee's protest, Washington first called attention to the fact that it was misdated, and then went on to say that he was not aware of having addressed to Lee any expressions that duty and the occasion had not warranted. But he promised that, as soon as circumstances should permit, Lee should have the opportunity of justifying himself to the army, to Congress, to America, and to the world in general, or of convincing them of his guilt.

This Lee answered twice: first, in a note which he dated the day of the battle, and again, with the correct date; and through both communications there sounds a curious echo of Conway's epistolary style when addressing his commander in chief. In his letter of the previous day he had, "with the greatest respect and veneration of General Washington," alluded to "those dirty earwigs, who will ever insinuate themselves near persons in high office." Now, in welcoming the opportunity of showing America the "sufficiency of her respective servants," he trusted that "temporary power of office and the tinsel dignity attending it" would not be able to "obfuscate the bright beams of truth." He proposed to retire from the army, but after reflecting on Washington's situation and his own, he recommended an immediate court-martial. Delay might make the collection of evidence difficult and also "bring on a paper war . . . for all are not my friends, nor all your admirers."

His wish was granted promptly.

HEADQUARTERS, ENGLISH TOWN, 30 June, 1778.
Sir,
Your letter by Colonel Fitzgerald and also one of this date have been received. I have sent Colonel Scammel, the Adjutant General, to put you in arrest, who will deliver to you a copy of the charges on which you will be tried. I am, Sir, your most obedient servant,

GEORGE WASHINGTON

The charges were (1) Disobedience of orders in not attacking the enemy on the 28th of June, agreeably to repeated instructions; (2)

Misbehavior before the enemy on the same day, by making an unnecessary, disorderly, and shameful retreat; (3) Disrespect to the commander in chief, in two letters dated the 1st of July and the 28th of June.

With Stirling as president, and four brigadiers and eight colonels as its other members, the court-martial convened at New Brunswick on July 4 and continued its hearings at Paramus, Peekskill, and North Castle, where, on August 12, after twenty-six sessions, it pronounced its verdict. The witnesses against the accused, twenty-six in all, were impressive in character. They were headed by Lafayette and von Steuben and included Wayne, the three other brigadier generals who had been under Lee's command that shameful morning, Captain L'Enfant of the engineers, Hamilton, Laurens, Dr. McHenry, and three other members of Washington's staff. Those for the defense were only half as many, but they were equally respectable: Knox and Duportail, Lieutenant Colonel Oswold, who had handled the artillery in so masterly a fashion, and some others whose troops had been involved in the retreat.

The testimony on the charge of cowardice was feeble. Nobody but Hamilton and Laurens appeared to have observed any positive symptoms of it; and Hamilton, who had proposed to Lee in the crisis of the battle that they die together, sword in hand, rather than retreat another foot, was shown to have been in a highly emotional state. Evidence of incapacity was strong, but there was none to show that Lee had actually issued any orders for the retreat, and Washington's final orders for an attack had included the phrase "unless there should be very strong reasons to the contrary," which had left that movement to Lee's decision. As to disrespect to the commander in chief, Lee's letters spoke for themselves. But, fortunately for him, his failure to report the retreat to Washington, a fault about which there could not be two opinions, had not been included in the charges.

Lee defended himself in a long and skillfully written document. He brazenly reminded the court that he had always opposed fighting a general action. With almost incredible effrontery he both took credit for having issued no orders for the retreat and at the same time maintained that only the retreat had averted a disaster and made possible the final victory; and he made much of the fact that in spite of unfavorable terrain, mixed orders, and the spontaneous retirement of his troops he had lost not a gun, a battalion, or even a single company.

He had expected, he said, praise for this exploit, not the bitter rebuke that had been given him. He had confidently expected to receive an apology and had waited for it for forty hours before writing his first letter, which he believed was only such as any member of the court might excusably have written in his circumstances. So much for the charge of disrespect. The witnesses against him he characterized as "the whole squadron of these negative gentlemen who have pranced about over reams of paper for purposes too obvious," and he distinguished von Steuben, L'Enfant, and some others whose evidence had been against him, with the insidious insults of which he was a master.

The court found him guilty on all three counts, except that the retreat, which had been characterized in the charges as "unnecessary, disorderly, and shameful," was described in the verdict as merely "unnecessary and in some instances disorderly." The sentence, however, was no more than suspension from command in the Continental service for one year, and even that was subject to the approval or disapproval of Congress. The partisans of Washington were furious, the army disgusted. Lee, for his part, complained loudly that a great wrong had been done him. If he were guilty, the court—as Henry Lee observed—should have sentenced him to death; if not guilty, he should have been acquitted, not stigmatized as incapable, a coward, or a traitor.

But the action of Congress remained to be taken, and in mid-September Lee obtained leave to go to Philadelphia, where he found many ready sympathizers among what John Laurens called "the old faction." To Rush, Lee had already written that Washington saw and knew almost as little of the battle at Monmouth as he did of the battle of Philippi, and in a later letter he called Washington's official report of the battle "from beginning to end a most abominable damn lie." He complained to Richard Henry Lee that he had been ruined for giving a victory to a man whose head was never intended for a sprig of laurel; and he wrote Aaron Burr, who was one of his champions, that he intended to go to his estate in Virginia and "learn to hoe tobacco, which I find is the best school to form a consummate general."

He overlooked few opportunities not only to attack and undermine Washington but to sow the seeds of discord throughout the country. When Conway, now completely discredited, sailed for France late in November, Lee sent to Gates a copy of an attack on Washington for his treatment of that crafty adventurer, asked the favor of the old cabal to get it published in the Boston papers, and warned him that there was "a mine" under Gates's feet. In a "Vindication to the Public," which he published in the *Philadelphia Packet*, he stated that since his management at Monmouth Court House had been so successful, he would do exactly the same thing in similar circumstances, and thus himself started the "paper war" against which he had had the insolence to warn Washington in July.

But vilification is a game that more than one can play at. Lee was soon smarting under spoken and printed charges that the British repulse at Charleston in 1776, for which he had taken the credit, had been accomplished in spite of his attempted mismanagement, and that he had disobeyed orders in not marching promptly to Washington's aid in the December of that year. A letter in the *New Jersey Gazette* ridiculed his record in Poland and Russia, said he was worse than Cataline, and anatomized his facial ugliness. Consequences of his other misdoings caught up with him. In reply to the insulting statements that Lee had put into his defense before the court-martial, von Steuben sent him an insulting challenge. Lee appears to have wormed out of it by apologizing, for there was no duel between the two. But John Laurens, who deemed it his duty as Washington's aide to call Lee to account for his criticisms of the commander in chief, had the satisfaction of giving him a slight wound in the side when they met with pistols, at six paces, in a convenient wood four miles outside Philadelphia.

Meanwhile Lee kept bombarding Congress not only with requests for action on his sentence but with restatements of his case and attacks on the fairness of his trial—a course of whose impropriety his long service in the British army must have made him fully cognizant. But Congress kept deferring the matter from week to week. Not until the 5th of December did they vote upon it. Then with Georgia, and Massachusetts under the guidance of Samuel Adams, voting "nay," and the votes of New Jersey, Maryland, and Virginia divided, the sentence of the court-martial was approved by the six "ayes" of Rhode Island, Connecticut, New York, Pennsylvania, and the two Carolinas. Furious at the news, Lee pointed to one of his dogs, exclaiming: "Oh, that I was that animal, that I might not call man my brother!"

Not long after, he retired to his farm in what is now West Virginia. There he diversified a life of squalid eccentricity, with little companionship but that of his horses and dogs, by assailing the reputations of Sullivan, Wayne, and even his former friend Joseph Reed. The following July he published in *The Maryland Journal and Baltimore Advertiser* something that he called "Queries Political and Military, Humbly Offered to the Consideration of the Public." The queries were twenty-five in number, the first eight of them being aimed at Congress, the rest directly or indirectly at Washington, to whom he referred as his "persecutor," presenting himself as the victim of Washington's jealous spite.

The "Queries" were received with general indignation. He was not recalled to active duty when the term of his sentence expired. Upon hearing that his name might be dropped from the army list for the sake of economy, he wrote to Congress that they must know little of him if they supposed he would accept their money after the "wicked and infamous sentence" that had been passed upon him. Congress retorted by informing him that they had no further use for his services, and it was in vain that Lee tried to apologize and wheedle his way out of the cul-de-sac in which his ill temper had landed him.

He lived on, mostly in his rural retirement, for only two years and some months longer, but long enough to see the triumph of the cause which his self-seeking and innate duplicity had done their utmost to ruin. He died on October 2, 1782, at Philadelphia, at a little inn

called the Conestoga Wagon, after a brief illness, at the age of
fifty-two. Bitterly fleering to the last, he had written in his will that
he did not wish to be buried in any churchyard, since he had kept
such bad company while living that he did not choose to continue it
when dead.

He was, however, buried in Christ Churchyard in Philadelphia.
The funeral service was held at the City Tavern and was an occasion
of importance. Mindful of the years he had spent in the American
service and willing to forget his dubious conduct, many officers were
among the large crowd that followed his body to the grave. More
than two generations were to pass before a collection of old papers
in an English country house yielded incontrovertible proof of his
traitorous double-dealing in "Mr. Lee's plan" to enable the British
to win the war.

3

Washington took no public notice of Lee's attacks upon him,
though he said that he felt that they ought to be answered. Otherwise tens of thousands of people who did not know the facts might
accept Lee's statements as true. Rivington's *Gazette* in New York
reprinted Lee's article on the battle at Monmouth and the trial; and
his presentation of himself as the persecuted victim of his commander
in chief's jealousy griped Washington severely. Unless Lee's trial at
Lee's own request could be considered in that light, Washington
wrote to Joseph Reed, he defied Lee to produce a single instance of
persecution. Since the trial began he had never even mentioned Lee
outside his military family if he could avoid doing so. But he felt no
inclination to answer him, and in the months since the battle he
was too busy on matters far more important.

The problem of cooperating with the French forces under d'Estaing
occupied his time and his thoughts throughout the remaining weeks
of July and the most of August. Never before had prospects been so
bright for the American cause. D'Estaing had arrived at the Delaware Capes only ten days too late to bottle up Earl Howe's warships
and the British transports in Delaware Bay. He had paused there
only long enough to send Monsieur Gérard, the first ambassador

from France to the United States, up the river to Philadelphia; and
when he anchored off Sandy Hook on July 11, the British in New
York faced the prospect of a siege and capture either by assault or
starvation.

The twelve great French ships of the line and five frigates—a total
of 834 guns—were far stronger than Earl Howe's squadron. If
d'Estaing could force the entrance to the harbor and land his four
thousand soldiers on Long Island, while Washington moved down
to Kingsbridge and occupied the line of the Harlem River, Clinton's
army might be so closely invested that it would be starved into surrender: it was reported to be already short of supplies. And if New
York were taken, Newport would fall almost of its own weight.

While still at Paramus, Washington sent his French-speaking aides,
Laurens and, after him, Hamilton, to arrange the preliminaries for a
joint attack. But Laurens, who narrowly escaped drowning in the
rough waters of the Shrewsbury River on the way, found the situation
of the French fleet much less promising than it had appeared at a
distance. Inside the Hook, Earl Howe had anchored his nine heavy
ships and a storeship armed with cannon right across the channel.
Soldiers from the army had volunteered eagerly to augment his crews,
and cannon had been mounted in batteries on the Hook itself.

A still more serious obstacle was the lack of a sufficient depth of
water to allow the larger French ships to cross the bar at the
entrance of the channel. Washington sent down four experienced
sea captains to act as pilots. D'Estaing offered a reward of fifty
thousand crowns to any man who would take the ships in. But none
was found who thought it possible, and the French soundings confirmed their judgment. It was a tantalizing situation: "the English
colors," wrote d'Estaing, "waving upon so great a crowd of masts
on the other side of a simple barrier of sand," and no way to get at
them.

The French ships, moreover, had been eighty-four days at sea
between Toulon and the Delaware Capes and were running short
of bread and even of water. Parties sent on shore to replenish supplies
of the latter found wells only at a considerable distance inland and
the inhabitants either unwilling to furnish wagons to haul it or

demanding such high prices for the use of them that Laurens proposed bringing water in a swift ship from the Delaware country. But even if its more pressing wants were supplied, d'Estaing's fleet, anchored as it was in open sea, could not keep its station if the weather turned foul.

He remained off the Hook for eleven days, captured twenty trading vessels and one or two sloops of war; then, convinced that the crossing of the bar presented an insuperable obstacle to operations against New York, he set sail for Newport. It was fortunate for the British that he did so. If he had stayed a little longer, he might have destroyed in detail the naval reinforcement from England, which, battered and dispersed by storms in crossing the Atlantic, began to drop in by twos and threes soon after the French fleet departed.

In the beginning of their consultations Washington had proposed Newport to d'Estaing as an alternative objective if New York should prove impracticable. Sullivan was in command in that sector. John Hancock joined him with seven thousand New England militia, and Washington sent him Greene and Lafayette as division commanders and two brigades of Continentals, with which to cooperate with d'Estaing's force. Unfortunately the Americans were ten days late at the rendezvous. Earl Howe's fleet appeared in the offing, and d'Estaing, though in the act of landing his four thousand soldiers, re-embarked them and sailed out to give battle. He was roughly handled both in the ensuing action and by a severe storm, refused to leave his troops with Sullivan, and put in at Boston for repairs. Sullivan, furiously angry, issued a general order in which he denounced the French for their halfhearted cooperation; the militia went home discouraged; and on learning that Earl Howe was bringing reinforcements to the Newport garrison, Sullivan and the Continentals fought a gallant rear guard action and retired to the mainland.

So, in anger and disillusionment, ended the first attempt at joint operations between the United States and their powerful ally. D'Estaing sailed for the West Indies, whither Clinton, in pursuance of orders from Germain, was sending a splendidly equipped expedition for the conquest of the island of St. Lucia. American patriots,

army and people alike, were disgusted. But North America had now
become only one of the theaters of a great European war, and as
Washington wrote philosophically that November: "It is a maxim
founded on the universal experience of mankind, that no nation is
to be trusted further than it is bound by its own interests."

Washington was used to disappointments. Few men had met with
more, and through no fault of his own. Want of men had prevented
his gathering the fruits of the Princeton campaign. The fog cost him
the victory at Germantown. Charles Lee's mismanagement—to give
it no worse a name—kept Monmouth from being decisive. And not
even Robert E. Lee learned better how to cope with disappointment.
It was well that Washington had done so. For until the last of the
hostilities that dragged through the next three years, the conduct and
fortunes of his French ally gave him little else to cope with.

Bending every effort to the collection of an army of 25,000 men
in 1779, he waited through the summer for d'Estaing to cooperate
with him in an attack on New York. But d'Estaing was busy with
West Indian conquests and found time only to join Lincoln in his
disastrous attempt to recapture Savannah, which had been taken
in the previous December by a British seaborne expedition from New
York. A mission to France by Lafayette resulted in the arrival of
Rochambeau in Rhode Island with an army of 6,000 men in the
May of 1780. But a British squadron promptly bottled him up there,
and a reinforcement of 4,000 was so thoroughly blockaded at Brest
that it never left port. It was midsummer of 1781 when John
Laurens's undiplomatic diplomacy at Versailles made the French
alliance effective through fresh supplies of hard money, clothing,
munitions and arms, and the full cooperation of the French fleet.

After the failure of the Newport operations Washington distributed his troops in cantonments all the way from Bound Brook
through Elizabeth, Ramapo, West Point, and Peekskill to Danbury
in Connecticut. Thus they could be readily concentrated whether
the enemy moved against New England, up the Hudson, or into
New Jersey. And thus most of the army remained, with headquarters at either West Point or Morristown, for the next two and a
half years. In October, 1779, the British evacuated Newport, and the

addition of its garrison brought Sir Henry Clinton's forces at New York up to more than 28,000 men. Washington often had less than 10,000 with which to oppose him. But aside from raiding the Connecticut coast towns, from New Haven to Norwalk, Clinton was well content to obey his orders and prosecute the war in the South. So far as major operations were concerned, the war in the northern theater was over.

All that broke the monotony of camp life for Washington's soldiers were Wayne's capture of Stony Point, Henry Lee's similar exploit at Paulus Hook, a sharp fight at Springfield in New Jersey, and a march toward Kingsbridge to check a British threat against Rochambeau in Rhode Island. Meanwhile the condition of the troops went from bad to worse. Their clothing, worn threadbare by the end of the Monmouth campaign, was reduced to rags a few months later. In huts like those at Valley Forge, the men huddled, three to a tattered blanket, through the terrible winter of 1779-80, when the Hudson froze so hard that artillery could be driven across the ice. Again they sometimes went five or six days without meat; and with a thousand Continental dollars worth only one in hard money, pay became practically nonexistent.

But the spirit of these men never faltered. When Savannah and Charleston fell, when Georgia and the two Carolinas were overrun by the enemy and Richmond was burned, the Continentals from North Carolina and Virginia, from Maryland and Delaware and Pennsylvania, marched southward eagerly to follow de Kalb, Greene, and Lafayette through the bitter campaigns that turned the British tactical victories into strategic defeats. The Pennsylvania troops mutinied at Morristown, to be sure. But never, probably, was another mutiny like theirs. They hanged the emissaries whom Clinton sent to bring them into the British service, and when, their grievances satisfied, they were allowed to go home, most of them re-enlisted and marched south under Wayne to join Lafayette in Virginia.

As at Valley Forge, Washington was untiring in his efforts to relieve the hardships and privations of his men. Unfortunately they could not, he wrote on one occasion, live on air like the chameleon, or suck their paws for sustenance through the winter as bears did.

When all else failed, he laid requisitions on the near-by counties through the local magistrates. These were filled punctually and in many counties exceeded. For nobody now dared to assail Washington openly in his position as commander in chief. Covert opposition to him never ceased in Congress. But the failure of an expedition against Castine, which Congress had undertaken without consulting him; the spectacular flight of Gates, Congress's appointee to the southern command, from the field of Camden; Lee's condemnation; and Mifflin's loss of reputation had combined with the success of his strategy at Valley Forge and the victory at Monmouth to make him pre-eminent in the minds of his countrymen. People might ask why they should exert themselves when six thousand French troops lay idle for months at Newport, and recruiting might suffer accordingly. Legislatures might shrink from levying taxes sufficient to support the war. The news from the South might be of an almost unbroken series of defeats. The fall of Charleston might be, as it was, the greatest disaster that ever befell American arms—considering the numbers of troops engaged in this war. But during the more than thirty months that Washington spent in watchful waiting for an opportunity to take the offensive there arose no general outcry for action such as forced his hand in 1777.

When, in August, 1781, that opportunity came, with the whole-hearted cooperation of the French fleet under de Grasse and the troops under Rochambeau, Washington was ready for it, and his army was ready. Their great march of four hundred miles from the Hudson to Yorktown in twenty-eight days—a stroke which, for boldness and swiftness, has been likened to Napoleon's famous march from Boulogne to Ulm in 1805—and their behavior at the siege that followed bear undeniable witness to the quality which their leader, the training of von Steuben, and the ordeal of Valley Forge had instilled in them.

Louis Philippe, Comte de Ségur, who was to distinguish himself in the wars of Napoleon thirty years later, visited their camp upon their return to the Hudson and wrote of them:

I had expected to see in this democratic camp unkempt soldiers and officers without training, all republicans devoid of that urbanity so common in our old civilized countries. I recalled the first days of their revolution, when ploughmen and artisans . . . had rushed on without any semblance of order . . . to give battle to the British phalanxes. . . . One may imagine how surprised I was when I saw a well-disciplined army presenting in every detail the very image of order, reason, training, and experience. The generals, their aides-de-camp and the other officers evinced in their behavior and their speech noble and decent manners and a natural kindness. . . . This dignity in every individual, this self respect which sprung from their love of liberty and their feeling of equality had not constituted small obstacles to their chief who had to rise above them without awakening jealousy and who had to bend their independence to discipline without stirring discontent. Any other man but Washington would have failed in the undertaking.

BIBLIOGRAPHY

ADAMS, CHARLES FRANCIS: *Studies Military and Diplomatic*, New York, 1911.

ADAMS, JOHN: *Familiar Letters of John Adams and His Wife*, Charles Francis Adams, ed., Boston, 1875.

ADAMS, RANDOLPH G.: *British Headquarters Maps and Sketches*, Ann Arbor, 1928.

American Archives, 5th Series, Vol. III, Washington, 1853.

ANDERSON, TROYER STEELE: *The Command of the Howe Brothers during the American Revolution*, New York and London, 1936.

ANDRÉ, JOHN: *Journal*, Tarrytown, N. Y., 1930.

AZOY, LT. COL. A. C. M.: Monmouth, the Battle That Was Won at Valley Forge, *Infantry Journal*, Vol. 46, No. 1.

BANCROFT, GEORGE: *History of the American Revolution, Epoch Fourth*, London, 1852.

——: *History of the United States of America*, New York, 1891.

BAURMEISTER, CARL LEOPOLD: *Letters to Colonel von Jungkenn Written during the Philadelphia Campaign, 1777-1778*, Bernhard A. Uhlendorf and Edna Vosper, eds., Philadelphia, 1937.

BEAN, THEODORE W.: *Washington at Valley Forge*, Morristown, 1876.

BEVERIDGE, ALBERT J.: *Life of John Marshall*, Boston and New York, 1916.

BOLTON, CHARLES KNOWLES: *The Private Soldier under Washington*, New York, 1902.

BOUDINOT, ELIAS: "Letters, 1775-1782," Ms. in Princeton University Library.

BOYD, JAMES: *Light Horse Harry Lee*, New York, 1931.

BOYD, THOMAS: *Mad Anthony Wayne*, New York and London, 1929.

BROOKS, NOAH: *Henry Knox, A Soldier of the Revolution*, New York and London, 1900.

BURK, REV. W. HERBERT, D. D.: *Making a Museum*, 1926.

BURR, AARON: *Memoirs*, Matthew L. Davis, ed., New York, 1858.

CARRINGTON, HENRY BEEBE, A.M., L.L.D.: *Battles of the American Revolution*, New York, 1876.

CHINARD, GILBERT: *George Washington as the French Knew Him*, Princeton, 1940.

CLINTON, SIR HENRY: "Papers," at the Clements Memorial Library, University of Michigan, Ann Arbor.

CONWAY, MONCURE DANIEL: *Life of Thomas Paine*, New York and London, 1893.

CORNER, GEORGE W.: *The Autobiography of Benjamin Rush*, Princeton, 1948.

CRESSWELL, NICHOLAS: *Journal, 1774-1777*, London, 1925.

CURTIS, EDWARD E., Ph. D.: *The British Army in the American Revolution*, New Haven, 1926.

CUSTIS, GEORGE WASHINGTON PARKE: *Memoirs of Washington*, New York, 1859.

DANIEL, HAWTHORNE: *For Want of a Nail*, New York, 1948.

DAWSON, HENRY BARTON: *Battles of the United States*, New York, 1858.

DESMOND, ALICE CURTIS: *Martha Washington, Our First Lady*, New York, 1947.

Dictionary of American Biography, New York, 1935.

Dictionary of National Biography, New York, 1885.

DRAKE, FRANCIS S.: *Life and Correspondence of Henry Knox, Major General in the American Revolutionary Army*, Boston, 1873.

DUNLAP, WILLIAM: *A History of the American Theatre*, New York, 1832.

ECHEVERIA, DURAND: "The French Image of America," Gift Thesis, Ms. in Princeton University Library.

ELLET, ELIZABETH FRIES: *Women of the American Revolution*, Philadelphia, 1900.

Encyclopaedia Britannica, 11th Edition, New York, 1911.

EWING, GEORGE: *Military Journal*, Yonkers, 1928.

FISKE, JOHN: *The American Revolution*, Boston and New York, 1902.

FITZPATRICK, JOHN C., L.H.D., Lit.D.: *George Washington, Colonial Traveler, 1732-1775*, Indianapolis, 1927.

————: *George Washington Himself*, Indianapolis, 1933.

————: *Writings of Washington*, Washington, 1923.

FORD, PAUL LEICESTER: *The True George Washington*, Philadelphia, 1897.

FORD, WORTHINGTON CHAUNCEY: *The Writings of Washington*, New York and London, 1890.

FORTESQUE, HONORABLE J. W.: *History of the British Army*, London, 1902.

"Frazer Family Record," Ms. in possession of Andrew Welsh Imbrie.

GERMAIN, LORD GEORGE: "Papers," at the Clements Memorial Library, University of Michigan, Ann Arbor, Michigan.

GLYN, ENSIGN THOMAS: "Journal" Ms. in Princeton University Library.

GODFREY, CARLOS E., M.D.: *The Commander-in-Chief's Guard*, Washington, D. C., 1904.

GOTTSCHALK, LOUIS: *Lafayette Joins the American Army*, Chicago, 1937.

———: *Lafayette and the Close of the American Revolution*, Chicago, 1942.

Grand Dictionnaire Universel, Paris.

Grand Encyclopédie, Paris.

GRAYDON, ALEXANDER: *Memoirs of His Own Time*, Philadelphia, 1846.

GREENE, FRANCIS VINTON: *General Greene*, New York, 1893.

———: *The Revolutionary War and the Military Policy of the United States*, New York, 1911.

GREENE, GEORGE WASHINGTON: *Life of Nathanael Greene, Major General in the Army of the Revolution*, New York, 1871.

HAMILTON, ALEXANDER: *Works*, Henry Cabot Lodge, ed., New York and London, 1904.

HATCH, LOUIS CLINTON: *The Administration of the American Revolutionary Army*, New York and London, 1904.

HELTZHEIMER, JACOB, "Diary", *Pennsylvania Magazine of History and Biography*, Vol. XVI.

HUDLESTON, F. J.: *Gentleman Johnny Burgoyne*, New York, 1927.

———: *Warriors in Undress*, Boston, 1926.

HUGHES, RUPERT: *George Washington, Savior of the States*, New York, 1930.

IRVING, WASHINGTON: *Life of George Washington*, New York, 1855.

JONES, JUDGE THOMAS: *History of New York During the Revolutionary War*, New York, 1879.

JORDAN, JOHN W.: "Military Hospitals at Bethlehem and Lititz during the American Revolution," *Pennsylvania Magazine*, Vol. XX.

KAPP, FRIEDRICH: *Life of Frederick William von Steuben*, New York, 1859.

KEMBLE, STEPHEN: *Kemble Papers*, New York, 1884.

KIDDER, FREDERIC: *History of the First New Hampshire Regiment in the War of the Revolution*, Albany, 1868.

KITE, ELIZABETH S.: *Beaumarchais and the War of American Independence*, Boston, 1918.

———: *Brigadier General Louis Lebègue Duportail*, Baltimore and Philadelphia, 1933.

KNOX, DUDLEY W.: *The Naval Genius of George Washington*, Boston, 1932.

KNOX, WILLIAM, *Letters*: Historical Mss. Commission, Dublin, 1909.

LAFAYETTE, GENERAL: *Memoirs, Correspondence, and Manuscripts*, London, 1837.

LAURENS, JOHN: *Army Correspondence in the Years 1777-8*, New York, 1857.

LEE, HENRY: *Memoirs of the War in the Southern Department of the United States*, Washington, 1827.

Lee Papers, Collections of the New York Historical Society, New York, 1874.

LOSSING, BENSON J.: *Pictorial Field Book of the Revolution*, New York, 1852.

LOWELL, EDWARD J.: *The Hessians and Other German Auxiliaries of Great Britain in the Revolutionary War*, New York, 1884.

LUNDIN, LEONARD: *Cockpit of the Revolution*, Princeton, 1940.

McHENRY, JAMES: *Papers*, New York, 1944.

McMICHAEL, JAMES: "Diary of Lieutenant James McMichael of the Pennsylvania Line," *Pennsylvania Magazine of History and Biography*, Vol. XVI.

MARSHALL, CHRISTOPHER, *Diary*, William Duane, ed., Albany, 1877.

MARSHALL, JOHN: *Life of Washington*, Philadelphia, 1804.

MAURICE, MAJOR GENERAL SIR FREDERICK, K.C.M.G., C. B., L.L.D.: *History of the Scots Guards*, London, 1934.

MELLICK, ANDREW J., JR.: *Lesser Crossroads*, H. G. Schmidt, ed., New Brunswick, 1948.

The Montrésor Journals, G. D. Scull, ed., New York, 1882.

MUHLENBERG, HENRY A.: *Life of Major General Peter Muhlenberg*, Philadelphia, 1849.

OBERHOLTZER, ELLIS PAXSON, PH.D.: *Life of Robert Morris*, New York and London, 1903.

PALMER, JOHN McAULAY: *General von Steuben*, New Haven, 1937.

PATRIDGE, BELLAMY: *Sir Billy Howe*, London and New York, 1932.

PATTERSON, SAMUEL WHITE: *Horatio Gates, Defender of American Liberties*, New York, 1941.

PEARSON, HESKETH: *Tom Paine, Friend of Mankind*, New York, 1937.

Pennsylvania Archives, 1760-1776, Vol. 4, Philadelphia, 1853.

PICKERING, OCTAVIUS: *Life of Timothy Pickering*, Boston, 1867.

Princeton Standard, Series III, No. 18.

REED, WILLIAM B.: *Life of Esther de Berdt, Afterwards Esther Reed*, Philadelphia, 1853.

REPPLIER, AGNES: *Philadelphia, the Place and the People*, New York, 1898.

RICHARDS, H. H. M., LITT.D.: *Valley Forge and the Pennsylvania Germans*, Pennsylvania German Society Proceedings, Vol. 26.

RUSH, BENJAMIN, M.D.: *A Memorial, 1745-1813*, Philadelphia, 1905.

RUSH, BENJAMIN, M. D.: *Directions for Preserving the Health of Soldiers*, Lancaster, 1777.

SABINE, LORENZO: *The American Loyalists*, Boston, 1847.

SACKVILLE, GEORGE GERMAIN: *Report on the Manuscripts of Mrs. Stopford Sackville of Drayton House, Northamptonshire*, London, 1904-1910.

SARGENT, WINTHROP: *Life and Career of Major John André*, New York, 1902.

SÉGUR, M. LE COMTE DE: *Memoirs, Souvenirs et Anecdotes*, Paris, 1859.

SERLE, AMBROSE: *American Journal*, E. H. Tatum, ed., San Marino, 1940.

SHERMAN, ANDREW: *Historic Morristown*, Morristown, 1905.

SHIPPEN, NANCY: *Her Journal Book*, Ethel Armes, ed., Philadelphia and London, 1935.

SMITH, FRANK: *Thomas Paine, Liberator*, New York, 1938.

Sparks Manuscript, in Princeton University Library.

SPARKS, JARED: *Correspondents of the American Revolution*, Boston, 1853.

———: *The Writings of Washington*, Boston, 1834.

STEDMAN, CHARLES: *History of the Origin, Progress, and Termination of the American War*, London, 1794.

STEINER, BERNARD C.: *Life and Correspondence of James McHenry*, Cleveland, 1907.

STEVENS, B. F.: *Facsimiles of Manuscripts in European Archives Relating to America*, London, 1890.

STILLÉ, CHARLES J.: *Major General Anthony Wayne and the Pennsylvania Line in the Continental Army*, Philadelphia, 1893.

STRYKER, WILLIAM S.: *The Battle of Monmouth*, William Starr Myers, Ph.D., ed., Princeton, 1927.

TAYLOR, FRANK H.: *Valley Forge, A Chronicle of American Heroism*, Philadelphia, 1911.

TOWER, CHARLEMAGNE, L.L.D.: *The Marquis de Lafayette in the American Revolution*, Philadelphia, 1901.

TREVELYAN, RT. HON. SIR GEORGE OTTO, BART.: *The American Revolution*, London, New York and Bombay, 1903.

TUCKERMAN, BAYARD: *Life of General Lafayette*, New York, 1889.

———: *Life of General Philip Schuyler*, New York, 1904.

Valley Forge Orderly Book of General George Weedon, New York, 1902.

VAN DOREN, CARL: *Benjamin Franklin*, New York, 1938.

———: *Mutiny in January*, New York, 1943.

———: *Secret History of the American Revolution*, New York, 1941.

WALDO, DR. ALBIGENCE, "Diary," *The Historical Magazine*, Vol. V.

WALPOLE, HORACE: *Letters*, P. Cunningham, ed., London, 1891.

WANDELL, SAMUEL H., and MINNEGERODE, MEADE: *Aaron Burr*, New York, 1925.

WASHINGTON, GEORGE, *Diaries*, 1771-1785, John C. Fitzpatrick, ed., Boston and New York, 1925.

WASHINGTON, GEORGE: *Revolutionary Orders*, Henry Whiting, ed., New York and London, 1844.

WHARTON, ANNE H.: *Life of Martha Washington*, New York, 1897.

WILDES, HENRY EMERSON: *Anthony Wayne, Trouble Shooter of the American Revolution*, New York, 1941.

WILKINSON, GENERAL JAMES: *Memoirs of My Own Times*, Philadelphia, 1816.

WISTER, SALLY, *Journal*, Albert Cook Myers, ed., Philadelphia, 1902.

INDEX

Achmutty, Miss (Mrs. John Montrésor), 180
Adams, Abigail, 8, 44
Adams, John, 20, 23, 44, 46, 53, 65, 128, 129, 161, 162, 168
Adams, Samuel, 236
Agnew, General, 68, 72
Albany, N. Y., 6, 9, 19, 28, 29, 40, 41, 76, 84
Alexander, Lady "Kitty," 145, 190, 204, 219
Alexander, William (*see* Stirling, Lord)
Allentown, N. J., 210, 211
Allentown, Pa., 84, 94
Amboy, N. J., 29, 32, 35, 36, 37, 204, 206
Amherst, General Lord Jeffrey, 164
André, Captain John, 52, 74, 86, 87, 169, 171, 178, 179, 208
Andromeda, H.M.S., 178
Anspach, Prince of, 21
Anspach troops, 59, 184
Arendt, Baron d', 76
Armand, Chevalier, 145
Armstrong, General John, 47, 55, 69
Arnold, Benedict, 4, 20, 21, 29, 31, 41, 142, 185, 190, 195
Articles of Confederation, 146
Artois, Comte d', 159
Augusta, H.M.S., 78
Austria, 159

Baltimore, Md., 5
Barren Hill, 183, 196
Barry, Commodore John, 111
Bavaria, 159
Baylor, Colonel, 46
Beaumarchais, Caron de, 158, 159
Bennington, Vt., battle of, 20, 46
Berkshire Hills, 23
Bethlehem, Pa., 47, 84, 101, 102, 112
Biddle, Mrs. Clement, 145

Biddle, Edward, 125
Billingsport, N. J., 67, 69, 75
Billy, Washington's servant, 116
Bland, Colonel, 46
Board of Treasury of the United States, 154
Board of War, 62, 130-131, 132, 142, 191
Bordentown, N. J., 4, 80, 154
Boston, Mass., 4, 28, 35, 42, 44, 191, 239; siege of, 18, 23, 158
Boudinot, Elias, 17, 146, 155, 156, 175, 191, 201
Bound Brook, N. J., 29, 30, 32, 34, 240
Braddock's expedition, 28, 135
Brandywine, battle of the (*see* Chad's Ford)
Brandywine Creek, 115, 121
British army, 3, 6, 9, 31; winter and spring, 1777, 32, 33, 35; New Jersey campaign, 36, 37; advance on Philadelphia, 40, 42, 44, 45, 47, 48, 50, 51, 53; Brandywine battle, 54-60; takes Philadelphia, 65; Germantown battle, 67-74; at Philadelphia, 75, 77, 81, 85-88, 96, 98, 103, 115, 117, 119-121, 167, 170, 171, 173, 176, 183, 184, 186; Monmouth campaign, 202, 203, 205, 207, 208, 211, 214-216, 221, 225, 227, 238-241
British fleet, 40, 67, 75, 78, 81, 85, 206, 224, 237, 238, 239
British Government, 39, 157, 165, 172, 200
Broglie, Comte de, 43, 165
Brunswick, Duke of, 210
Bucks County, Pa., 44, 117
Bullion's tavern, 30
Bunch of Grapes, tavern, Philadelphia, 170
Bunker Hill, battle of, 87, 119